SERVICE SHEETS
1948 to 1966 'Bantam'
D1 - D3 - D5 - D7
Rigid – Spring Frame
Swing Arm
125cc – 150cc – 175cc

A Floyd Clymer Publication
Published in 2021 by VelocePress.com

INTRODUCTION

Welcome to the world of digital publishing ~ the book you now hold in your hand was printed using the latest state of the art digital technology. The advent of print-on-demand has forever changed the publishing process, never has information been so accessible and it is our hope that this book serves your informational needs for years to come. If this is your first exposure to digital publishing, we hope that you are pleased with the results. Many more titles of interest to the classic automobile and motorcycle enthusiast, collector and restorer are available via our website at www.VelocePress.com. We hope that you find this title as interesting as we do.

NOTE FROM THE PUBLISHER

The information presented is true and complete to the best of our knowledge. All recommendations are made without any guarantees on the part of the author or the publisher, who also disclaim all liability incurred with the use of this information.

TRADEMARKS

We recognize that some words, model names and designations, for example, mentioned herein are the property of the trademark holder. We use them for identification purposes only. This is not an official publication.

INFORMATION ON THE USE OF THIS PUBLICATION

This manual is an invaluable resource for those interested in performing their own maintenance. However, in today's information age we are constantly subject to changes in common practice, new technology, availability of improved materials and increased awareness of chemical toxicity. As such, it is advised that the user consult with an experienced professional prior to undertaking any procedure described herein. While every care has been taken to ensure correctness of information, it is obviously not possible to guarantee complete freedom from errors or omissions or to accept liability arising from such errors or omissions. Therefore, any individual that uses the information contained within, or elects to perform or participate in do-it-yourself repairs or modifications acknowledges that there is a risk factor involved and that the publisher or its associates cannot be held responsible for personal injury or property damage resulting from the use of the information or the outcome of such procedures.

WARNING!

One final word of advice, this publication is intended to be used as a reference guide, and when in doubt the reader should consult with a qualified technician.

BSA 'SERVICE SHEETS'

UNDERSTANDING AND INTERPRETING THE 1945 AND ONWARDS PUBLICATIONS

In 1945, after the war had ended, BSA resumed production of their civilian line of motorcycles. However, they continued their pre-war practice of publishing repair, overhaul and technical information in the form of individual 'Service Sheets'. It should be noted that BSA never intended that these service sheets would be distributed to the general public, they were 'dealer only' publications and, as such, the print quality was at times somewhat questionable. It was not until the early 1960's that BSA eventually started publishing model specific workshop manuals that were available to the general public. Consequently, these 'Service Sheets' were the only publications available for the maintenance and repair of BSA models that were manufactured through the early 1960's.

At some point in the 1930's, BSA adopted the practice of identifying their various model types by 'groups' and the models manufactured from 1945 through the mid 1960's were in Groups A, B, C, D and M. The service sheets that were associated to a particular group were identified numerically and, while there were some exceptions due to overlapping data between models, in general terms the numbers relate to a particular model group. They are as follows: The 200 series of service sheets were applicable to Group A models, the 300 series to Group B, the 400 series to Group C, the 500 series to Group D and the 600 series to Group M. In addition, there were a 700 series applicable to mechanical maintenance and an 800 series for electronic service and wiring diagrams. Both the 700 and 800 series of service sheets contained information that was not model specific but was applicable across multiple model groups. Finally, there were a 900 series for the BSA Dandy and a 1000 series for the BSA Sunbeam and Triumph Tigress scooter.

Unfortunately, as these service sheets were issued individually and at random times, the numbering sequence within any group is, at times, illogical and not necessarily consecutive. Consequently, assembling those individual sheets into a publication that serves as a model specific workshop manual is a somewhat difficult task and owners of BSA motor cycles are subjected to considerable confusion surrounding the appropriate selection from the multitude of reprints that have recently flooded the on-line marketplace. Many of the reprints found on internet websites are from 'bedroom sellers' at enticingly low prices by individuals that really have no idea what they are selling. Many are nothing more than poor quality comb-bound photocopies that are scanned and printed complete with greasy pages and thumbprints and, as such, are deceptively described as 'pre-owned', 'used' or even 'refurbished'! In addition, they are often advertised for the incorrect series and/or model years of motorcycles.

The most complete compilation of the 1945 and onwards service sheets was issued by BSA in the form of a 'dealer only' ring binder that contained all of the individual service sheets totaling to almost 500 pages, it is extremely scarce and difficult to find. It is this ring bound publication that was used to create this 'Service Sheet' manual'.

'D' GROUP SERVICE SHEET MANUAL 1948-1966 (D1 to D7)

This manual includes the 27 service sheets (84 pages) published by BSA under part number 00-4020. However, an additional 15 service sheets have been added from that 'dealer only' publication, to produce a single manual containing 42 service sheets (150 pages) that cover the 1948 to 1966 rigid, spring frame, swing arm D1, D3, D5 and D7 Bantam. Obviously, as the 1966 D10 and the 1968 to 1970 D14 models share many mechanical similarities with the D7, this manual will also be of use to owners of those later models. Please note that service sheets other than those in the 500 series that are included in this publication may also contain data that is applicable to 'other' model groups, as that was the original intention.

For additional information the reader is directed to **'The Book of the BSA Bantam'** (ISBN 9781588502100) which covers all Bantam models from 1948 to 1971.

GENERAL INDEX

PAGE	SHEET	SUBJECT	PAGE	SHEET	SUBJECT
3		Supplement	68	708	Carburetter
11	412C	Suspension	76	708B	Carburetter
12	501	Engine	77	708C	Carburetter
13	501A	Gearbox	81	709	Fault Diagnosis
14	502	Lube	82	710	Chain
15	503	Engine	84	710X	Frames by model
17	504	Engine	101	711	Special Tools
20	505	Engine	109	711A	Special Tools
27	506	Engine	113	711B	Special Tools
35	507	Gearbox	120	714	Spokes
37	508	Hubs	124	805	Battery
44	509	Forks	128	806	Lights
48	510	Technical Data	131	807	Horn
49	511	Technical Data	133	808B	Wiring
50	514	Suspension	137	808E	Wiring
52	515	Hubs	139	808L	Wiring
57	516	Forks	141	810	Alternator
60	612	Brakes	145	810A	Alternator
62	702	Technical Data	149	811	Lamps
64	703	Technical Data	151	812	Alternator
66	704	Technical Data	155	812A	Alternator
			159	815	Battery

SUPPLEMENT

The wiring diagrams on the following pages are included as they are presented in a logical year/model format and in some cases they are more legible than those in the Service Sheets. The appropriate BSA Service Sheet number is referenced on each diagram

For the sake of completeness, the late model 1967-1970 wiring diagram is also included.

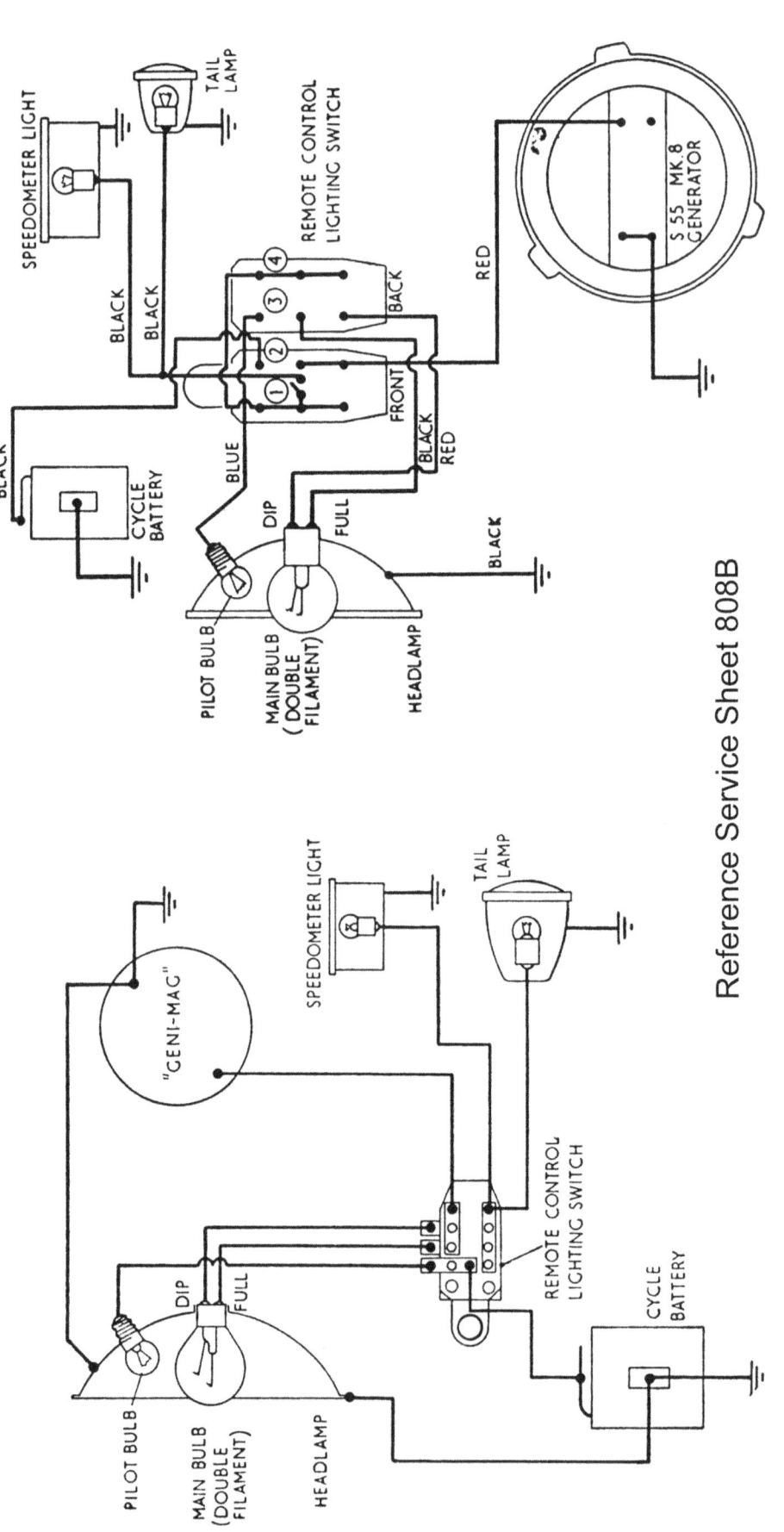

Reference Service Sheet 808B

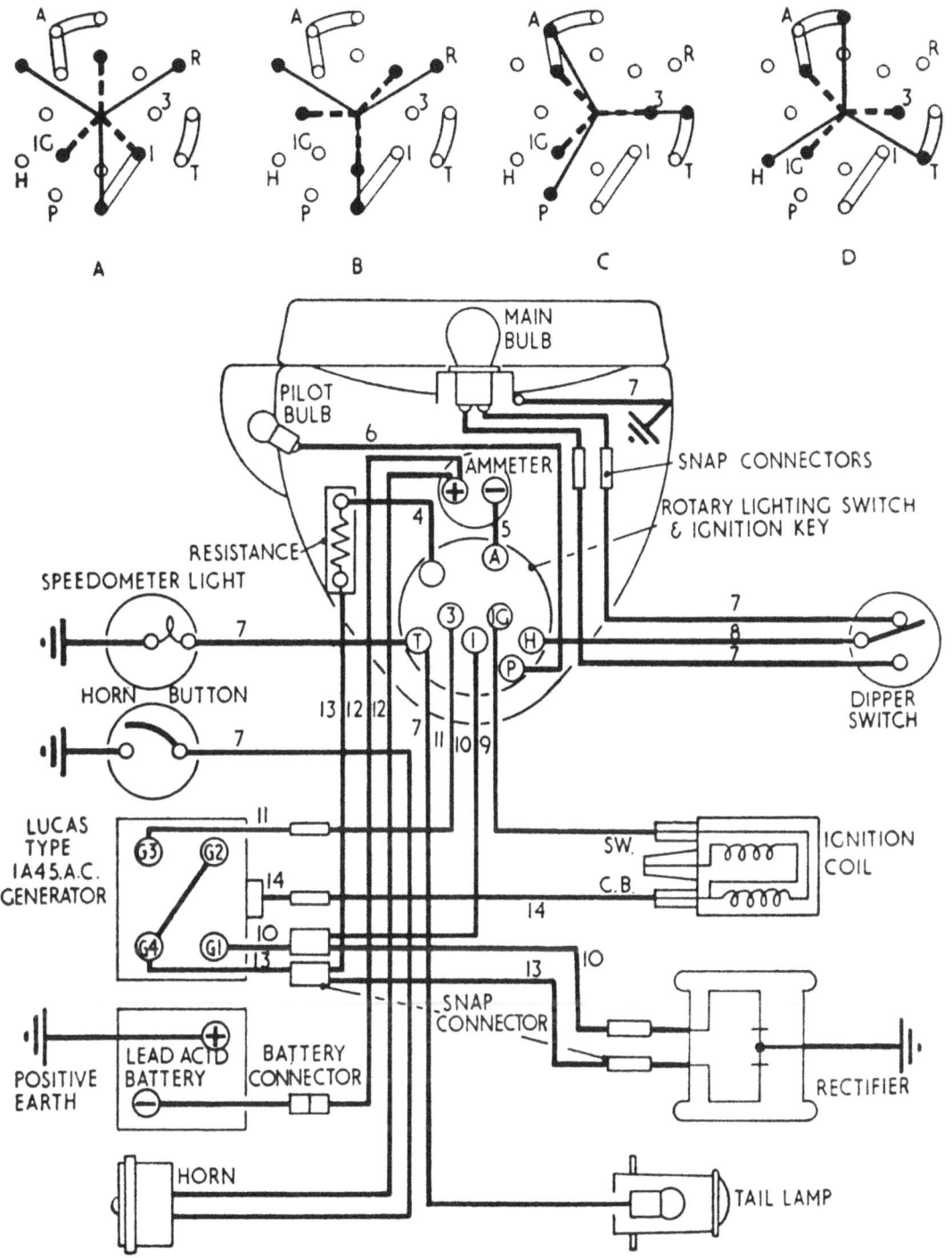

Wiring diagram for 1950-3 Model D1 Bantams with Lucas a.c. generator and Lucas SSP575P headlamp with headlamp lighting switch

This diagram applies to 123 cm³ Bantams with Lucas battery-lighting (rectifier) and coil ignition, provided as an alternative to the Wipac direct-lighting equipment

- 4. Brown and yellow
- 5. Brown and blue
- 6. Red and black
- 7. Black
- 8. Blue
- 9. White
- 10. Purple
- 11. Green
- 12. Brown
- 13. Yellow
- 14. White and black

Reference Service Sheet 808B

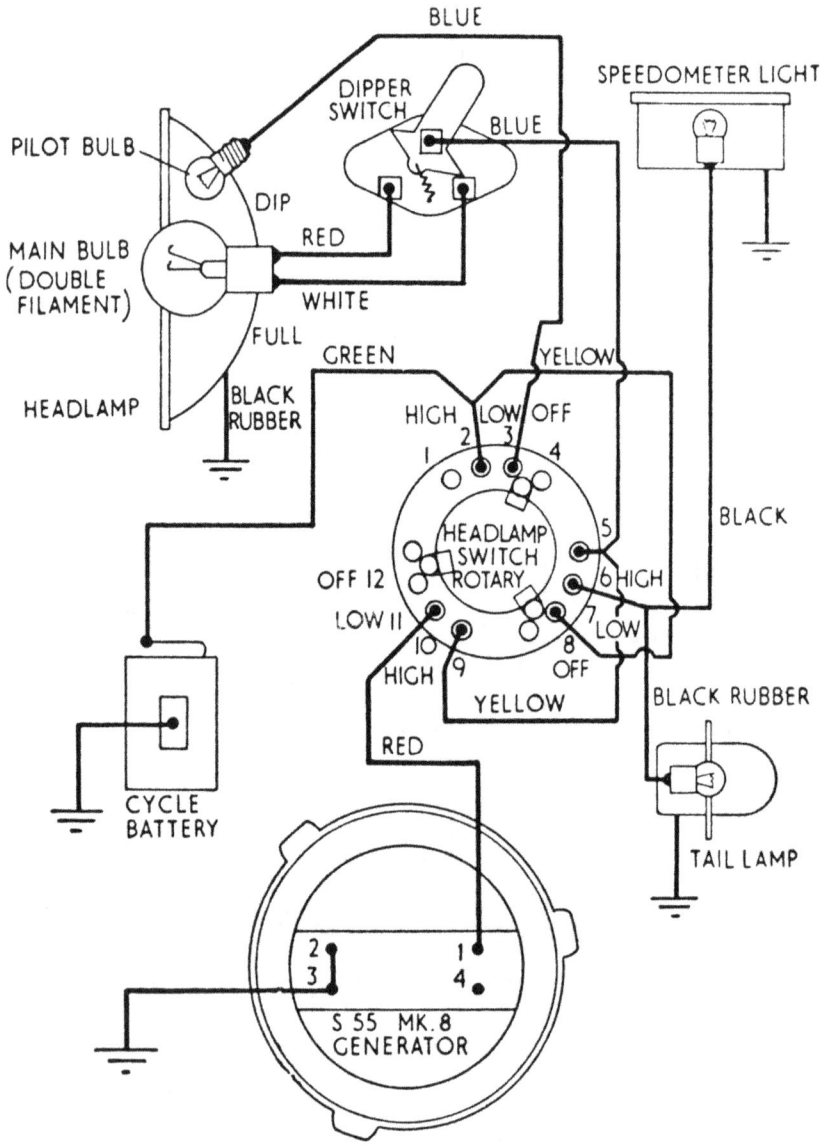

Wiring diagram for 1952–61 Models D1 and D3 Bantams with Wipac a.c./d.c. S55/Mk. 8 generator and Wipac 1-58F headlamp with headlamp lighting switch

This diagram applies to 123 cm³ and 148 cm³ Bantams with Wipac direct lighting from January, 1952, to 1959 inclusive

Reference Service Sheet 808B

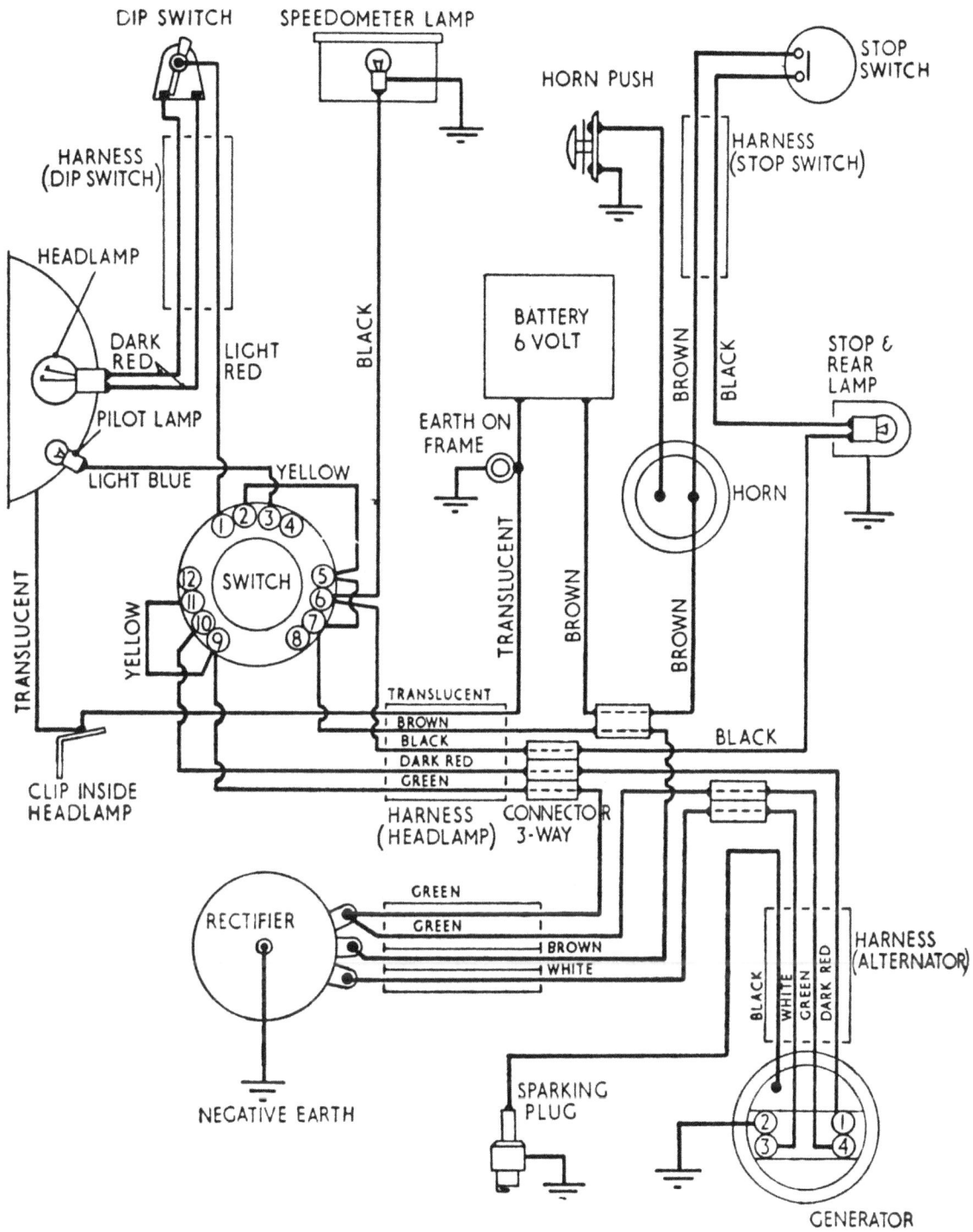

Wiring diagram for 1954-61 Models D1, D3, D5 Bantams
with Wipac 02143 headlamp and Wipac a.c./d.c. S55/Mk. 8
generator

On late 1954 and all 1955-61 battery lighting models the battery positive terminal is earthed and a three-bulb stop-tail lamp is fitted. On 1960-1 models the Wipac type 0213 headlamp was replaced by a Wipac type SO891 headlamp with a "pre-focus" main bulb. The above diagram, however, applies to all models

Reference Service Sheet 808B

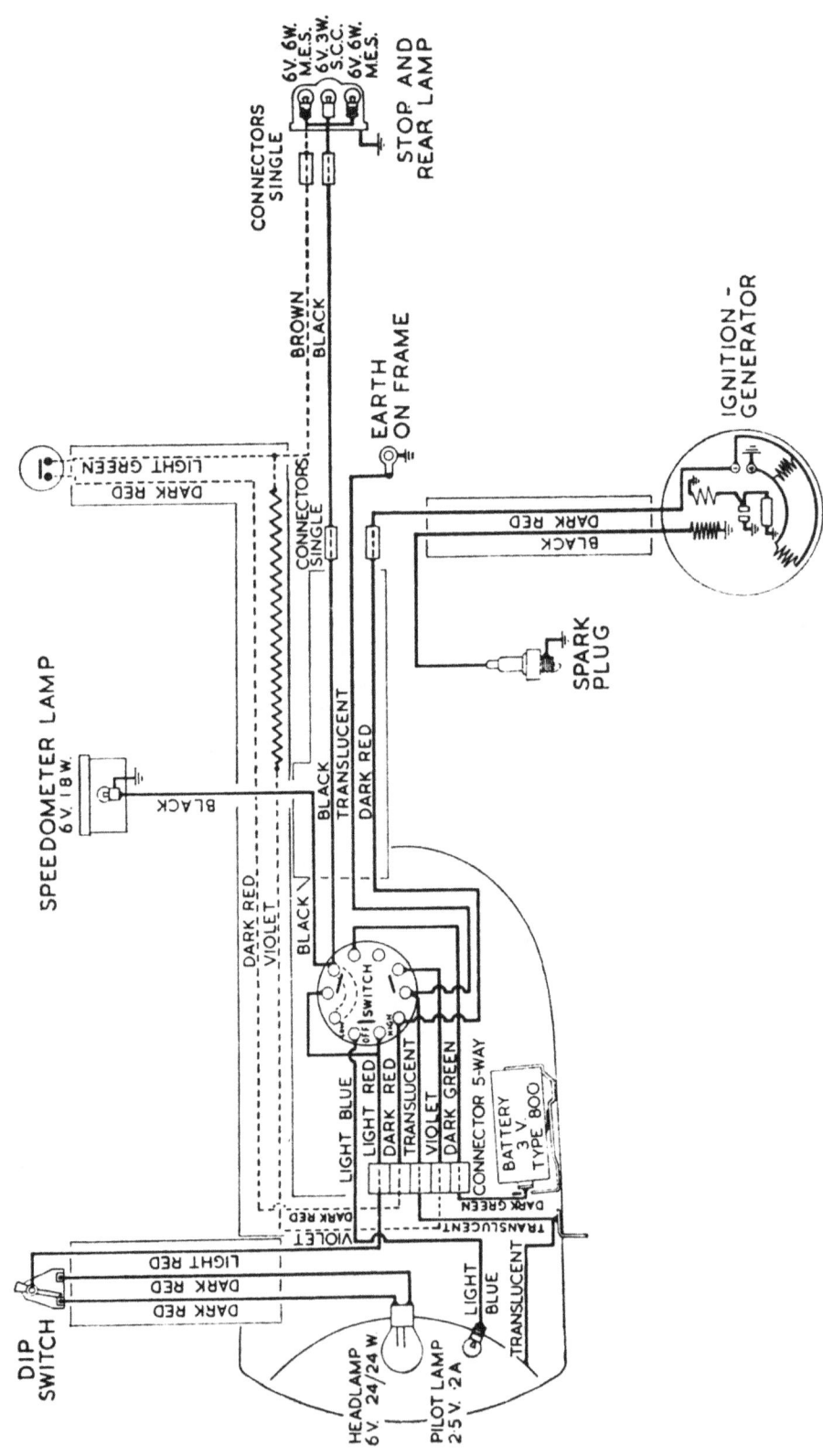

Wiring diagram for 1962-5 direct lighting Models D7, D7D/L with Wipac a.c./d.c. S55/Mk. 8 generator and Wipac SO856 headlamp

Reference Service Sheet 808E

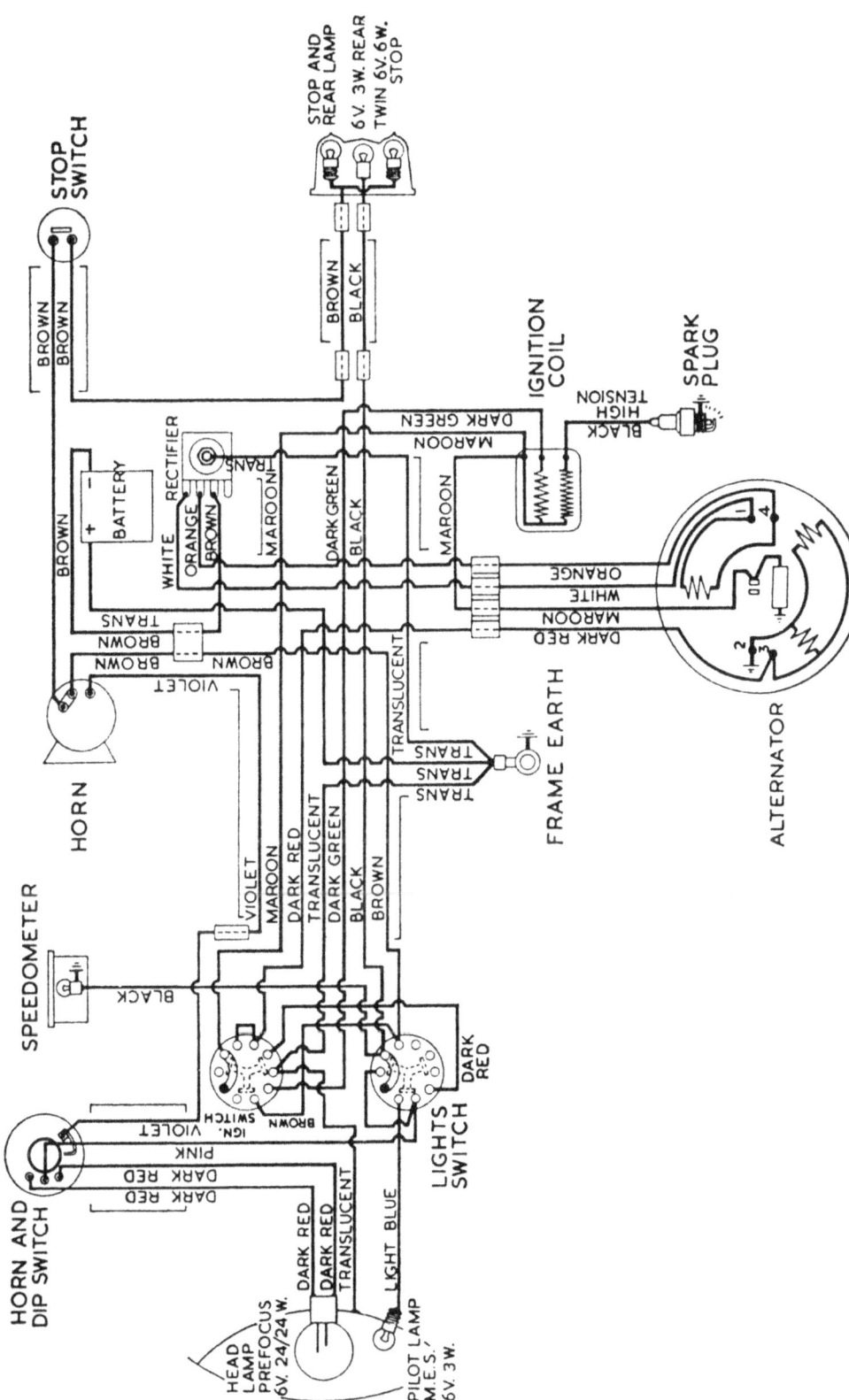

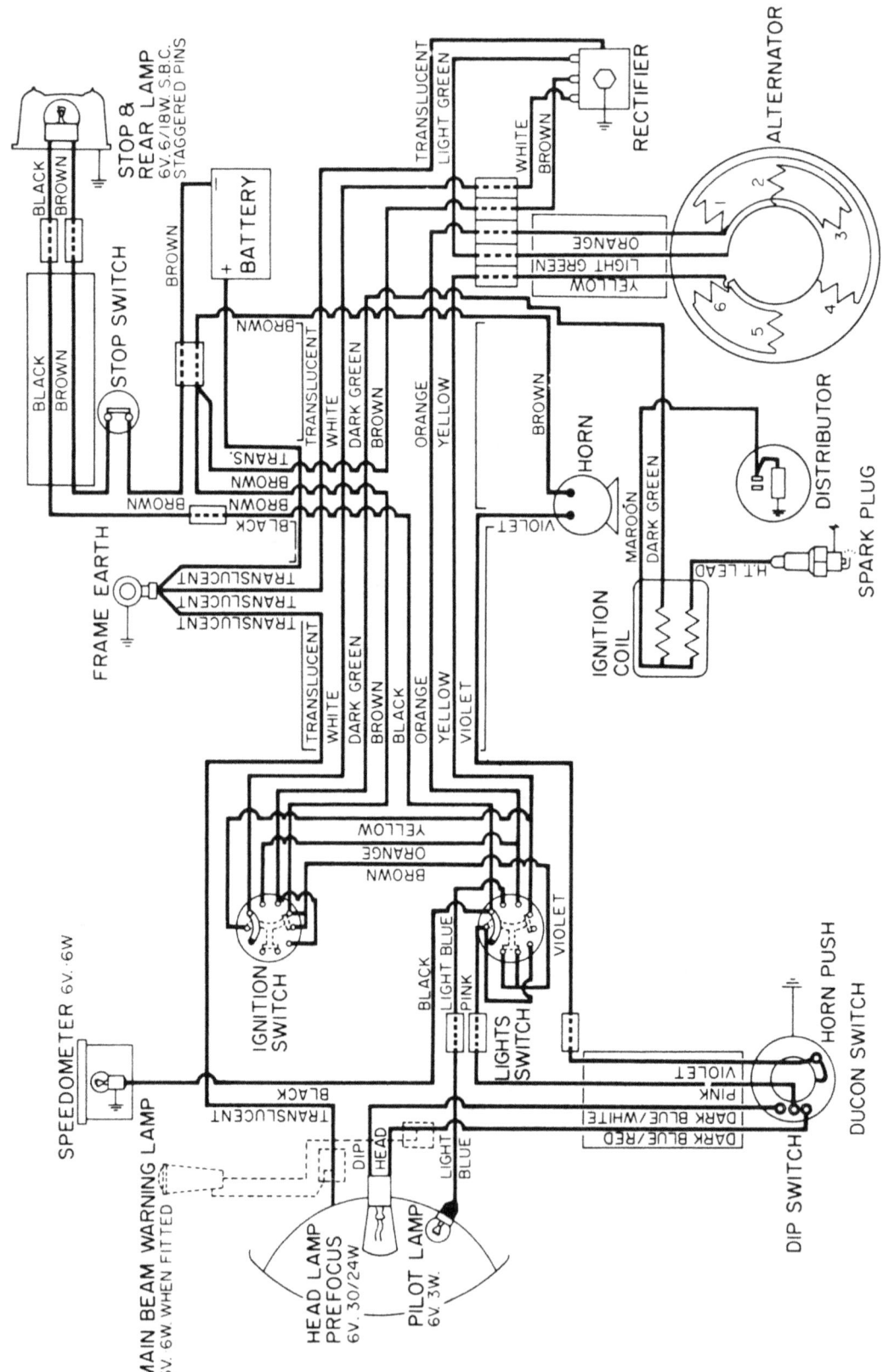

Wiring diagram for 1967–70 coil-ignition and battery-lighting models D10, D14, and Bantam 175

Note that some cable colours (notably those from the generator) have changed from those on the preceding diagrams

BSA SERVICE SHEET No. 412C

D3, D5, D7, C12, C15 and B40 SWINGING ARM MODELS
REAR SUSPENSION

FRAME

The silent bloc bushes fitted to the rear suspension swinging arm are unlikely to need replacement for some considerable time. If it is found necessary to renew them, first remove the suspension units by detaching the top pivot bolts and the bottom retaining nuts.

Remove the rear wheel and chainguard. Undo the fork spindle nut and tap out the spindle, using a suitable drift.

Lift the rear fork until it is clear of the side plates; it can then be turned and pulled away from the rear.

After the central distance piece has been displaced the bushes can be removed with a suitable drift.

DISMANTLING THE SUSPENSION UNITS

Early C12 models were fitted with a damper spring of 100 lb./inch rate, this was later increased to 124 lb./inch.

The 124 lb./inch spring, part number 29-4570 can be fitted to early machines where it is considered necessary.

The spring is retained by circlips fitted at its base and a service tool, part number 61-5064 has been introduced to facilitate removal.

The tool is assembled as shown in Fig. C46 and when the nut is screwed down sufficiently the spring is compressed thus releasing the circlips. The circlips can be extracted through the apertures in the tool and the spring comes away when the tool is removed.

Reassembly is in the reverse order.

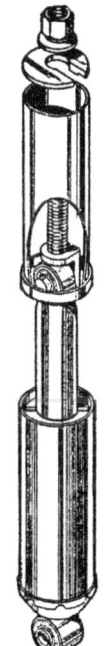

Fig. C46.

B.S.A. MOTOR CYCLES LTD., Service Department, Armoury Road, Birmingham 11.
Printed in England at the B.S.A. Press

BSA SERVICE SHEET No. 501

Revised June, 1959.

"D" Group Engine and Gearbox (Exploded View)

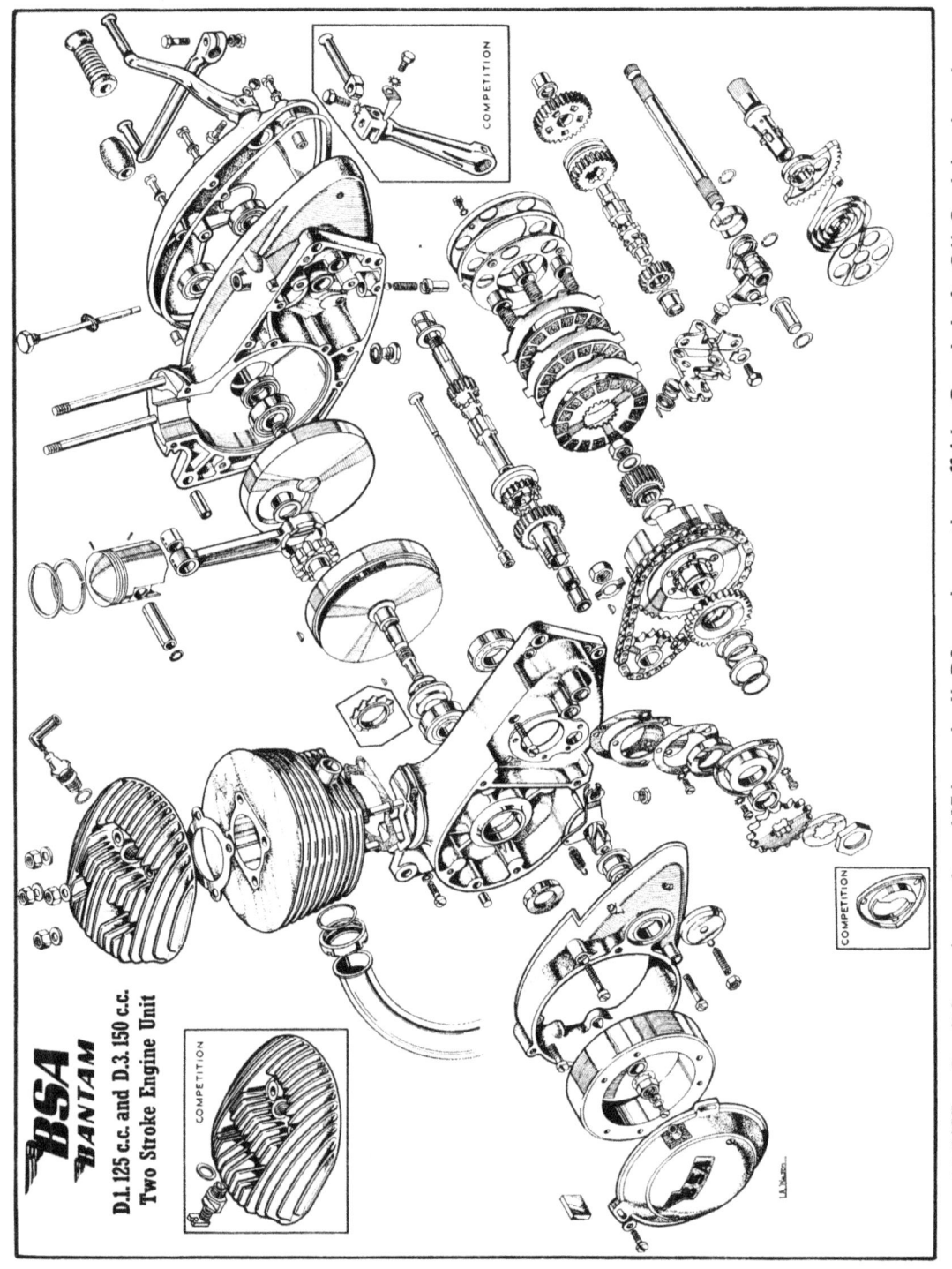

NOTE.—On D1 engines after 1954, and all D3 engines, the offside Crankshaft Oil Seal is placed next to the flywheel instead of between the two bearings.

B.S.A. MOTOR CYCLES LIMITED,
Service Dept., Waverley Works, Birmingham. 10.
(PRINTED IN ENGLAND)

BSA SERVICE SHEET No. 501A

D GROUP GEAR RATIOS

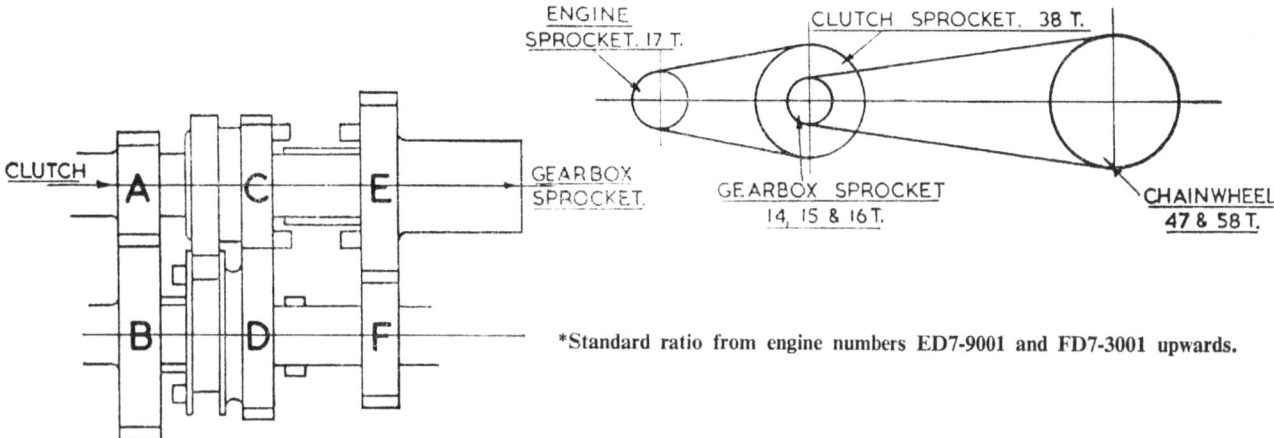

*Standard ratio from engine numbers ED7-9001 and FD7-3001 upwards.

		STANDARD RATIO		*STANDARD RATIO		CLOSE RATIO	
	GEAR REFERENCE LETTER ON DIAGRAM	COMPONENT NUMBER	NO. OF TEETH	COMPONENT NUMBER	NO. OF TEETH	COMPONENT NUMBER	NO. OF TEETH
	A	90–1345	15	90–1345	15	90–1489	19
	B	90–0082	32	90–0082	32	90–0448	28
	C	90–1357	22	90–1357	22	90–1357	22
	D	90–1360	25	90–1360	25	90–1492	25
	E	90–0065	28	90–1582	26	90–0474	24
	F	90–1358	19	90–1584	21	90–1495	23

GEARBOX SPROCKET	CHAINWHEEL					
16	46	TOP SECOND BOTTOM		6.426 10.73 20.2	6.426 9.189 16.96	6.426 7.62 9.89
15	46	TOP SECOND BOTTOM		6.85 11.43 21.5	6.85 9.79 18.08	6.85 8.124 10.54
14	46	TOP SECOND BOTTOM		7.34 12.25 23.04	7.34 10.49 19.37	7.34 8.70 11.3
16	47	TOP SECOND BOTTOM		6.58 10.85 20.41	6.58 9.38 17.07	6.58 7.78 10.1
15	47	TOP SECOND BOTTOM		7.0 11.69 21.98	7.0 10.01 18.48	7.0 8.3 10.78
14	47	TOP SECOND BOTTOM		7.5 12.52 23.55	7.5 10.725 19.8	7.5 8.9 11.53
INTERNAL RATIOS		TOP SECOND BOTTOM		1.0 1.67 3.14	1.0 1.43 2.64	1.0 1.186 1.54

D5 and D7 models prior to frame number D7-5885 used 46T rear chainwheel. Later D7 models used 47T chainwheel.
'A' refers to mainshaft with gear cut direct on to shaft.
'F' is the layshaft complete with gear.

B.S.A. MOTOR CYCLES LTD., Service Dept., Armoury Road, Birmingham 11

PRINTED IN ENGLAND   THE B.S.A. PRESS

BSA SERVICE SHEET No. 502

MODELS D1, D3, D5 AND D7

THE PETROIL LUBRICATION SYSTEM

The correct lubrication of the two-stroke engine fitted to these models depends upon a certain quantity of oil being mixed with the petrol. It is preferable for this to be done before the fuel is poured into the tank, and a number of filling stations now supply 'petroil' mixture ready for use. Failing this, the oil and petrol should be thoroughly mixed in a separate container. If this is not possible, the petrol should be put into the tank first and the oil added, after which the machine should be rocked to and fro.

The petrol tap must be turned off when the machine is parked. Failure to do this may result in the carburettor float chamber becoming filled with oil if allowed to stand for a long period.

While the engine is running, oil is induced into the crankcase through the carburettor in the form of oil mist mixed with the fuel supply. As the piston descends, compressing the charge in the crankcase, most of the oil mist separates out and is deposited in the crankcase as liquid oil which lubricates the big-end and main bearings. The petrol and air mixture passes up through the transfer ports into the combustion chamber.

Surplus oil is carried by the action of the fuel transfer to the combustion chamber, where it serves as an upper cylinder lubricant, and is eventually burned by the heat of combustion.

There is no point in increasing the proportion of oil to petrol above that recommended, since any excess of oil is merely transferred to the combustion chamber where it is burnt. A higher proportion of oil in the charge means a lower proportion of petrol and therefore a less suitable combustible mixture.

A measure for oil is incorporated in the filler cap, that on earlier models being approximately 5 in. long while the later type is approximately $6\frac{1}{4}$ in. long. Two and a half of the former, or two of the latter measures must be used with each gallon of petrol. Both these quantities correspond to 1 part of oil to 20 parts of petrol and this will provide adequate lubrication throughout the life of the engine.

If the special two-stroke self-mixing oils are used, the proportion should be increased to 1 to 16, which equals half a pint to one gallon of petrol.

RECOMMENDED ENGINE OILS

CASTROL XXL	or TWO-STROKE SELF-MIX OIL
MOBILOIL BB	or MOBILMIX TT
SHELL X100–40	or PETROILER MIX No. 2T
B.P. ENERGOL 40	or ENERGOL TWO-STROKE OIL
ESSO EXTRA 40/50	or ESSO TWO-STROKE MOTOR OIL

Models D5 and D7

On models D5 and D7 the main engine bearings are lubricated by oil transfer from the gearbox. It is therefore essential that the following undiluted oils be used in the gearbox.

RECOMMENDED GEARBOX OILS

CASTROL XXL
SHELL X100–40
ESSO EXTRA 40/50
MOBILOIL BB
ENERGOL 40

B.S.A. MOTOR CYCLES LTD., Service Department, Armoury Road, Birmingham 11

B.S.A. PRESS

BSA SERVICE SHEET No. 503

MODELS D1, D3, D5 AND D7
ENGINE ADJUSTMENTS WHICH CAN BE CARRIED OUT WITHOUT DISMANTLING

Contact Breaker Points

Access to the contact breaker mechanism is obtained by removing the small cap in the centre of the generator cover. On early Wipac models this cap is retained by a spring clip as shown in Fig. D1, but on all other models two small retaining screws are used.

D7 Models

On D7 models, access to the contact breaker and clutch adjuster, can be obtained after the pear-shaped cover on the left-hand side of the engine has been removed by taking out the three screws.

The contact points must be maintained in good condition and kept free from oil and dirt. They should be cleaned occasionally by passing a piece of smooth clean paper between the points and with-

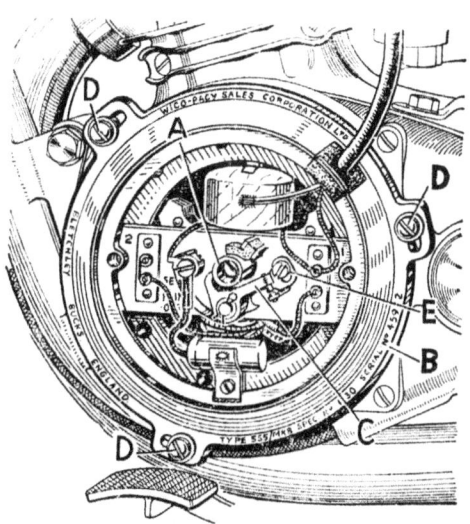

Fig. D1. *Wipac Equipment.*

drawing it when the points are closed. If the points are burnt they should be cleaned with very fine emery cloth, and then wiped with a petrol-soaked rag. This is easier carried out if the rocker arm complete is removed. On Wipac magnetos the spring clip on the end of the rocker arm spindle must be removed and the terminal at the end of the spring disconnected to allow the rocker arm to be detached. On Lucas generators the terminal post nuts should be slackened so that the slotted end of the spring can be removed from the post, thus permitting the rocker to be withdrawn from the spindle.

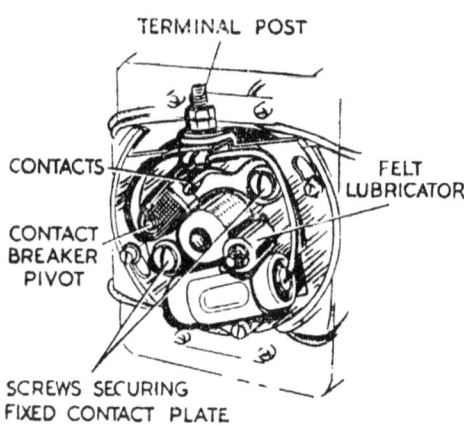

Fig. D1a. *Lucas Equipment.*

It is most important that the correct contact breaker gap is maintained. Rotate the engine until the points are fully open and then check the gap with feeler gauges. The gap should be .015 in. for Wipac and .012 in. for Lucas equipment.

If the gap is incorrect the points must be re-adjusted. Slacken the screws securing the fixed contact plate (E) Fig. D1, for Wipac, and Fig. D1a for Lucas equipment. Move the plate until the contact gap is correct then tighten the securing screws and re-check the gap. Early Wipac models have an eccentric headed screw at (F) Fig. D1, to facilitate movement of the plate, but on all other models the plate is simply pushed backwards or forwards.

B.S.A. Service Sheet No. 503 (contd.)

Ignition Timing

Before checking the ignition timing the contact breaker gap must always be checked, as this affects the ignition setting. Rotate the engine until it is at top dead centre, as ascertained by a suitable rod inserted through the plug hole. Turn the engine backwards until the piston has descended $\frac{5}{32}$ in. for D1 and D3 models, $\frac{1}{16}$ in. for D5 and D7 models and the contact points should then be just on the point of opening, i.e. not more than .002 in. apart. This is best determined by inserting a piece of very fine paper (such as cigarette paper) between the points. The paper will be only lightly gripped when the points are just on the point of opening.

If the setting is not correct the three screws in slotted holes (D) Fig. D1, should be slackened, thus permitting the complete contact breaker back plate to be rotated until the correct setting is obtained. Rotating the plate in a clockwise direction advances the ignition. On Lucas models the contact breaker back plate is retained by four screws in slotted holes, as shown in Fig. D1a, but the procedure is identical.

Sparking Plug

The sparking plug is of such importance in satisfactory engine performance that it is advantageous to give proper attention to this component. It is poor economy to use any but the most efficient plug. The better plug will soon pay for itself by effecting more complete combustion and loss of power due to partially unburned fuel will be eliminated. The plug most suited to the requirements of this engine is the Champion L10S. Remove the sparking plug every 1,000 miles (1,500 km.) or so, for inspection. If the carburation system is in correct adjustment the sparking plug points should remain clean almost indefinitely. An

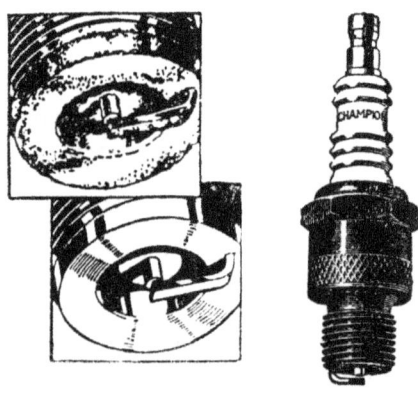

Fig. D2. *The Sparking Plug.*

over-rich mixture will, however, cause the formation of a sooty deposit on the points and, later, outside the plug body (as upper view, Fig. D2). If therefore such a deposit is found, clean it off carefully and check your carburetter. Too large a proportion of oil in the petroil mixture will also cause plug fouling. The continued use of leaded fuel may also eventually produce a deposit on the plug—this time of a greyish colour.

A light deposit due to any of these causes can easily be cleaned off, but if it is allowed to accumulate, particularly inside the body, the plug may spark internally with an adverse effect on engine performance—if, indeed, it does not stop the engine altogether—and the plug should be taken to a garage for cleaning. If eventually the cleaning process fails to restore the plug to its original condition of efficiency, it should be replaced by a new one.

When inspecting a plug, also check the gap between the points. This should be .018—.020 in. (.44—.50 mm), and adjustment should be made by bending the side wire. Never attempt to move the centre electrode.

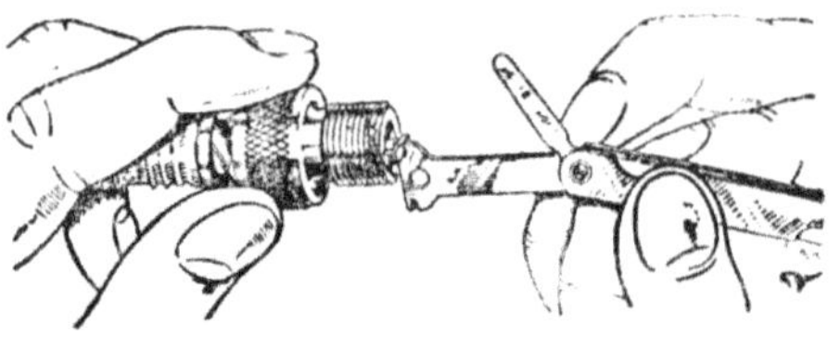

Fig. D3. *Setting the Plug Points.*

B.S.A. MOTOR CYCLES LTD., Service Department, Armoury Road, Birmingham 11.

B.S.A. PRESS.

BSA SERVICE SHEET No. 504

Models D1, D3, D5 and D7

ENGINE DISMANTLING FOR DECARBONISING

Decarbonising should be carried out at regular intervals of about three thousand miles (5,000 km.) if consistent results are to be expected. The symptoms indicating an excessive deposit of carbon are undue roughness of the engine and a tendency to "pink" under load, erratic running with excessive four- and eight-stroking, and an appreciable falling off in power. This latter item is particularly noticeable when the exhaust port becomes fouled with carbon as it causes an obstuction to the free escape of the exhaust gas, and interferes with the correct scavenging of the cylinder which is so necessary for the efficient transfer of combustible mixture from the crankcase.

Before commencing to decarbonise the engine it is necessary to slacken the two bolts holding the petrol tank to the steering head, and to remove entirely the rear petrol tank securing bolt which passes through the frame, and carries the earth wire of the electrical system. Disconnect the petrol pipe from the tank tap, after turning fuel off at tap and raise the rear of the tank about 1 in. to allow the removal of the cylinder barrel over the long securing studs.

Removal of Cylinder

First remove the carburettor from its stub at the rear of the cylinder by releasing the clip bolt by means of which it is attached. The exhaust pipe must also be disconnected by releasing the union nut at the front of the cylinder barrel by means of the special "C" spanner included in the toolkit. If this nut should prove unduly obstinate, a few drops of penetrating oil should be applied to the threaded portion immediately above the nut and a little time should be allowed for this to act before attempting to unscrew the nut. Disconnect the high-tension lead from the sparking plug and unscrew the latter.

The cylinder head and barrel are attached to the crankcase by means of four long studs and when the four nuts on the top of the cylinder head are removed, the head can easily be lifted clear, followed by the cylinder barrel. Take care when removing the latter to support the piston as it emerges from the end of the bore in order that it may not be damaged as it falls clear.

Piston

Place the cylinder head and barrel on one side on a bench and examine the piston. It should not be necessary to remove this from the connecting rod, but if it should be desired to do this for any reason, first remove the circlip from one end of the gudgeon pin using a pair of pointed-nose pliers or some suitable instrument to lever the circlip out. Then holding the piston firmly in the hand, tap the gudgeon pin out from the other end. If it is too tight to move, it can be released by warming the piston by means of a rag soaked in hot water and wrung out. Application of this rag will cause the aluminium alloy of the piston to expand more than the steel gudgeon pin, thus releasing the latter which can then be freely pushed or tapped out. Mark the inside of the piston skirt to indicate the front of the piston as originally fitted.

B.S.A. Service Sheet No. 504 (contd.)

Scrape any carbon which has accumulated on the crown of the piston, taking care not to damage the relatively soft surface of the metal itself, and after removing all the carbon, polish lightly with fine emery cloth if desired and finally wipe clean with an oil rag.

Piston Rings

Now examine the piston rings noting that these are located in their grooves by means of pegs which engage in the piston ring gaps. If in good condition, the rings will be found to present a uniformly smooth metallic surface over their entire peripheries, and if they are in this condition and obviously have a certain amount of "springiness" as evidenced by the fact that their free gap is considerably greater than the closed gap when in the bore (see Service Sheet No. 506) they should not be disturbed. If, on the other hand, the rings show signs of heat as evidenced by brown or more highly discoloured patches, they should be replaced by new rings, and in this case particular attention should be paid to the fit of the ends of the rings on their locating pegs in the piston ring grooves, and they should also be checked in the bore to ensure that they have an adequate gap. These points will not arise if genuine B.S.A. spares are fitted as the gaps on these are already correct when the rings are sent out, but if for any reason genuine B.S.A. spares are not obtainable, these points must receive careful attention. First place the ring in the cylinder bore in a position where it is clear of the ports and, making certain that it is square by pressing the skirt of the piston against it or a suitable bar of material of the correct diameter, examine the gap which should be not less than .008 in. (.2 mm.). Having satisfied yourself on this point, place the ring in its groove on the piston and make certain that it is free without perceptible up and down play. If it is not free and the groove itself is clean, rub the ring down on a piece of fine emery cloth laid on a dead flat surface, using a rotary motion of the arm to ensure uniform pressure on the ring. As soon as ring is found to be free in its groove, wipe it absolutely clean and fit it into position.

Check also that there is sufficient clearance between the inner portion of the gap and the locating peg in the groove. Do this by closing the ring in its groove by finger pressure until there is no gap, thus showing that there is clearance at the peg underneath. If the gap will not close, indicating that the steps are binding on the peg, ease the steps gently with a dead smooth file. If the piston has been removed from the connecting rod refit it, first putting a smear of oil on the gudgeon pin, not forgetting a new circlip to replace the one which was removed. Note that the piston ring gaps should face towards the rear on D1 models and towards the front on D3, D5 and D7 models. Then put a piece of clean rag over the piston and crankcase mouth and turn your attention to the cylinder barrel and head.

Cylinder Head and Ports

Remove all carbon deposit from the cylinder head, bearing in mind again that the aluminium is soft and easily damaged if the decarbonising tool is carelessly applied, and carefully wipe clean to ensure the removal of all loose particles. Most of the carbon deposit likely to have accumulated in the cylinder will be in the exhaust port, and this is most important as explained above. Scrape this out carefully, taking care not to let the tool slip into the bore and damage the surface of the latter. Examine the transfer and inlet ports for the presence of carbon, although this is unlikely to be heavy, and finally wipe the ports and the cylinder bore absolutely clean.

B.S.A. Service Sheet No. 504 (contd.)

Big-end Bearing

While the cylinder is off it is as well to test the big-end bearing for wear. This is done by taking hold of the connecting rod stem and pulling it upwards until the crank is at top dead centre. Then holding it in this position try gently but firmly to pull and push the connecting rod in the direction of its travel in order to feel whether there is any play. If the big-end is in a sound condition there should be no play in this direction, although it may be possible to rock the rod sideways, i.e. at right angles to the axis of the machine. If vertical play is perceptible in the big-end it must be decided whether the amount in evidence is permissible or not. The assembly is not likely to require replacement, however, provided that the machine has been carefully used and adequately lubricated, for the big-end bearing is of ample dimensions for the work it has to do. But if for any reason the big-end bearing has deteriorated as the result of neglect or abuse, it should be replaced.

Reassembly

Before attempting to replace the cylinder barrel over the piston, smear the latter generously with engine oil and then place it over the piston, carefully manipulating the rings into the end of the bore and seeing that they enter freely without the application of force. As soon as the cylinder barrel is home, replace the cylinder head and put the washers and nuts on the four holding down bolts. Tighten the nuts in diagonal order so as to avoid distortion.

Examine the sparking plug (see Service Sheet No. 503) and refit if sound.

Before refitting, the exhaust pipe and silencer should be examined for freedom from carbon and cleaned if necessary. Refit the exhaust pipe and carburettor, lower the rear of the tank into position and insert the long securing bolt, after passing it through the earth connection tag attached to the electric wiring harness. Ensure that face of tag is clean and free from dirt or corrosion so that it makes a good contact.

Tighten up rear and front tank securing bolts.

B.S.A. MOTOR CYCLES LTD., Service Department, Armoury Road, Birmingham 11

B.S.A. PRESS

BSA SERVICE SHEET No. 505

MODELS D1, D3 PLUNGER, D3, D5 & D7 SWINGING ARM
REMOVING ENGINE-GEAR UNIT FROM FRAME
AND COMPLETE DISMANTLING

Removing the Unit

Disconnect the clutch and carburettor controls, the petrol pipe, plug lead, and the electrical connections from the flywheel generator. Take off the rear chain and chainguard. In the case of the D3 swinging arm model with battery lighting, the rectifier is bolted to the chainguard, but there is no need to remove the guard completely. After the front and rear fixing bolts have been removed it can be suspended out of the way by means of a stout wire hooked over the top frame member.

Using the "C" spanner provided in the tool kit; unscrew the exhaust pipe union nut and remove the pipe.

Take off the nuts on the engine bolts and withdraw the bolts. The engine can now be lifted from the frame.

Dismantling

Drain off the oil from both the engine and gearbox units by removing the large hexagonal nut under the gearbox, adjacent to the domed primary chaincase cover and the smaller hexagon nut on the nearside front underside of the engine. The gearbox oil also serves the oilbath for the primary chain and the primary chaincase is drained automatically by the removal of the gearbox drain plug.

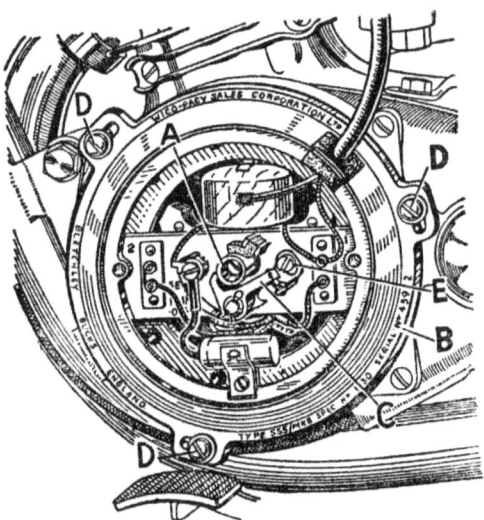

Fig. D4. *The contact breaker mechanism.*

B.S.A. Service Sheet No. 505 (contd.)

Flywheel Generator (Wico-Pacy)

On the nearside of the engine, three cheese-headed screws (D) Fig. D4, slotted for withdrawal with a screwdriver and located in elongated slots, and one screw (A) in the centre of the contact breaker mechanism, hold the ignition coil and contact breaker assembly cover in position.

Model D7.—The model D7 differs slightly from the other "D" Group machines in that to obtain access to the generator, the pear-shaped cover on the left-hand side of the unit must be removed by taking out the three screws, after this, the procedure for dismantling is identical.

Note that the screw (A) Fig. D4, in the centre of the contact breaker mechanism also secures the contact breaker cam which is keyed on to the mainshaft. The cam will fall from the shaft as the large alloy cover is withdrawn, and care must be taken to see that neither the cam nor its key is lost during this operation.

The right-hand threaded nut holding the flywheel must now be unscrewed to allow the withdrawal of the flywheel. Service Tool number 61-3188 is used for this operation (Fig. D5). Note that a large shakeproof washer is fitted between the nut and flywheel boss.

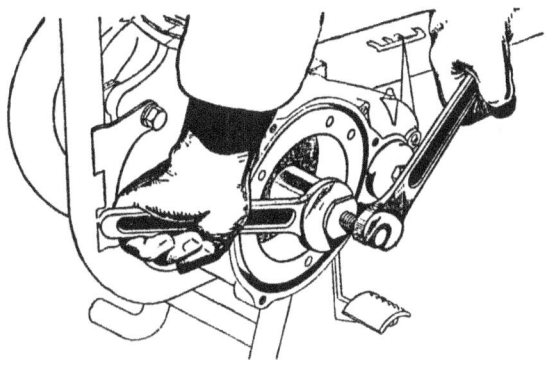

Fig. D5. *Removing the generator flywheel with service tool 61-3188.*

When the flywheel is withdrawn it should be placed in its correct position in the ignition assembly unit to ensure that the magnetic properties of the flywheel are retained, or alternatively place a circular steel plate to cover all the magnets in the wheel for the same purpose. *Failure to do so may entail loss of electrical efficiency.*

On machines with Wico-Pacy equipment, two short screws inside at (A), and three long screws outside at (B) Fig. D6, secure the alloy flywheel housing cover in position.

When Lucas equipment is fitted, the cover is retained by three long screws only.

With the cover removed, the rear drive sprocket and gear position indicator are revealed. This indicator is not fitted to later models, its place being taken by a thrust pad, part number 90-0759. On the inside of the cover is the clutch push rod operating lever, mounted behind the adjusting screw (C) Fig. D6.

Pull out the clutch push rod, part number 90-0099 and the rubber oil seal washer, part number 90-0132, from the centre of the sprocket. Unscrew the sprocket securing nut, first bending back the tab of the locking washer. This nut is left-hand threaded. Remove the nut, washer and sprocket, and take off the gear indicator lever (if fitted).

B.S.A. Service Sheet No. 505 (contd.)

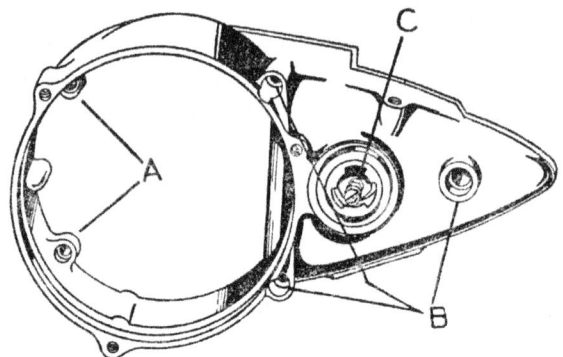

Fig. D6.

Primary Drive Cover

On the offside of the engine the change-speed foot pedal is splined on its shaft and held in position by a pinch bolt (C) Fig. D7. Unscrew and withdraw the pinch bolt and take off the pedal. Now take off the kickstart pedal, this also is fitted to a splined shaft and held in position by a pinch bolt (B) Fig. D7.

By unscrewing the five cheese-headed screws (D), two long ones at the front of the alloy primary drive cover, and three at the rear, this cover can be taken off, revealing the engine sprocket, non-adjustable primary chain, clutch assembly, kickstarter quadrant and clock-type spring.

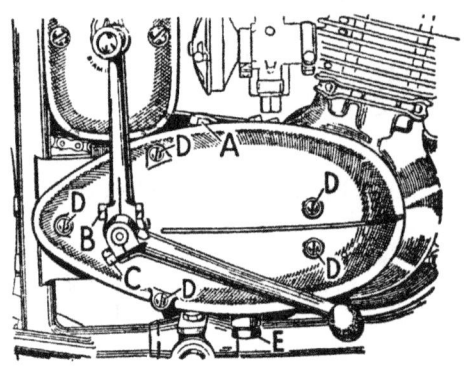

Fig. D7.

The keyed engine sprocket, part number 90–0120, is held on its taper shaft by means of a right-hand threaded nut and double tab washer, one tab of which must be turned back from the engine sprocket securing nut before unscrewing. The second tab is turned over on to a flat on the engine sprocket and need not be touched. Unscrew the nut and take off the tab washer.

Now remove the primary chain by releasing its spring link and using Service Tool number 61–3198, pull the engine sprocket from its tapered keyed shaft. Take care not to lose the key as the sprocket is withdrawn.

B.S.A. Service Sheet No. 505 (contd.)

Clutch

Using Service Tool number 61-3191 compress the clutch springs to allow the large plate retaining circlip and the clutch plate assembly to be removed (Fig. D8). Take out the clutch plates and withdraw the mushroom-headed clutch push rod, part number 90-0098, from the centre of the mainshaft.

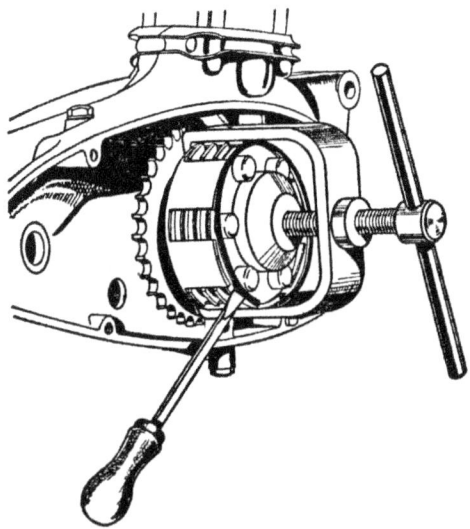

Fig. D8. *Removing the clutch plate circlip with Service Tool number 61-3191.*

The clutch hub nut has a right-hand thread and its removal allows Service Tool number 61-3256 to be used to draw the clutch hub from the splined mainshaft. The centre of the hub has a brass thrust washer, part number 90-0283, in a recess, and the whole hub revolves on a central brass bush, part number 90-0076, which is a sliding fit on the mainshaft and is inserted from the rear, or kickstart ratchet side of the assembly.

Crankcase

Before the crankcase halves can be parted the cylinder and piston must be removed. The procedure is detailed under "Engine Dismantling for Decarbonising", Service Sheet No. 504.

Removal of the eleven cheese-headed countersunk screws, seven short ones along the bottom and rear of crankcase, two long screws and two further screws on the cylinder base will allow the crankcase to be parted. Later models have two additional screws which must also be removed. One is situated just below the rear drive sprocket and the other on the drive side of the crankcase behind the top run of the primary chain.

The front and top rear frame bolt holes in the crankcase are dowelled and great care must be taken in parting the cases to ensure that damage does not occur to either case if leverage is applied at any point by means of a screwdriver or lever.

The mainshaft runs on three ballraces, two on the drive side, part number 89-3023 (inner), and part number 90-0010 (outer), and one on the timing or generator side, part number 89-3023. The two larger races may be pressed out to the inside of the cases, after these have been warmed, and the small race to the outside. Note that on engines after DD-101 and BD3-5138 a circlip has been incorporated between the oil seal, part number 90-0147, and the main bearing on the generator side, the oil seal being outside the bearing.

On the drive side, the oil seal, part number 90-0749, is located inside both bearings on D1 engines after 1954 and all D3 engines. Earlier models have the oil seal, part number 90-0284, between the two main bearings. Take note of the number and thickness of any shims fitted either side of the flywheel assembly; and also of the crankshaft distance collar between the flywheels and bearing on the generator side. This collar has been replaced by an oil drag fan on later models.

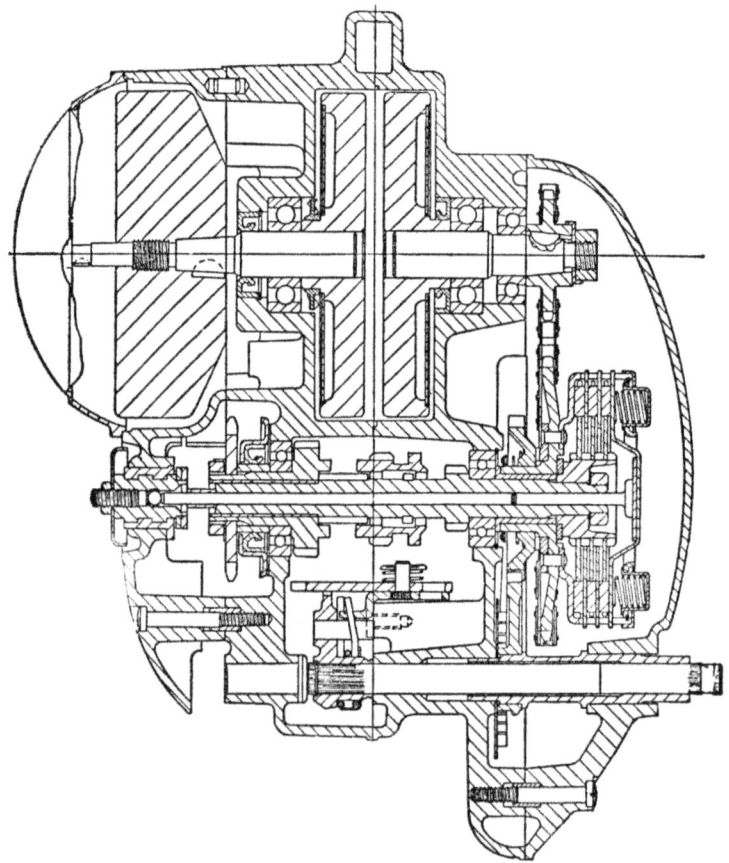

Fig. D8A. *Horizontal section of engine unit.*

Flywheel Assembly

It is advisable at this stage to test the big-end bearing for wear. This is done by taking hold of the connecting rod stem and pulling it upwards until the crank is at top dead centre. Then holding it in this position try gently but firmly to pull and push the connecting rod in the direction of its travel in order to feel whether there is any play.

If the big-end is in a sound condition there should be no play in this direction, although it may be possible to rock the rod sideways, i.e. at right-angles to the axis of the machine. If vertical play is perceptible in the big-end it must be decided whether the amount

B.S.A. Service Sheet No. 505 (contd.)

in evidence is permissible or not. The bearing is not likely to need replacing however, provided that the machine has been carefully used and adequately lubricated, for it is of ample dimensions for the work it has to do. But if for any reason the big-end bearing has deteriorated as the result of neglect or abuse, it should be replaced.

If it has been decided that the big-end bearing must be replaced the flywheels should now be parted, using Service Tool number 61-3206 (Fig. D9). Place the flywheels in the bolster and position the stripping bars, Service Tool number 61-3208. Use the punch Service Tool number 61-3209 to drive out the crankpin. Take off the uppermost flywheel and reverse the lower one in the bolster. Again using Service Tool number 61-3209 drive out the crankpin.

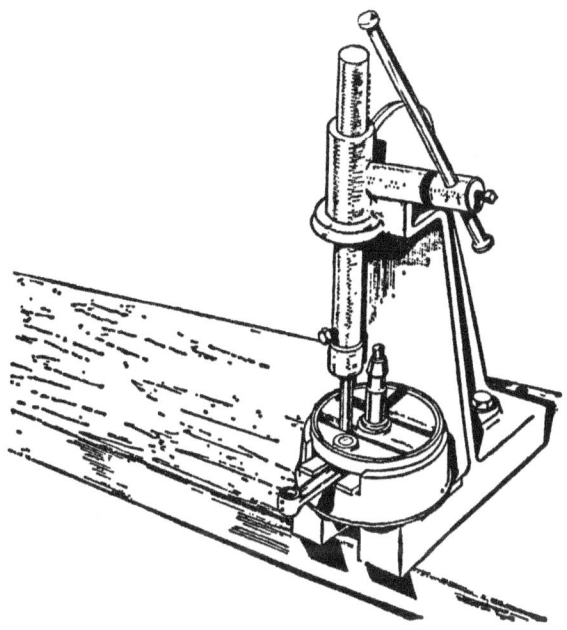

Fig. D9. *Parting the flywheels with Service Tool 61-3206.*

Kickstarter Mechanism

The kickstart ratchet spring, part number 90-0039, is secured in position by a circlip and pressed metal collar. Take off the circlip and collar and remove the kickstarter ratchet pinion.

Gearbox (*see also Service Sheet No. 506*)

The gearbox control shaft carries on its serrated end inside the case a gear selector claw (G) Fig. D16, part number 90-0190. This is held in position by a circlip, part number 90-0051, and fitted around the boss of this claw is a double-ended coil spring. This is housed inside a metal cover (K) part number 90-0054. The two ends of the spring fit one either side of a peg driven into the claw, and also pass over a projection on the bridge piece of the gear selector mechanism, thus acting as a centralizing device for the claw.

The bridge piece, part number 90-0056, is secured by two ¼ in. bolts (B) and locking washers to the alloy case, and carries the gear selector quadrant, on a central pin positioned by a spring and plate.

B.S.A. Service Sheet No. 505 (contd.)

The end of the gear selector quadrant is located in a spring-loaded plunger, part number 90–0047, pressed into the bottom of the alloy case (A) Fig. D16.

The mainshaft oil seal housing (D) Fig. D12, part number 90–0072, is held in position on the gearbox end of the drive side crankcase half by three $\frac{3}{16}$ in. screws and shakeproof washers, which, when removed, reveal a plate (A), part number 90–0133, held by two $\frac{3}{16}$ in. screws and washers. This plate functions as a positioning plate for the gearbox mainshaft ballrace and layshaft phosphor bronze bush.

The mainshaft oil seal housing contains the gearbox sprocket distance sleeve, part number 90–0071, (F), and an oil seal of the spring-loaded type, part number 89–3006 (E).

Clutch Control

The flywheel generator alloy cover (Fig. D6), carries the clutch actuating lever and quick-action screw, part number 90–0180. If this mechanism needs attention, remove the metal cover, part number 90–0106, which acts as a dust cover to the clutch lever actuating screw, then remove the extension spring, part number 19–0122, from the actuating lever and press out the lever and screw from the case. In the centre of the screw is a steel ball, adjusting screw, part number 90–0105, and locknut, part number 89–0366.

This completes the dismantling of the engine and gearbox unit.

Removal of Lucas Generator

The dismantling of the engine unit is identical with the exception of the removal of the generator.

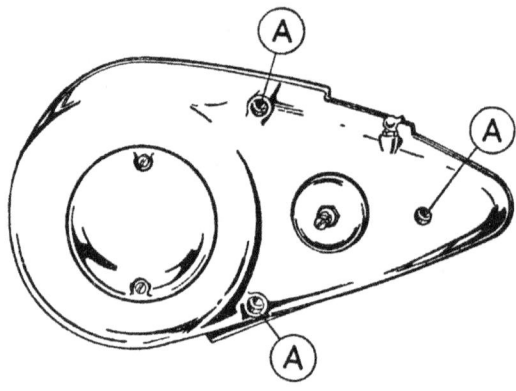

Fig. D10.

Remove the three screws (A) Fig. D10, and take off the cover.

Take off the four ¼ in. nuts holding the stator and remove the centre bolt securing the cam and rotor.

Insert the extractor, tool number 90–0297, screw up tight to remove the rotor from the mainshaft.

B.S.A. MOTOR CYCLES LTD., Service Department, Armoury Road, Birmingham 11.

B.S.A. PRESS

BSA SERVICE SHEET No. 506

MODELS D1, D3, D5 AND D7
RE-ASSEMBLY OF THE ENGINE-GEARBOX UNIT

Crankcase

If new ball races and bushes are to be inserted, warm the two crankcase halves suitably support them to avoid damage, and press in the new parts in their appropriate positions. When dealing with a D1 engine manufactured before 1955, do not forget that the oil seal part number 90-0284, is located between the two drive-side main bearings. Later D1 and all D3 and D5 engines have a different oil seal part number 90-0749, and this is placed next to the flywheels, inside both bearings.

On the generator side, the oil seal part number 90-0147, should be fitted outside the main bearing. Care must be taken not to press in the seal too far, so as to obscure the oil passage to the main bearing. Engines after numbers DD-101 and BD3-5138 have a circlip between the oil seal and bearing. This means that the oil seal is located approximately 0.10 in. further out, and the parallel portion of the flywheel spindle is extended by this amount. If the later type crankcase assembly part number 90-0826, is used to replace a 1954 D3 crankcase assembly part number 90-0777, the circlip should be removed and the oil seal placed closer to the bearing, unless a later type flywheel and con-rod assembly part number 90-0823, or a flywheel spindle part number 90-0821, is fitted at the same time.

Replace the spring-loaded ball socket (A) Fig. D16 in its recess in the bottom of the offside crankcase.

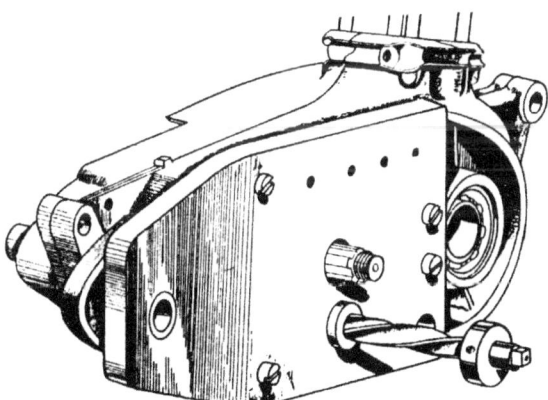

Fig. D11. *Line Reaming the Gearbox Bushes with Service Tool 61-3199.*

If the gearbox phosphor bronze bushes have been renewed, bolt the two crankcase halves together and line-ream the bushes, using Service Tool 61-3199 and reamer number 61-3205 (Fig. D11). Make sure that **all s**warf is removed after this operation.

B.S.A. Service Sheet No. 506 (contd.)

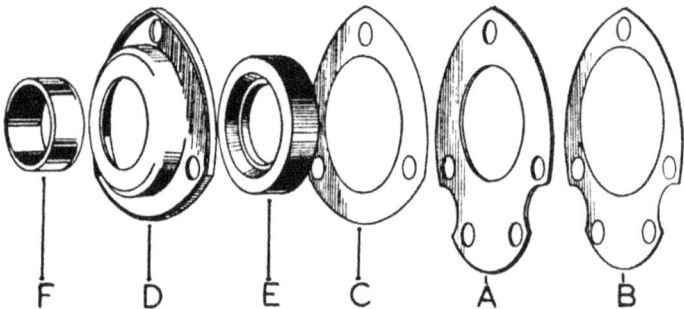

Fig. D11a. *The Oil Seal Assembly.*

Next secure the gearbox mainshaft ball race and layshaft bush retaining end plate (A) Fig. D11a, part number 90–0133, on the nearside case with its two 3/16 in. cheese-headed screws, followed by the triangular oil seal housing washer (C) part number 90–0073, the mainshaft oil seal housing (D) part number 90–0072, and the oil seal (E) part number 89–3006, with the steel sleeve (F) part number 90–0071, in the centre of the assembly. Note that a gasket (B) is fitted between the end plate and the crankcase.

The following details are intended to assist people who wish to complete their own flywheel repairs. Owners are reminded, however, that fully reconditioned and guaranteed flywheel assemblies are avilable through the B.S.A. Exchange Replacement Service and can be purchased from appointed B.S.A. Dealers or Stockists.

This Service is recommended in view of the skill and specialised equipment necessary to make a first-class job.

Flywheel Assembly

The 1955 pattern flywheel spindles 90–0821 (nearside) and 90–0505 (offside), can be used as replacements in all earlier engines having a Wipac generator. For Lucas equipment, flywheel spindles 90–0605 (nearside) and 90–0505 (offside) should be used. When fitted to

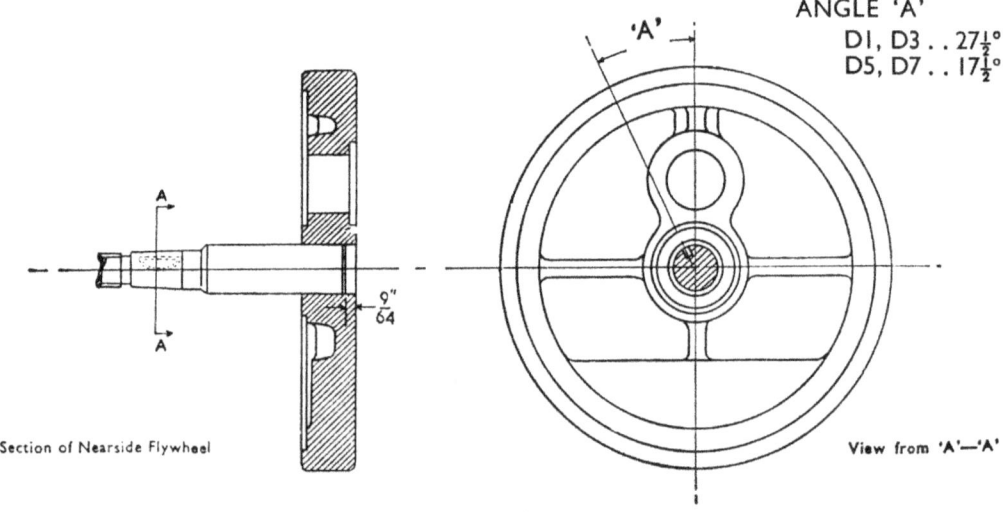

Fig. D12.

B.S.A. Service Sheet No. 506 (contd.)

flywheel assemblies which have the narrow type of big-end bearing ($\frac{1}{4} \times \frac{1}{4}$ in. rollers), these spindles must be assembled so that they are recessed 9/64 in. from the inside faces of the flywheels. With the wide big-end bearing ($\frac{1}{4} \times \frac{3}{8}$ in. rollers), the spindles must be assembled flush with the faces of the big-end recesses in the flywheels. The nearside spindle on all models must be located as shown in Fig. D12.

It is not advisable to attempt to take up wear in the big-end assembly by fitting over-size rollers, since the connecting rod, rollers, and crankpin are carefully matched before leaving the Works. We strongly recommend that a complete replacement assembly be used.

To assemble place the nearside flywheel in bolster, Service Tool 61-3206, and using a suitable hand press insert one side of the new crankpin. Postition the second flywheel over the crankpin and using bridge piece Service Tool 61-3210 press the flywheel on to the crankpin as illustrated in Fig. D13.

The flywheel will now be only approximately aligned and further steps must be taken to ensure that the wheels and shafts are brought within necessary limits. Two of the actual or similar bearings used in the engine should be fitted to the main shafts and the assembly mounted in vee-blocks as in Fig. D14.

Fig. D13—Reassembly of the Flywheels.   Fig. D14—Checking Flywheel Alignment.

Using a dial micrometer the accuracy of the assembly can be measured. Any necessary corrections should be done by the careful use of a mallet or lead hammer applied to the flywheels and the wheels should be brought within the limit of .004 in. on the rims and .006 in. on the inner faces. Shafts should be trued to within .002 in. maximum.

The big-end assembly having been renewed and the flywheels checked for balance and concentricity, replace the flywheel side plates into their recesses and secure by "dot" punching the edge of the flywheels over the edges of the sheet metal plates (Fig. D15). NOTE:—No side plates are used on the D5.

RE-CHECK THE FLYWHEELS FOR TRUTH.

B.S.A. Service Sheet No. 506 (contd.)

The next step is to check the end float of the flywheel assembly in the crankcase, and adjust if necessary. Shim washers of various thicknesses are supplied for this purpose.

Place a .010 in. shim on the offside spindle, and insert the latter through the main bearings and oil seal in the offside crankcase. Fit the distance collar part number 90-0243, or the oil drag fan part number 90-0750, in position over the nearside spindle. The nearside crankcase should then be replaced, and the two halves screwed together temporily. Measure the amount of end float on the flywheel assembly, which should be .004 to .006 in. Remove the nearside crankcase and fit any shims which may be required on the nearside spindle, next to the flywheel.

If the flywheel assembly has not been disturbed, replace the original shims in their original positions.

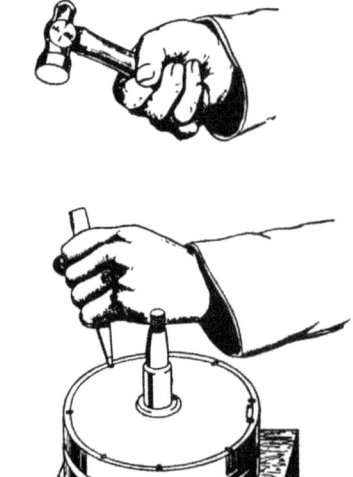

Fig. D15.

Later models with engine prefix letters DD, DDB or ED5, use shims only between the left-hand flywheel and the bearing, these are available in sizes .003/.004/.005/.010 in.

Gearbox

Now fit the gear quadrant selector mechanism to the offside crankcase. Engage the quadrant with the spring-loaded locating plunger in the bottom of the case, (A) Fig. D16, the quadrant to be at its innermost position in relation to the plunger; this is bottom gear. Secure in position by fitting the two bolts (B) with their tab locking washers, turning over the tabs to lock the bolts.

Next pass the splined end of the gearbox mainshaft through the offside ballrace already placed in its recess, followed by the mainshaft sliding gear (C), and then the mainshaft primary gear.

Now place the large layshaft gear (D), (this is the gear having the centre machined to engage with the dogs of the selector gear) concave side downward against the phosphor bronze bush in the bottom of the case in mesh with the small mainshaft pinion.

Engage the two central selecting or sliding gears, one already in position on the mainshaft, so that the small dog on the gear selector arm (E) enters the track machined on the side of the lower or layshaft gear (F), the upperside of this gear track engaging with the solid machined ring on the mainshaft sliding gear (C).

Insert the layshaft through the lower gears and engage the gear train (see Fig. D16).

B.S.A. Service Sheet No. 506 (contd.)

Next pass the footchange pedal lever shaft with its spring-loaded claw assembled (G) through its bearing hole in the offside case. Engage the ends of the spring attached to the claw on either side of the projection on the gear selector mechanism, securing the bridge piece between the two bolts, the claw facing the gears.

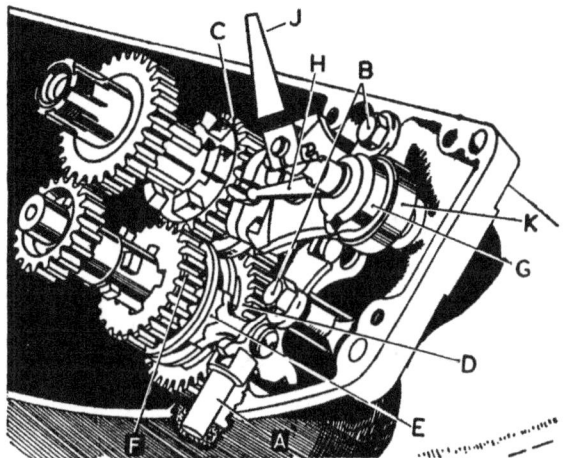

Fig. D16. *The Gear Cluster.*

Apply jointing compound evenly to the edge of one crankcase and allow it to become "tacky". Insert the gear position indicator spindle (H), into its bearing hole in the nearside crankcase, and attach the indicator lever (J), to the outer end of the spindle, pointing upwards. Place the nearside crankcase in position, passing the engine mainshaft and gearbox pinion sleeve through their respective races, taking care that the ball end of the inside gear indicator lever enters its recess on the gear selector arm. Later models do not have this indicator, its place being taken by a thrust pad.

Secure the two crankcase halves together by means of the eleven cheese-headed screws (thirteen on later models), tightening them evenly all round to avoid distortion. Note that a spring washer is fitted behind the head of each screw.

Place the kickstarter clock-type return spring, part number 90-0089, in position on the kickstart quadrant shaft, then slide the circular distance plate, part number 90-0090 on to the quadrant shaft against the spring between the spring and the alloy case. Insert the assembly on to the gear selector shaft, placing one end of the spring into the recess at the rear of the case above the dowel hole. Give one turn of tension to the spring and push the kickstart quadrant home into its recess in wall of alloy case with the quadrant against its stop below the dowel hole.

Clutch and Transmission

Enter the clutch chainwheel with its centre bush in position, flange at the rear, on to the splined end of the gearbox shaft, which is projecting through the case, having previously assembled the ratchet and spring on to the shaft (see Fig. D17).

B.S.A. Service Sheet No. 506 (contd.)

Place the thrust washer into its recess on the inside of the clutch chainwheel assembly, slide the clutch hub, part number 90–0028, on to the splines and secure by the large nut, part number 21-0007. Enter the mushroom-headed clutch push rod, part number 90–0098, to the hole in the centre of the shaft.

Fig. D17. *The Clutch (exploded view).*

The clutch plates are now inserted into the centre of the chainwheel assembly, cork plate first then steel plate in sequence, the last plate being the domed clutch actuating plate, part number 90–0037 (Fig. D17).

Next insert the six springs into the spring cups and place them in the holes in the spring plate, part number 90–0341, the raised centre of the plate outwards. Using Service Too, number 61–3191, compress the springs, and place the large circlip, part number 90–0027, into its groove on the inside of clutch plate housing (Fig. D8, Service Sheet No. 505).

The crankshaft sprocket should now be placed on its taper-keyed engine shaft, followed by the double tab washer, part number 90–0121, one tab resting on the flat on the engine sprocket. Screw the securing nut, up tightly, and turn the second tab over on to the nut face.

Place primary chain over the sprockets and fit the spring link. Now fit the dome-shaped alloy primary chain cover with a cemented paper washer on the jointing face, over the primary drive assembly, passing the kickstart quadrant shaft through its hole in rear of the cover. Secure with five cheese-headed screws, the two longest screws in the front holes in the cover. Note that each screw is fitted with a fibre washer.

Fit kickstart pedal and foot gearchange lever to their respective shafts.

Now turn the unit round and insert the second clutch push rod, part number 90–0099, into the hole in gearbox mainshaft. Slide the rubber oil seal washer, part number 90–0132, on to the rod.

The gearbox sprocket, is pushed on to the splines projecting through the gearbox end of the nearside case, then secured by nut and splined washer, the edge of which is turned over on to the nut as a locking device.

B.S.A. Service Sheet No. 506 (contd.)

The flywheel generator alloy cover carries the clutch actuating lever and quick-action mechanism, which is pressed into this cover from the inside when the cover has been warmed. A flat on the collar of the actuating screw positions this part in the cover (Fig. D18).

In the centre of the quick-action screw is a ball and adjusting screw, part number 90–0105, with locknut, part number 89–0366. The metal cover, part number 90–0106, presses over the quick-action screw from the outside of the cover. Attach the extension spring, part number 90–0122, to its hole in the lever and the hole in the inside of the cover.

Place the crankcase outer cover, in position on the nearside case. This cover carries the clutch operating lever and adjuster. Five cheese-headed screws, two inside and three outside, secure the cover to the crankcase.

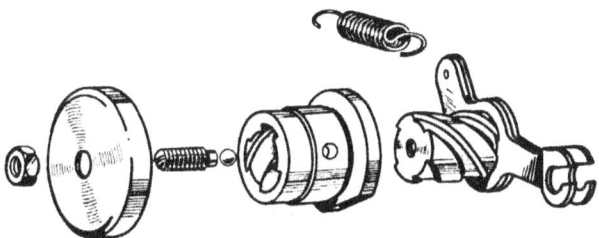

Fig. D18. *The Clutch Actuating Mechanism.*

Flywheel Generator (Wico-Pacy)

Place flywheel on the keyed-taper of the engine mainshaft, followed by the large shakeproof washer, and tighten the nut. Make sure key has not fallen out.

Now insert the electrical ignition unit carrying the plug lead into its recess. Three elongated ears on the outside of this unit allow the screws to be passed through the unit securing it to the flywheel cover (Fig. D4).

The "make and break" cam is now inserted into the centre of this unit on to the keyed end of the engine mainshaft and secured by a 3/16 in. screw and spring washer.

Variation of the ignition timing is obtained by moving the whole unit to and fro' on the elongated slots on the outside of the unit. Adjust "make and break" points if necessary. See Service Sheet No. 503. Set the ignition timing so that the points are just breaking with the piston 5/32 in. (3.75 mm.) before top dead centre.

The watertight cover is now placed in position and secured by the two screws.

The remainder of the unit is assembled as after decarbonisation (see Service Sheet No. 504).

B.S.A. Service Sheet No. 506 (contd.)

Reassembly of the Lucas Generator

The procedure for reassembly of the Lucas generator is merely the reverse to that described on Service Sheet No. 505 for dismantling, but the following should be specially noted:—
Provision is made for the easy removal and replacement of the steady bearing and bearing plate; the cam and steady bearing journal are both press-fits on to the rotor shaft and can be removed by means of a suitable extractor of standard pattern. On reassembly, it is imperative that the cam is correctly fitted in relation to the rotor shaft or the performance of the machine will be adversely affected when the engine is run with the ingition switch in the "emergency start" position.

The following precaution must be taken in order that the steady bearing is correctly aligned. During the re-fitting operation, the four contact plate fixing screws should be slackened off and should not be re-tightened until the remainder of the re-fitting operations are completed, i.e. the alternator fixing bolts and the rotor retaining bolt should be fully tightened before finally tightening the contact plate fixing screws. The fixing screw holes in the contact plate are drilled oversize and providing the foregoing precautions are observed the contact plate will automatically align the steady bearing with the rotor shaft.

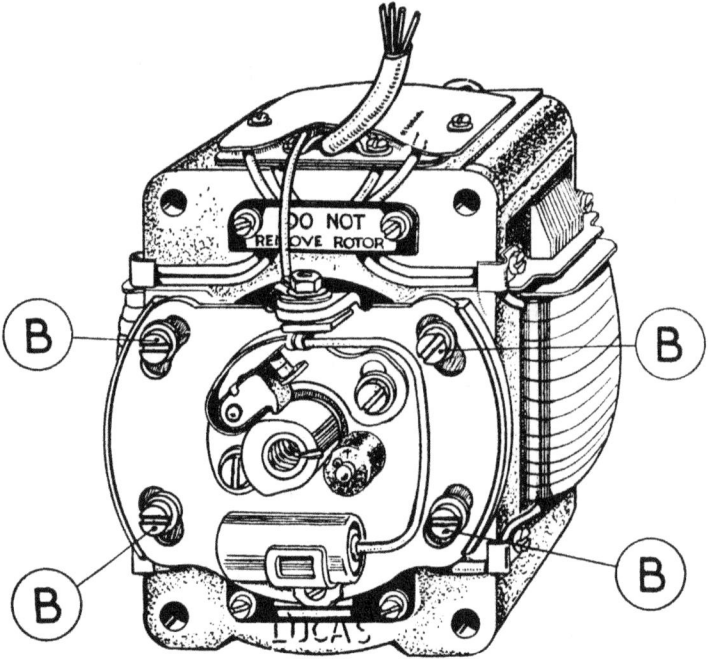

Fig. D18a.

Timing with the Lucas Generator

Variation of the ignition timing is obtained by slackening off the four screws (B) Fig. D18a, and turning the timing control in the desired direction.

Movement in an anti-clockwise direction will retard the spark, and in a clockwise direction will advance the spark.

B.S.A. MOTOR CYCLES LTD., Service Department, Armoury Road, Birmingham 11.

Printed in England   B.S.A. Press

BSA SERVICE SHEET No. 507

Models D1, D3, D5, and D7
PRIMARY TRANSMISSION

Clutch Adjustment

There must always be a slight amount of play in the clutch withdrawal mechanism in the gearbox, or a short length of free cable at the handlebar lever end. If the play becomes excessive, difficulty will be experienced in changing gear, as the clutch may not fully disengage, in which case the control should be adjusted.

The clutch adjustment will be found at the left-hand end of the gearbox mainshaft (Fig. D21) and it consists of an adjusting pin (A) screwed into the clutch withdrawal quick thread sleeve and a locknut (B) to secure it in position. This adjusting pin presses against the clutch withdrawal rod with a steel ball interposed. (On the model D.7. the adjuster is concealed underneath the pear shaped cover on the left-hand side of the engine.)

The withdrawal mechanism must at all times be so adjusted that there is a slight amount of play between the pin, the steel ball and the operating rod, in order to ensure that the clutch springs may exert their full pressure on the driving and driven plates. If there is not sufficient play there will be a tendency for the clutch to slip continually owing to reduced spring pressure, and this in turn will cause over-heating and serious damage to the clutch itself.

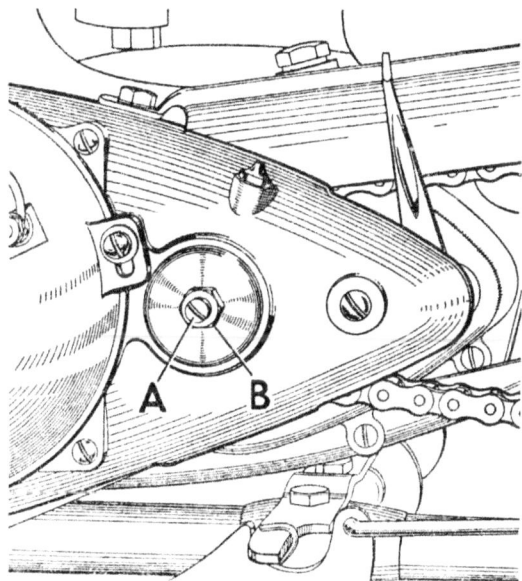

Fig. D 21 — Clutch control adjustment

To adjust, release the locknut and holding it with a spanner turn the adjusting pin back one or two turns with a screwdriver. Then, still holding the locknut with a spanner, screw the adjusting pin gently in until it is felt to meet some resistance. Then unscrew it half-a-turn and holding it in this position retighten the locknut. If the adjustment is correctly made in this manner, it will be found that there is a small amount of free play at the clutch lever on the left handlebar before this is felt to take up the spring pressure during the action of declutching.

B.S.A. Service Sheet No. 507 (cont.)

Front Chain

The front chain runs on short fixed centres and adjustment for tension is neither required nor provided for.

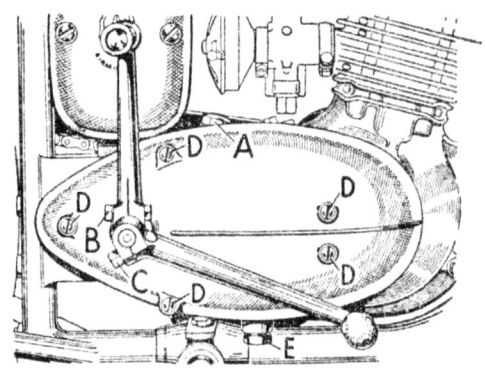

Fig. D 19

This chain will run for many thousands of miles before examination is required. This operation involves the removal of the primary chain cover (Fig. D19) after the kick-starter and gear change pedals, both of which are mounted on splines and locked by pinch bolts ("B" and "C" respectively) have been removed together with the five securing screws ("D"). The normal up and down play on the front chain is up to $\frac{3}{8}$ in. (1 cm.) and the maximum permissible, indicating that the chain is unduly worn and requires replacement, is about $\frac{3}{4}$ in. (2 cm.).

Remember when replacing a chain fitted with a detachable connecting link, that the spring fastener must always be put on with the closed end facing the forward direction of travel i.e. on the top run of the chain.

B.S.A. MOTOR CYCLES LTD.
Service Dept., Armoury Road,
Birmingham, 11
Printed in England.

BSA SERVICE SHEET No. 508

MODELS D1, D3, D5 AND C10L

DISMANTLING AND RE-ASSEMBLY OF THE HUBS AND BRAKES

FRONT WHEEL

To remove the front wheel from the forks, disconnect the brake cable at the brake arm on the cover plate, by removing the ¼ in. diameter round head bolt and nut holding the "U" shaped cable clip. Unscrew the cable adjuster, withdraw the cable and place it out of the way.

Unscrew the two spindle nuts, using the plug spanner, and remove the three mudguard stay bolts on the left-hand fork end bracket. (The latter is not necessary on earlier models, where the mudguard is attached to the outer fork tubes). Lift the left-hand lower fork leg away from the spindle, and pull the wheel away from the right-hand leg, so that the brake anchor plate clears it. The wheel will then drop out.

FRONT BRAKE

Unscrew and remove the spindle nut securing the cover plate. The plate can now be withdrawn and the brake shoes examined. It is not advisable to remove the shoes from the cover plate unless the linings require renewal.

If it is necessary to remove the shoes, first take off the brake lever (A) Fig. D22, and tap in the cam (B) until the cam plate clears the shoes. Insert a screwdriver between the brake shoes adjacent to the fulcrum pin (C) and twist the screwdriver. Place a small lever, (D) between the shoe and the anchor plate and lever the shoe upwards until the spring tension is released. The shoes can then be lifted from the cover plate.

If the shoes require re-lining, see Service Sheet No. 612.

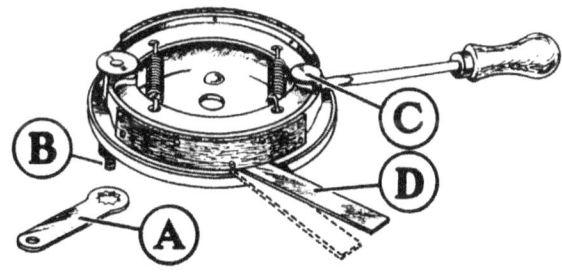

Fig. D22.

B.S.A. Service Sheet No. 508 (contd.)

FRONT WHEEL BEARINGS (Standard Model)

If it is necessary to remove the bearings for examination or cleaning, unscrew the locknut (L) and spindle nut (A) Fig. D23, and tap the spindle right through, using a hide mallet and soft drift to prevent damage to the threads.

The dust caps (B) can be prised off with the aid of a screwdriver between the cap and the edge of the spoke flange. Care should be taken to work the caps off a little at a time, to avoid distortion. Next unscrew the lock ring (G) securing the outer ring of the ball journal on the brake side. This ring has a left-hand thread.

Take out the felt washers (C) and (H) and the plain steel washers (D).

The ball journals can now be inspected, but they should not be removed unless new ones are required.

If it is necessary to renew the journals the hub should be supported at the brake drum end. With the aid of a suitable soft drift applied to the inner ring of the ball journal,(E) Fig. D23, drive the journal in towards the centre of the hub. This will cause the brake drum side journal to be driven out. When it is clear of the hub, take out the distance piece (F) and pass a drift through the hub until contact is made with the other journal, in order to drive it out.

Note:—This procedure is possible only on machines after engine number YD-2850. Earlier models have no deep counterbore in the hub and the journals must be driven out from opposite ends after the distance piece (F) has been displaced slightly to allow a soft drift to be applied to the inner ring of the race.

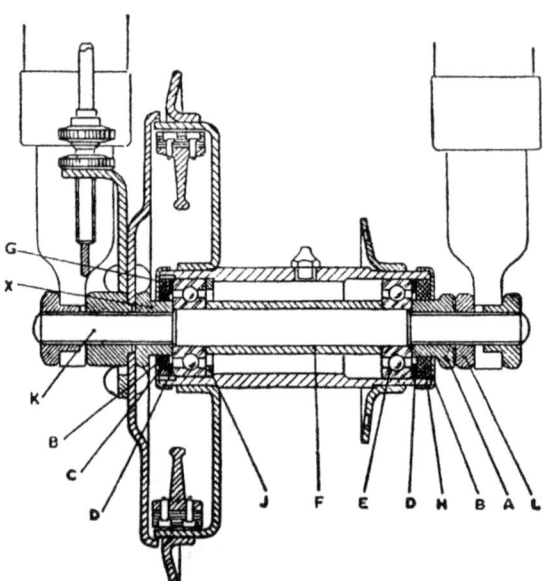

Fig. D23.

B.S.A. Service Sheet No. 508 (contd.)

COMPETITION MODELS

The front hubs are fitted with adjustable taper-roller bearings as illustrated in Fig. D23a, but instructions for removing the wheel and dismantling the brake are identical with those for standard machines.

To dismantle the bearings, unscrew the two locknuts (M) and (N), remove the brake plate washer (P) and bearing distance piece (R), prise off the dust caps (S), and take out the felt washers (T). The spindle may now be withdrawn from the brake drum side, leaving only the bearings, felt retaining cups (U) and bearing abutment rings (V) and (W) in the

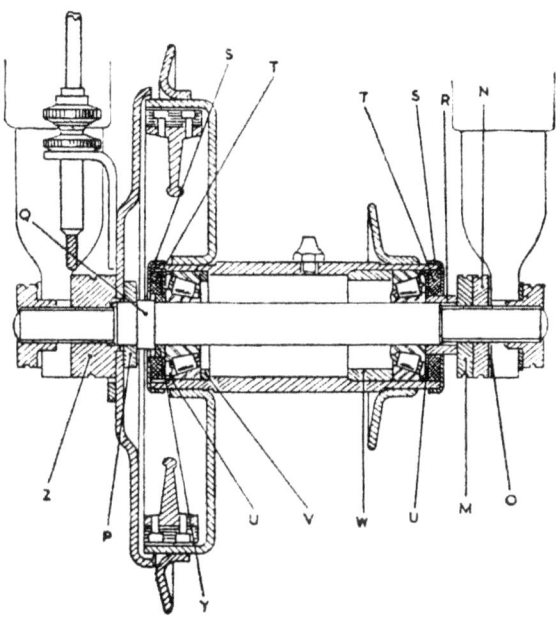

Fig. D23a.

hub. With the hub suitably supported at the brake drum end and a soft drift applied against the abutment ring (V), the ring itself, the bearing and the retaining cup (U) may be driven out in one operation, during which the drift should be moved around the circumference of the abutment ring to ensure even extraction. The hub may now be turned over and the same procedure adopted for removal of the corresponding parts in the other side of the hub.

Note:—The front spindle assembly of the early competition models differed slightly in that the spindle itself had no fixed collar (Q), brake plate washer (P) or bearing thrust washer (Y). These parts replace a shaped nut which was screwed along the brake drum side threaded end of the spindle, tight against the spindle shoulder. Also, a shaped nut was used in the place of the existing distance piece (R) and nut (M). These points should be borne in mind when dismantling and reassembling, but the procedure otherwise is the same as for the current type hub described.

B.S.A. Service Sheet No. 508 (contd.)

REAR WHEEL

To remove the rear wheel from the frame, disconnect the brake rod by unscrewing the knurled adjusting nut and lift the rod out of the way.

Uncouple the chain at the connecting link, and run the chain off the sprockets after first placing a clean piece of paper or other suitable material underneath the machine to protect the chain from road or floor grit.

Disconnect the speedometer drive by unscrewing the locknut on the speedometer gearbox.

Slacken off the spindle nuts sufficiently to draw the wheel out of the fork ends. Lean the machine over and draw the wheel out under the left-hand chainstay.

REAR BRAKE

The brake cover plate and shoes are identical with those of the front wheel, and the instructions given for removal will apply equally to the rear brake.

REAR BEARINGS

The rear wheel hub is identical with that in the front wheel except that a speedometer drive gearbox is fitted to the offside. This is held in position by a plain washer and an additional locknut; after removing the locknut the gearbox can be drawn straight off the hub barrel. The instructions given for removal of the front hub bearings will apply equally to the rear hub, except that on spring frame models the inner locknut (corresponding to "L" on Fig. D23) is replaced with a plain distance collar.

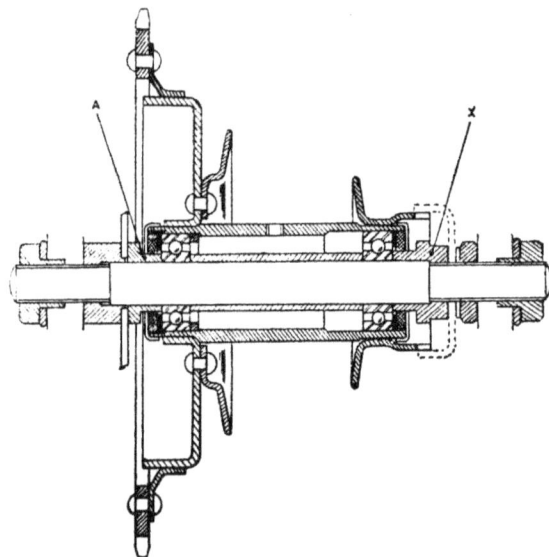

Fig. D23b.

Note:—On later spring frame models (1958 onwards) the distance collar is omitted; correct positionig of the speedometer gearbox allowed for by the shape of the spindle nut (x), Fig. D23b.

B.S.A. Service Sheet No. 508 (contd.

The rear hub spindle assembly is also different in other respects, but removal of the wheel and dismantling of the brake is the same as for earlier models, as also is the procedure for removing the speedometer gearbox. After these operations have been carried out, the spindle can be tapped through from the brake drum side, as the part (A) Fig. 23b, is merely a distance piece; which will then fall away. From this stage, dismantling is again the same as for earlier models.

REASSEMBLY OF THE HUBS

The following applies to all hubs, except the front hub on competition models, and refer to the illustration Fig. D23, unless otherwise stated. If new ball journals are to be fitted first place the distance piece (J) in position in the hub barrel, brake drum side, and press in the hub journal, taking care to see that it is square to the housing. Insert one plain steel washer (D) and then screw in the lock ring (G). This has a left-hand thread. Reverse the hub, insert the inner distance sleeve (F), and push the spindle (K) through the bearing and distance sleeve. At this stage, if the hub has been cleaned out, it should be re-packed with grease. Place the second journal in position and press it into the housing until the inner distance sleeve is firmly gripped, and remove the spindle. Replace the other plain washer (D), felt washers (C) and dust caps (B), and re-insert the spindle so that the "fixed" nut is on the brake drum side, except on the rear hubs of the later spring frame models; where it should be on the opposite side.

The "fixed" nut is marked (X) on both illustrations, Fig.s D23 and D23b, and has been left undisturbed on the spindle throughout all the previously mentioned operations. If, for any reason, it has been slackened; it should be retightened firmly against the shoulder of the spindle. The "fixed" nut is located on the longer-threaded end of the spindles fitted to all front wheels and the later type spring frame rear wheel. On the rear wheels fitted to pre-1953 spring frame models and all rigid frame rear wheels the "fixed" nut is located on the shorter-threaded end of the spindle.

The spindle nut (A) may now be replaced and thoroughly tightened, except on the later spring frame rear hub where it is necessary to replace the distance collar (A) Fig. D23b, and the brake cover plate complete with shoes, before finally tightening down with the brake cover plate nut. In each case the tightening of the nut will lock together the spindle, the inner rings of the journals, and the sleeve (F). This assembly should rotate freely in the ball races if the journals have been pressed in squarely. On the ohter wheels, the brake cover plate and its nut should now be replaced, and the nut sequrely tightened. It should be noted that in each case the brake cover plate nut has a spigot which must be correctly located in the centre hole of the brake plate before the nut is tightened. The locknut (L) should now be replaced and tightened against the spindle nut (A) — front hub and rigid frame rear hub only.

Refitting of the speedometer drive gearbox will now complete the reassembly. This may be placed straight over the wheel spindle on the rigid frame models and on the lates spring frame models, making sure the driving dogs are located correctly in the recesses in the end of the hub barrel. The plain washer and the outer locknut should then be replaced and tightened securely. On earlier spring frame models the plain distance collar must be replaced before the speedometer drive gearbox is refitted.

Where a speedometer is not fitted, a plain hub-end cap (part number 90-6029) should be fitted in place of the speedo gearbox.

B.S.A. Service Sheet No. 508 (contd.)

REASSEMBLY (Competition Front Hub)

All references will be to Fig. D23a.

Place the distance piece (v) in position in the brake drum side of the hub barrel and press the outer ring only of the taper-roller race firmly and squarely up to it. Reverse the hub, place in the distance piece (w) and press in the outer ring of the other race in the same manner.

Take the hub bearing thrust washer (Y) and slide it along almost the full length of the spindle, up to the spindle shoulder. Place the remainder of the brake drum side bearing (inner ring complete with cage and rollers) in position, backing it up to the thrust washer. Insert the spindle into the hub from the brake drum side, re-pack the hub with grease and slide into position the remainder of the other bearing. Press in the felt retainers (U), followed by the felt grease seals (T), and press on the dust caps (S). Owing to the "fixed" nut used on early spindles, the brake side bearing and oil seal assembly must be positioned in the hub before the spindle is inserted. Refit the bearing distance piece (R) and screw on to the spindle the nuts (M) and (N), locking them together when the correct bearing adjustment is obtained. Over-tightening of the hub bearings will cause rapid wear and when the wheel is refitted into the forks, just perceptible play (about 1/32 in.) should be felt at the rim.

Replace the brake plate washer (P) and the brake cover plate and its nut (Z), the spigot of which must be correctly located through the hole in the centre of the brake cover plate, before tightening securely.

SPECIAL NOTE (All Front Wheels)

The dimension over the front hub locknuts, inside the fork ends, must be maintained between 4.910–4.920 in. To adjust, use shims part number 90-5545 as required, between locknut and bearing abutment nut. On competition models the shims can be interposed at point (O) Fig. D23a, to avoid disturbing the bearing adjustment. It will be necessary to add shims periodically, as bearing wear progresses, and after each re-adjustment.

REPLACING THE WHEELS

Reassembly of the wheels is the reverse procedure to removal, except that care must be taken to locate the brake plate anchorages correctly, over the lower fork sliding member in the case of the front wheel, and over the fork end stud in the case of the rear wheel. Care must also be taken to see that the speedometer gearbox is lined up to the cable. Sharp bends in the cable will result in fracture of the inner wire.

Couple up the brakes and chain, adjust the wheels in the fork ends, lock securely, and finally adjust the brakes by means of their respective knurled thumb screws.

REAR CHAIN ADJUSTMENT

The rear chain is adjusted by means of screw adjusters in the fork ends behind the wheel spindle. Slacken off the nuts (A) Fig. D23c, and screw the adjusters (B) in or out until the chain tension is correct with an up and down movement of three-quarters of an inch (2 cm.). Make sure that the adjustment is equal on both sides of the wheel so that the latter is in correct alignment in the frame. This can be done either by glancing along the line of both wheels when the front wheel is set straight, or by means of a long straight-edge or the edge

B.S.A. Service Sheet No. 508 (contd.)

of a plank placed along the sides of the wheels. The straight-edge should touch both walls of both tyres.

After adjusting retighten the nuts (A).

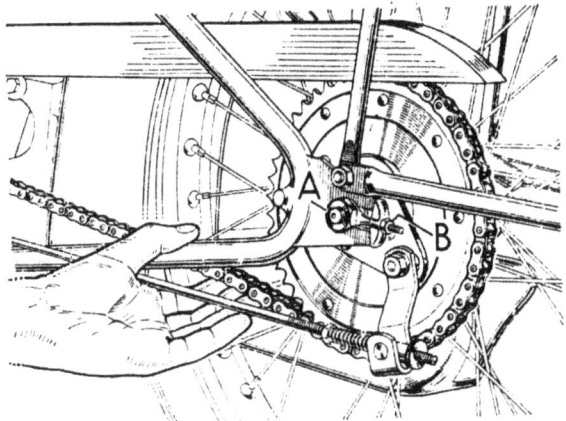

Fig. D23c.

On spring frame machines the rear chain should be adjusted when the machine is on its stand and the rear wheel in its lowest position. The adjustment should the be made so that the chain has a total up and down movement of ½ in. in the centre of the chain run at its tightest point.

In the case of the D3 and D5 swinging arm models, the movement should be ¾ in. (2 cm.) again with the machine on its stand.

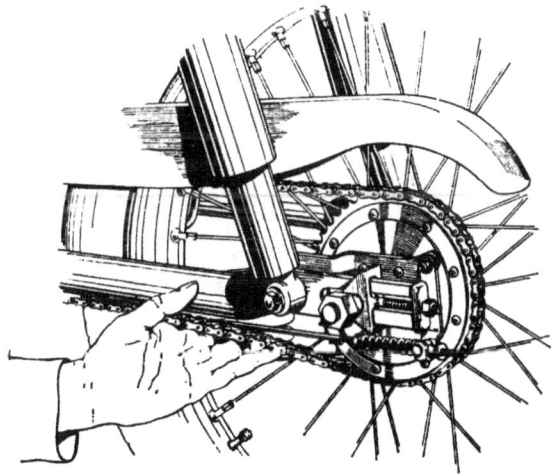

Fig. D23d.

B.S.A. MOTOR CYCLES LTD., Service Department, Armoury Road, Birmingham 11.
Printed in England
B.S.A. PRESS

BSA SERVICE SHEET No. 509

Models D1, D3, D5 and C10L — up to 1956
(for C10L 1956 onwards, please see Service Sheet No. 706)

REMOVAL AND DISMANTLING OF THE FRONT FORKS AND STEERING HEAD

Remove the front wheel as described in Service Sheet No. 508.

If only attention to the sliding members and bushes is required it is not necessary to dismantle the top part of the fork assembly but the mudguard must be unbolted from the lower fork members. On early D1 models the mudguard is attached to the upper fork tubes and removal is only necessary if the forks are to be completely dismantled.

Free the top end of the telescopic gaiters from the oil seal holders (B) Fig. D25, and slide the gaiters down the lower tubes. Remove the locking clips engaging in the top groove of the oil seal holders, which can then be unscrewed. On early models these clips are secured by the mudguard stay studs and later by the grease nipples which are screwed into the outer fork tube. Very early D1 models have no locking clips and the fork bushes on these models are non-detachable.

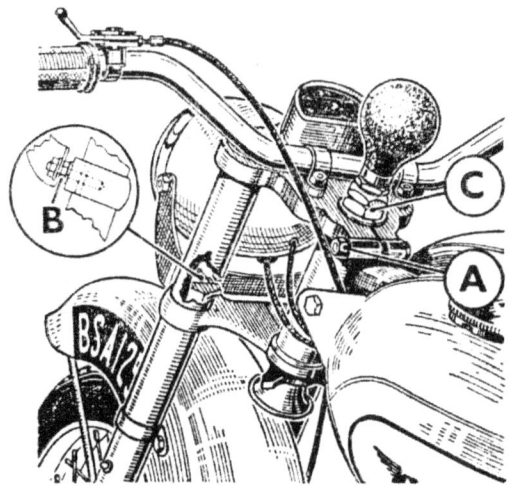

FIG. D24. *Front fork and steering head.*

Remove the two small nuts (A) Fig. D25, from the top of the two large nuts in the top yoke. On D3 and C10L models the small domed caps must first be removed. They should be levered up with the tang of a file inserted in the small hole in the edge of the dome. The sliding members complete with their springs can then be withdrawn from the bottom of the fixed tubes.

To detach the springs, hold the lower leg in a vice, as shown in Fig. D26, and using a small punch tap the spring from its thread. The spring can be removed from its upper end housing in a similar manner. Some models have a rubber tube fitted inside the spring to increase the resistance of the fork, and this can only be removed if one end of the spring is detached.

With the sliding tubes removed the lower fork bushes can be withdrawn. Removal of the grease nipples in the side of the outer legs will allow the fork bush distance piece

B.S.A. Service Sheet No. 509 (contd.)

and top bush to be pulled out of the fork outer tube with the aid of a spoke or other similar tool. On D1 models before frame No. YD1-57331 the fork bushes are non-detachable and if they show signs of wear then the fork outer tubes complete must be replaced by the later type.

Detach the clutch cable from the handlebar lever and remove the headlamp switch handlebar lever, when fitted. Removal of the four nuts beneath the fork top yoke which retain the handlebar clips or aluminium cover plate will allow the handlebars to be lifted away from the top yoke. If a bulb type horn is fitted in the streering head this should be removed before the handlebars.

From this point onwards the dismantling procedure for the D1 fork is slightly different from that for the other models and will be described first.

Remove the two nuts (D) Fig. D27, together with washers (E) and the two locknuts (C). Remove the headlamp from its bracket and lower it to the full extent of the wiring harness. This will allow access to the underside of the top yoke so that the speedometer cables can be disconnected and the instrument removed.

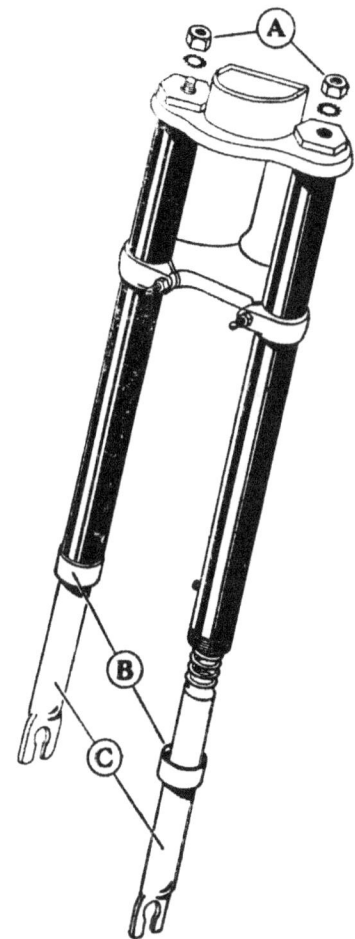

Fig. D25.

FIG. D26. *Removing the front fork springs.*

Slackening off the pinch bolt at the back of the top yoke will permit the yoke to be removed and placed aside, noting that it will be necessary to hold the lower part of the fork in position to prevent the balls of the lower head bearing dropping away. Pull the headlamp cowl assembly (when fitted) off the fork outer tubes and lift the headlamp over the forks so that it is resting securely on the petrol tank. As the remainder of the fork is withdrawn from the frame head a piece of clean rag should be held underneath the bottom yoke to catch any ball bearings which may escape.

B.S.A. Service Sheet No. 509 (contd.)

To remove the outer fork tubes place the assembly on a bench and slacken the pinch nuts (A) Fig. D28, in the bottom yoke. Expand the slots in the yoke by inserting a screwdriver as shown in Fig. D28 and draw the tubes down until they are resting on the large washers. Replace the nuts (D) and tap gently to remove the washers. The fork outer tubes can now be withdrawn.

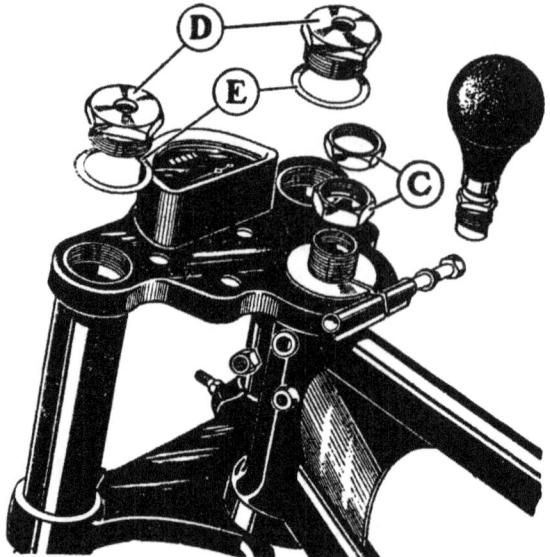

The trumpet part of the horn (when fitted) can be removed by unscrewing the slotted collar (B) Fig. D28.

On D3, D5 and C10L models the outer tubes are a taper fit in the top yoke and they should be freed by undoing the pinch nuts (A) Fig. D28, in the lower yoke and slackening the top nuts (D) Fig. D27, by about two turns. A sharp tap on the head of the nut with a hide mallet will free the tube and dismantling can then proceed as for the D1.

Fig. D27.

To remove the top yoke it is not necessary to undo the castellated sleeve nut on the fork stem and this will hold the lower part of the fork in position until it is ready to be removed.

When the forks have been dismantled the bearing cups can be removed from the frame head by screwing in Service Tool 61-3060 and driving them out from the opposite end with a suitable punch. Do not disturb the cups unless they are pitted or otherwise damaged.

Reassembly

New cups in the steering head should be driven in carefully and squarely to avoid damage and obtain correct alignment. This can best be done with a hide mallet. Grease the cups and place twenty-four $\frac{3}{16}$ in. balls in each cup.

Assembly can then be carried out in the reverse order to dismantling. Do not forget the rubber washers at the bottom of the headlamp cowl tubes (when fitted), the washers on top of the main fork tubes (D1 models), and the dust cover over the top bearing.

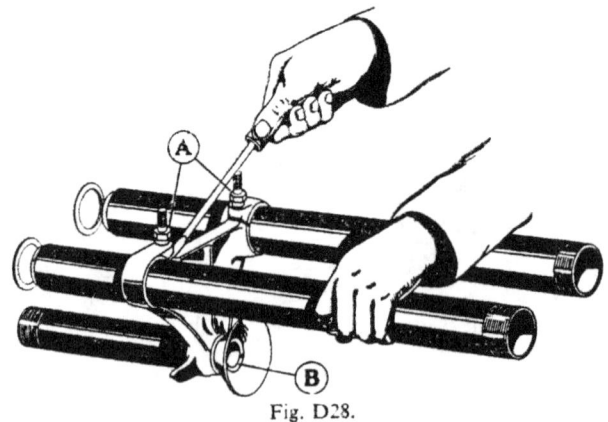

Fig. D28.

B.S.A. Service Sheet No. 509 (contd.)

On D1 models, when replacing the nuts (c) Fig. D27, ensure that the thicker of the two nuts is at the bottom with its recess facing downwards.

D1 Steering Head Adjustment

The method of adjusting the steering head bearings on the D1 models is different to that for the other models. The forks should be completely assembled but only the large nuts (D) Fig. D27, should be tightened, after ensuring that the mudguard stay studs on the fork outer tubes are facing each other and in line. Where the mudguard is attached to the sliding tubes, the two grease nipples should be facing outwards. Tighten down the lower of the two nuts (c) Fig. D24, until the forks rotate freely but have no up and down play. Secure the lower nut by means of the locknut and then check to ensure that the bearing is not over-tightened. A "lumpy" feeling as the forks are turned indicates that the adjustment is too tight. When this adjustment is completed the top yoke clamp nut (A) Fig. D24, and the lower clamp nuts (B) should be tightened securely.

D3 and C10L Steering Head Adjustment

Fig. D29.

The fork can be completely assembled and all the nuts fully tightened before the steering head adjustment is carried out. The fork should be assembled so that the headlamp cowl tubes are held firmly between the top and bottom fork yokes, with the rubber washers at the lower end of the tubes and the steel washers on top. The fork nuts can then be fully tightened with the exception of the stem nuts and the pinch bolt at the rear of the top yoke. The castellated sleeve nut (B) Fig. D29, should then be screwed down with the aid of Service Tool, part number 61-3002, or other similar tool until the forks rotate freely but without up and down play. Tighten the pinch bolt nut (c) to secure the sleeve nut and replace the top cap (A). Check that the bearing adjustment is still correct and replace the handlebar assembly.

Sliding Tube Reassembly (all models)

Place the upper bushes in the outer tubes and push them up as far as they will go with the aid of the distance tube. Line up the holes in the distance tubes with the grease nipple holes in the outer tubes and screw in the nipples. Position the telescopic gaiters on the lower tubes together with the oil seal holders and lower fork bushes. Take care that the oil seals are not damaged as they pass over the springs. Grease the springs and sliding members, then pass them up into the outer tubes. Position the lower bushes and screw up the oil seal holders. Secure the upper end of the springs in position by means of the nuts (A) Fig. D25, making sure that the fork ends are correctly positioned to receive the wheel spindle, before tightening the nuts. When the oil seal holders are fully tightened they should be secured by the small locking tabs which engage in the top groove of the holders. Make sure that the curved portion of the tab engages properly in the groove before it is tightened down.

B.S.A. MOTOR CYCLES LTD., Service Department, Armoury Road, Birmingham 11

B.S.A. PRESS

BSA SERVICE SHEET No. 510

MODELS D1, D3, D5 and D7

USEFUL DATA

Petrol tank capacity (approx.)	1¾ galls. (8 litres). D5 and D7 2 galls.
"Petroil" mixture	2 filler cap measures per gallon petrol with 6¼" filler. 2½ filler cap measures per gallon petrol with 5" filler.
Gearbox capacity	¾ pint (425 c.c.).
Bore	D1 — 52 mm. D3 — 57 mm. D5 and D7 — 61.5 mm
Stroke	58 mm.
Capacity (swept volume)	D1 — 123 c.c. D3 — 148 c.c. D5 and D7 — 174 c.c.
Piston ring gap	Max. .013 in. (.325 mm.). Min. .009 in. (.225 mm.).
Ignition timing	Piston distance before t.d.c. with points just opening, 5/32 in. (3.75 mm.). D1 and D3 1/16" (1.587 m.m.) D5 and D7
Plug point gap	.015 in. to .018 in. (.38 to .45 mm.).

Gear ratios		Standard	Competition	D5 and D7
	Top	7.0 to 1.	8.64 to 1.	6.48
	Second	11.7 to 1.	14.45 to 1.	10.74
	First	22.0 to 1.	27.1 to 1.	20.2

Tyre size, Front	2.75 × 19. D5 and D7, 3.00 × 18.
Rear	Standard 2.75 × 19; Comp., 3.25 × 19; D5 and D7, 3.00 × 18.
Tyre pressures, Front	16 lbs. sq. in. (1.125 kg. per sq. cm.). D5 and D7, 16 lbs. p.s.i.
(Standard Model) Rear	20–22 lbs. sq. in. (1.55 kg. per sq. cm.). D5 and D7, 24 lbs. p.s.i.
Front chain (.375in. × .225in.)	50 Links.
Rear chain (½ in. × .205 in.)	
Standard, Rigid Frame	116 Links.
Spring Frame	117 Links (D3, D5 121 Links. D7 S/Arm—120 Links.
Comp., Rigid Frame	122 Links.
Spring Frame	123 Links.
Standard carburetter jet	D1 — 75. D3 — 90. D5 and D7 — 140.
Jet needle position	2nd notch from top. D5 and D7, 4th.

B.S.A. MOTOR CYCLES LTD.,
Service Dept., Armoury Road, Birmingham, 11.
Printed in England.

BSA SERVICE SHEET No. 511

MODELS D1 AND D3

WORKSHOP DATA

(All dimensions in inches, finished size)

	Maximum	Minimum
Cylinder bore, D1	2.048	2.047
Cylinder bore, D3	2.245	2.244
Con-rod little-end bore	.4693	.469
Con-rod big-end bore	1.3487	1.3484
Crankpin diameter	.7968	.7965
Chainwheel bush	.8135	.8125
Primary drive gear bore	.501	.500
Mainshaft diameter	.499	.498
Layshaft bush bore	.501	.500
Layshaft bearing diameter	.4995	.4990
Kickstart spindle diameter (large)	.7793	.7788
Bore for kickstart spindle in primary chain cover	.7815	.7805
Kickstart sleeve diameter (small)	.6858	.6853
Bore in crankcase for kickstart sleeve	.688	.687
Gearchange shaft diameter (outer end)	.497	.496
Kickstart sleeve bore	.5005	.4995
Gearchange shaft diameter (inner end)	.499	.498
Bore in crankcase for gearchange shaft	.5005	.4995
Bore in crankcase for gear indicator spindle	.502	.500
Kickstart ratchet pinion bore	1.063	1.062
Chainwheel bearing diameter for ratchet pinion	1.060	1.059
Layshaft bearing diameter for 32 tooth gear	.5935	.593

BEARINGS

Location	Crankshaft (2)	Crankshaft (1)	Gearbox	Gearbox Mainshaft
B.S.A. Part No.	89-3023	90-10	90-12	90-11
Hoffman No.	LS.8	117	S.9	LS.7
Skefco No.	RLS.6	6203	EE.8	RLS.5
Ransome & Marles No.	LJ.3/4	LJ.17	KLNJ 7/8"	LJ. 5/8"
British Timkin No.	—	—	—	—
Fischer No.	LS.8	6203	EE.8	LS.7

B.S.A. MOTOR CYCLES LTD., Service Department, Armoury Road, Birmingham 11

B.S.A. PRESS   PRINTED IN ENGLAND

BSA SERVICE SHEET No. 514

This Sheet supersedes No. 814

"D" and "C" Group Models
PLUNGER TYPE REAR SUSPENSION

DISMANTLING

First remove the rear wheel, see Service Sheet number 410 for "C" Group models and number 508 for "D" Group models. "C" Group part numbers are shown in brackets where they differ from "D" Group part numbers.

Disconnect the rear mudguard stays, and take out the pinch bolts at the top and bottom of the rear suspension columns. The centre column, part number 90-4117, Fig. D27, can now be driven out using a soft drift so as to avoid damage to the end of the column.

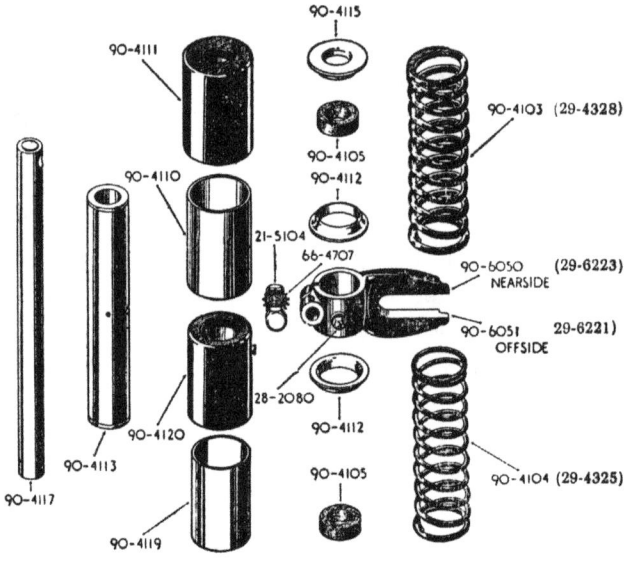

Fig. D27.

Grip the upper and lower shrouds firmly with both hands, compress the springs and lift out the suspension assembly.

Remove the shroud and springs from the sliding member, part number 90-4113. Carefully note the position of the steel washers and rubber bushes for subsequent assembly.

The bushes in the sliding member can now be examined for wear. If they require renewal, the tube complete with bushes must be replaced.

Unscrew the pinch bolt locknut, part number 21-5104, and take out the bolt. Insert a screwdriver into the slot, in the fork end 90-6051 (29-6221), the tube can then be withdrawn.

When replacing the tube ensure that the hole in the side of the tube lines up with the grease nipple in the fork end.

Note that the nearside fork end carries an anchor lug for the brake cover plate. On "C" Group models the head of the right-hand fork end clamping bolt is employed to secure the brake cover plate.

REASSEMBLY

Replace the shroud and springs on the sliding member in the reverse order to that of dismantling.

Take up the assembly and place the lower shroud in the frame lug. Press down on the upper shroud to compress the springs, and slide the assembly between the lugs Fig. D28).

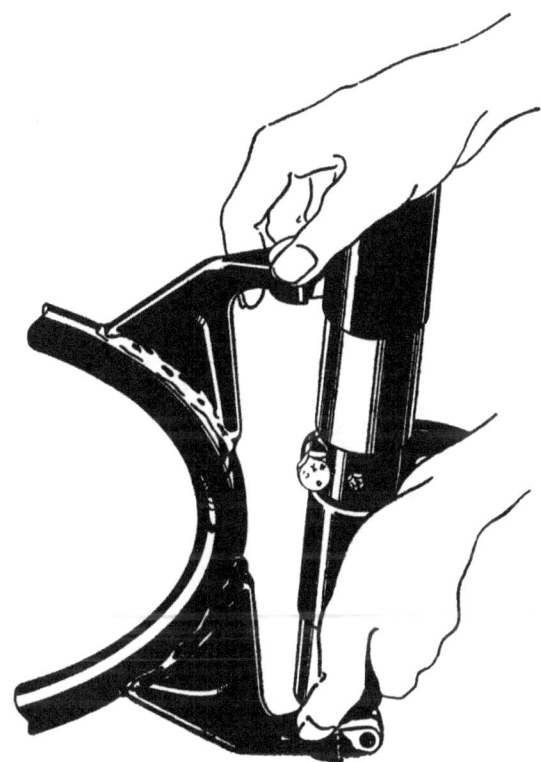

Fig. D28.

Use the champher on the lower end of the centre column to locate the assembly correctly in the frame top and bottom lugs. Insert the column from the top, ensuring that the slots are in line with the pich bolt hole.

Replace the pinch bolts, mudguard stays and rear wheel, couple up the brake and adjust.

Finally, check over all nuts and bolts for tightness.

B.S.A. MOTOR CYCLES LTD., Service Department, Armoury Road, Birmingham 11.
B.S.A. Press

BSA SERVICE SHEET No. 515

October, 1959

Model D7

DISMANTLING AND REASSEMBLY OF HUBS AND BRAKES

Both wheels are fitted with ball journal bearings which do not require adjustment   The bearings are packed with grease during assembly and this should last until the machine is in need of a major overhaul.

Front Wheel Removal

With the machine on its centre stand place a box or small wooden trestle underneath the crankcase so that the front wheel is clear of the ground.

Disconnect the brake cable by removing the nut (A) and the screw (B) Fig. D29 at the brake drum end. Slacken the torque arm nut (C) on the cover plate and remove the end caps (D) by unscrewing the four bolts (two in each cap) and as the last bolt is removed support the wheel to avoid damage to the screw threads on the bolt or the screwed sockets.   The wheel will now be free.

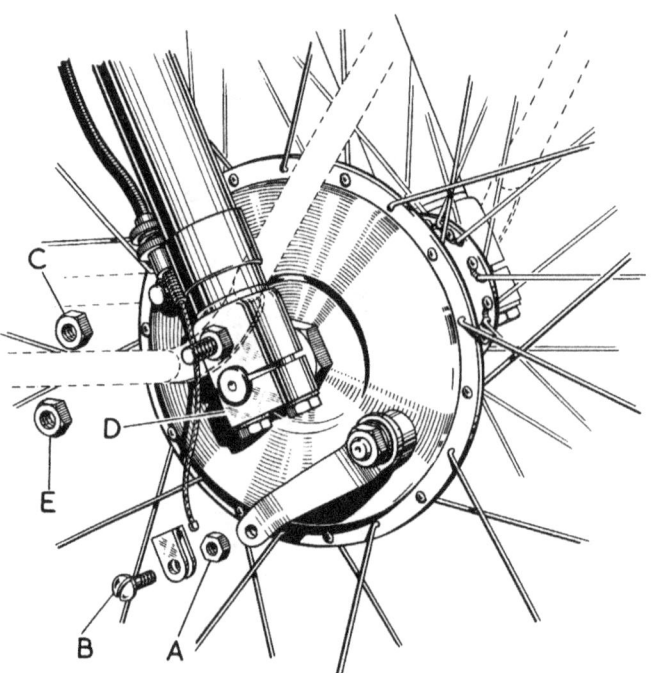

Fig. D29. Front Wheel Removal.

Front Hub Dismantling

Unscrew the large nut (F) Fig. D30 on the spindle.   This will be facilitated if the brake is applied by using a short length of tubing, such as a box spanner, over the brake arm.

Take off the cover plate complete with the brake shoes, cam and fulcrum pin.

B.S.A. SERVICE SHEET No. 515 (contd.)

The bearing retainer (G) which is now exposed has a left-hand thread and can be removed by unscrewing in a clockwise direction with a peg spanner, Part No. 61-3644.

Drive out the right-hand or brake side bearing by striking the left-hand side of the spindle with a mallet or copper hammer. If neither of these is available the bearing can be driven out with an ordinary hammer if a piece of hard wood is placed against the end of the spindle to protect it.

To remove the left-hand side bearing prise out the circlip (H) and, using a suitable piece of tube, drive out the bearing and dust cover from the right-hand side.

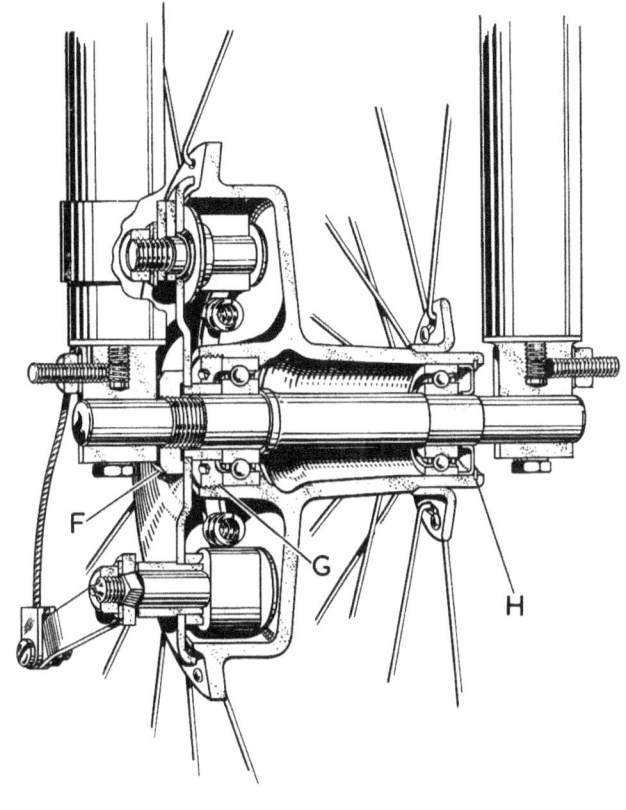

Fig. D30.

Fitting New Bearings

Place the bearing squarely in position on the right-hand side and drive in using a piece of tubing on the outer ring of the bearing. When it is resting on the abutment face in the hub, screw in the lockring using a peg spanner and turning anti-clockwise (left-hand thread).

Insert the spindle, screwed end first from the left-hand side, and tap it gently home so that the bearing inner ring is seated against the shoulder on the spindle.

Place the left-hand bearing over the spindle and drive it into the housing until the dust cap just clears the circlip groove, and replace the dust cap and circlip.

Brake Shoes

Before replacing the cover plate make sure that the brake linings are fit for further use and that cam spindle is quite free in the cover plate.

Replacement shoes may be obtained through the medium of your Dealer from the B.S.A. Exchange Replacement Service, and can be fitted by springing the old ones off the fulcrum and cam spindles then springing the new ones on in like manner.

B.S.A. SERVICE SHEET No. 515 (contd.)

Replacing the Wheel

Make sure that the cover plate nut (F) Fig. D30 is securely tightened, engage the torque arm bolt of the cover plate in the clip on the right-hand fork leg and replace the fork end clips. Before finally tightening the clip bolts pull the wheel towards the right-hand fork leg.

Replace the brake cable adjuster, clevis pin and split pin and check over the bolts for tightness.

Rear Wheel Removal

With the machine on its stand, disconnect the rear chain at the spring link, place a sheet of paper on the ground under the run of the chain and wind the chain off the rear sprocket on to the paper but leaving it over the gearbox sprocket.

Take off the brake rod adjusting nut (A) Fig. D31 and remove the torque arm bolt (B). Disconnect the speedometer cable by unscrewing the union nut at the end of the cable. The inner cable can then be lifted out of the gearbox drive.

Unscrew the spindle nuts (C) Fig. D31 and pull the wheel out of the fork ends, at the same time freeing the brake rod from the swivel pin on the lever. Tilt the machine over slightly towards the left-hand side and remove the wheel from the right-hand side.

Rear Wheel Dismantling

Unscrew the large nuts (A) Fig. D32 on the spindle, locking the spindle in the same way as described for the front wheel. Remove the brake cover plate complete with shoes and then the speedometer drive gearbox from the right-hand side. (Note the distance piece and driving dogs).

Next unscrew the bearing retainer (B) which has a right-hand thread and is therefore removed by using a peg spanner in an anti-clockwise direction.

Drive the spindle through the bearing on the brake side so driving out the right-hand bearing.

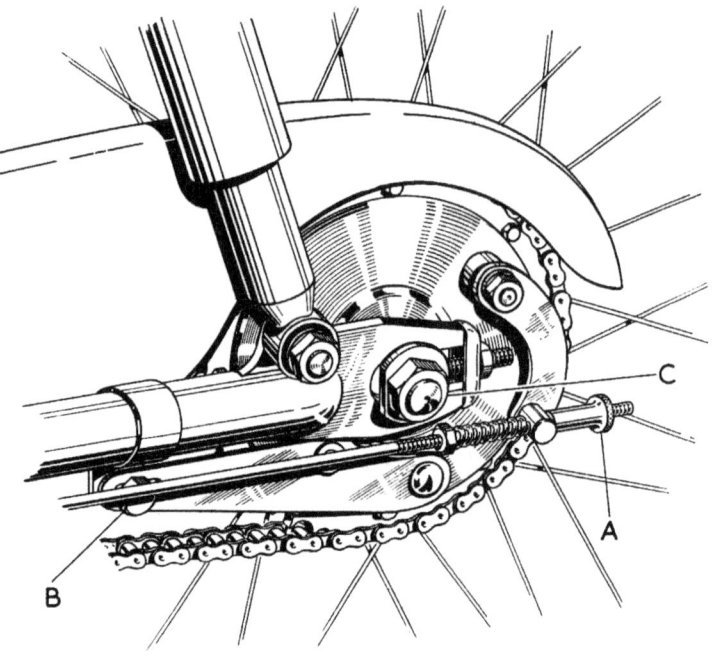

Fig. D31.

The brake-side bearing can now be driven out from the opposite side using a drift against the outer race of the bearing.

B.S.A. SERVICE SHEET No. 515 (contd.)

Fitting New Bearings

New bearings can be fitted in the reverse order but care must be taken to see that the locking washer is in place behind the drive-side bearing and that the bearing is seated well up to the abutment in the hub shell and the shoulder on the spindle.

After fitting the drive-side bearing and its retainer, insert the spindle from the right-hand side, drive in the right-hand bearing to the shoulder on the spindle, slide the distance piece (C) Fig. D32 over the right-hand side of the spindle, then the speedometer gearbox taking care to mesh the driving dogs and screw on the spindle locknut. This nut can be finally tightened after the brake cover plate is fitted.

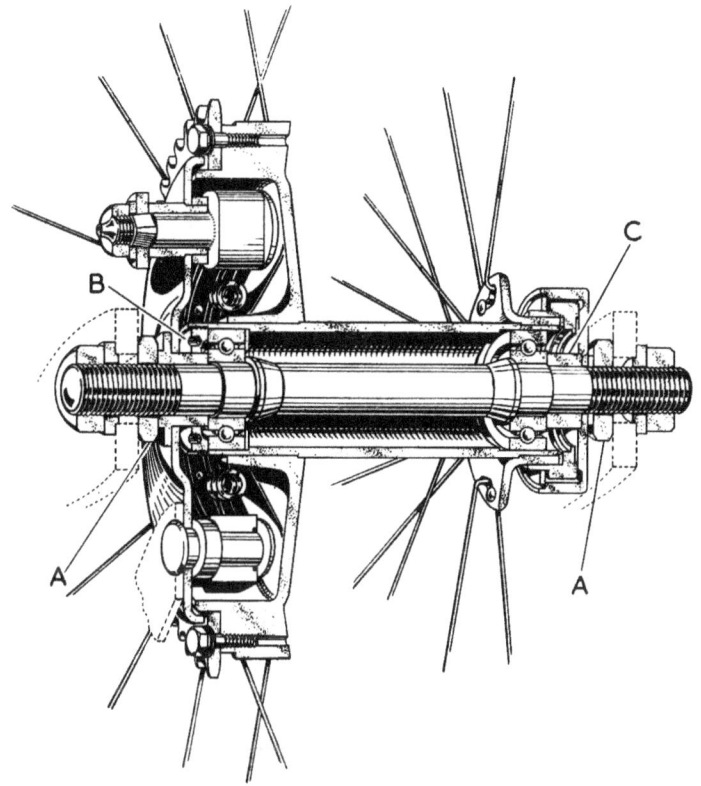

Fig. D32.

Brake Shoes

These are dealt with in the same manner as described for the front wheel and are interchangeable with the front shoes. After replacing the cover plate and nut, tighten the locknut on the speedometer drive.

Chainwheel

This is registered on to the brake drum and secured by eight bolts and spring washers.

Rear Wheel Replacement

Procedure is the reverse of that for removal, but care should be taken to see that the wheel is in alignment with the front. This is done by placing a straight edge against the wheels which must touch the front and rear of both tyres. The spring on the chain connecting link must also be fitted with the open end towards the rear wheel when on the top run of the chain. All nuts must be securely tightened.

B.S.A. SERVICE SHEET No. 515 (contd.)

Front Mudguard

If the front forks or steering head is to be dismantled, it will be necessary to remove the front mudguard. This is done by taking out the two bolts and nuts on the bridge piece midway up the fork legs, and then the two nuts (E) Fig. D29 on each side of the fork ends holding the stays. Spring the stays over the studs and drop the guard down out of the forks.

Rear Chain

The rear chain should be adjusted when the machine is on its stand and the rear wheel in its lowest position.

Adjustment should then be made so that the chain has a total up and down movement of $\frac{3}{4}$ inch in the centre of the chain run at its tightest point.

To carry out the adjustment slacken off the outer spindle nuts and the nut securing the brake torque arm to the frame. Screwing the adjuster nut in will tighten the chain but it is essential that both adjusters are screwed in or out the same amount in order to maintain correct wheel alignment.

When the chain adjustment has been corrected, care should be taken to see that all the nuts and bolts are securely tightened.

B.S.A. MOTOR CYCLES LTD., Service Department, Waverley Works, Birmingham, 10.

BSA SERVICE SHEET No. 516

MODEL D7

FRONT FORKS AND STEERING HEAD

Remove the front wheel and mudguard as described in Service Sheet No. 515.

Prise out the top cap (A) Fig. D33 and unscrew the ⅜ in. nut holding the top spring scroll.

Place a suitable tin underneath the fork end, take out the drain plug (B) and slacken the pinch bolt (C) in the bottom fork yoke.

To release the main tube from the taper in the top yoke pull the lower sliding member out to its fullest extent, unscrew and take out the top nut and screw in Service Tool No. 61-3350. Give the end of the tool a sharp blow with a hammer and draw the leg down through the bottom yoke.

Repeat for the other leg.

Place each leg in turn in a vice, gripping it on the flats of the fork end and unscrew the oil seal holder with Service Tool No. 61-3633.

The main tube can now be drawn upwards from the sliding member complete with the two bearing bushes, leaving the restrictor rod and spring still attached to the lower member. These need not be disturbed unless they are to be replaced.

Replacing Bushes

The lower bush is a press fit on to the main tube and the replacement must be fitted with the chamfered holes in line with the holes in the tube.

To remove the old bush, prise open the joint in the bush with a thin chisel or screwdriver and then tap the bush off.

The upper bush is a push fit in the lower sliding member and is retained in place by a washer and the top oil seal holder.

No difficulty will be experienced in replacing the top bush.

Reassembly

After fitting the new lower bush, slide the upper bush over the main tube with the flange uppermost, and apply a light coating of oil. Pass the tube over the spring and restrictor rod and slide into the lower member.

Holding the assembly in the vice by the fork ends, place the large washer in position over the flange on the top bush and screw on the oil seal holder with Service Tool No. 61-3633.

Take the assembly out of the vice and pass it up through the bottom

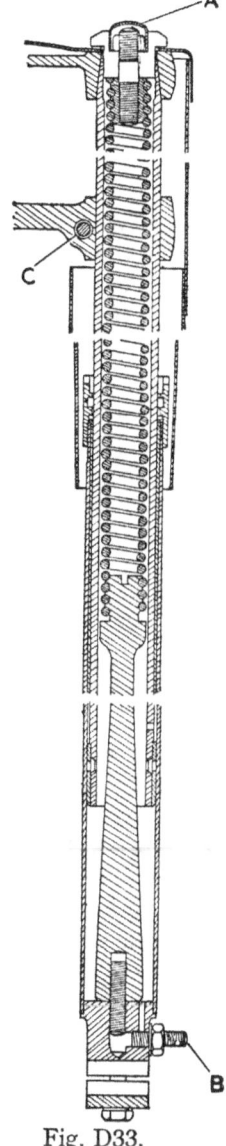

Fig. D33.
Front Fork Section

B.S.A. SERVICE SHEET No. 516 (contd.)

fork yoke, place the top washer in position then screw on the large top nut and secure over the stud of the spring scroll.

The ⅜ in. nut can now be refitted together with the top cap. Repeat the operation for the other leg.

Finally replace the mudguard and front wheel.

Steering Head

To adjust the steering head bearings place a weight on the saddle so that the front wheel is clear of the ground when the machine is on its stand.

Slacken the pinch bolt (A) Fig. D34 and adjust the nut (B) until the forks move freely from side to side without evidence of play in the bearings.

Take great care not to over tighten the nut (B) as this is liable to indent the bearings in the races.

When the adjustment is correct tighten the pinch bolt (A) securely and re-check the adjustment.

Dismantle the Steering Head

If the only attention required is examination or replacement of the head bearings there is no need to dismantle the forks completely, but the lighting cables to the headlamp will have to be broken at the couplings or sufficient slack obtained to move the forks away from the frame.

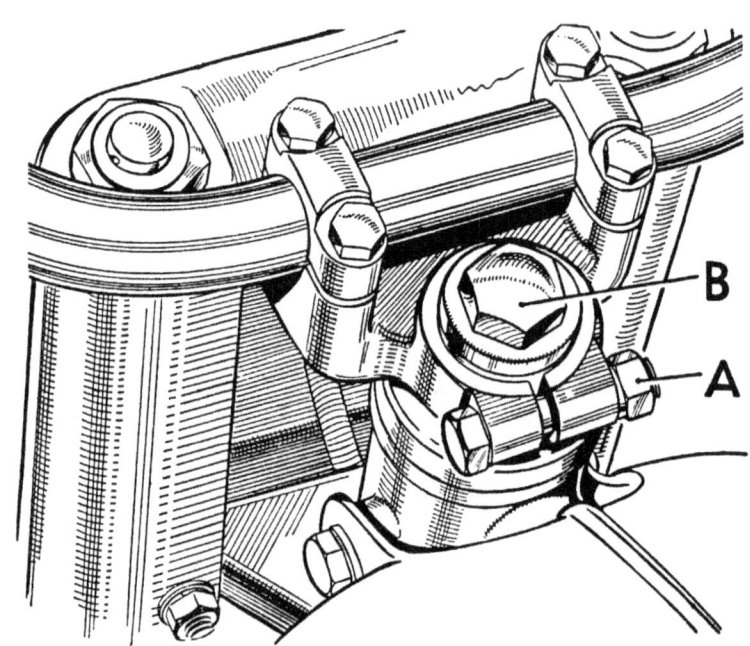

Model D7. Front Fork and steering head

Fig. D34.

Remove the top caps from the forks, unscrew the ⅜ in. nut and the large nuts holding the main tubes.

Slacken the pinch bolt (A) Fig. D34 and take off the nut (B).

Undo the four bolts holding the handlebar clips, place a piece of cloth on the tank, remove the handlebar from the clips and lay it on the cloth.

Take off the top yoke cover, support the forks underneath and remove the top yoke by striking alternately each side underneath the handlebar clips.

After the top yoke has been removed, the steering column and forks can be drawn out of the frame but a suitable tray or container should be held underneath the column to catch the ball bearings which will be released.

B.S.A. SERVICE SHEET No. 516 (contd.)

The cups, cones and balls should be clean and free from indentations or pitting. The top and bottom cups are identical, Part No. 65-4465, the bottom cone or crown race is Part No. 40-5027, and the top cone is Part No. 65-5319.

If new cups are fitted care must be taken to see that they are seated well down and square with the housing.

Reassembly

Apply a coating of grease to the steering head cups and insert 24 balls, 3/16 in. dia. in each cup.

Slide the column up through the steering head tube, being careful not to displace the balls, place the top cone in position, then the top yoke, and screw on the nut (B) Fig. D34.

Replace the top yoke cover, the ⅜ in. nuts and the large nuts and washers and the handlebar, adjusting the steering head as previously described.

Finally recouple the headlamp wiring and check the lighting.

B.S.A. MOTOR CYCLES LTD., Service Department, Armoury Road Birmingham 11.
THE B.S.A. PRESS

BSA SERVICE SHEET No. 612

Reprinted Sept. 1960

All Models

BRAKE RELINING

Brake Shoe Removal and Replacement

After the brake plate has been removed from the wheel, the brake cam lever A (Fig. M40) should be detached and the cam spindle B pushed in slightly to allow the shoes to clear the brake plate. Insert a screwdriver between the brake shoes at the fulcrum pin C and twist the screwdriver.

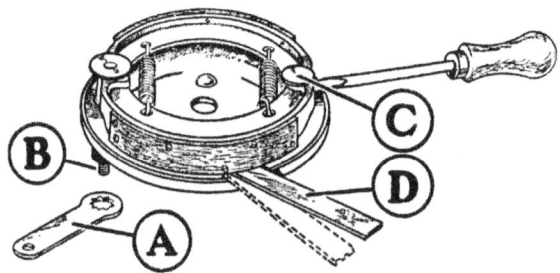

Fig. M40. Removing the Brake Shoes

Place a small lever D between one of the shoes and the cover plate and lever the shoe away from the cover plate until the spring pressure is released. Both shoes can then be lifted from the brake plate.

The shoes can be replaced by the reverse procedure. Hook the springs on to the shoes and place the ends of the shoes in position on the fulcrum pin and cam lever. Then push the shoes outwards until the springs pull them into their correct position.

NOTE: The brake shoe springs are quite strong and care should be taken that the fingers are not trapped by the brake shoes during these operations.

Brake Shoe Relining

With the shoes removed the linings can best be removed by drilling away the heads of the rivets and punching the shanks out to the inside of the shoe with a suitable drift.

New linings are die pressed to suit the curvature of the shoes, but will require drilling and counter-boring for the rivets. Position the lining and hold it in place at one end by means of clamps. Using the holes in the shoes as guides, drill holes of the correct size for the rivets adjacent to the clamp. Turn the shoe over, and counterbore the holes just drilled sufficiently deep so that the rivet heads will stand below the lining surface; this is important, since the rivets will otherwise score the brake drum.

B.S.A. Service Sheet No. 612 (continued)

Insert the rivets into the holes and rivet them over on the inside of the shoe. This is easily accomplished by holding in a vice a short length of rod, whose diameter is equal to that of the rivet head, and using it as an anvil upon which to rest the rivet head while hammering the shank over. (See Fig. M41.) This will also make sure that the rivets do not stand proud of the lining.

Move the clamps to the next pair of holes, taking care that the lining is kept in firm contact with the shoe the whole time, and repeat the above procedure. When the lining is finally riveted down, bevel off the ends of the linings and file off any local high spots.

Precautions to be observed when fitting the relined shoes to the hubs are given in the Service Sheet on Hubs and Brakes.

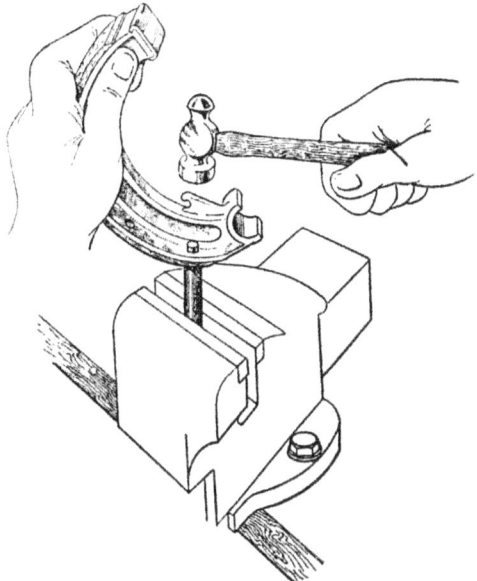

Fig. M41. Riveting the Linings

Works reconditioned brake shoes can be obtained through the medium of your Dealer from the B.S.A. Exchange Replacement Service.

B.S.A. MOTOR CYCLES LTD.
Service Dept., Waverley Works, Birmingham 10
Printed in England.

BSA SERVICE SHEET No. 702

Reprinted June, 1959.

ALL MODELS

WORKSHOP DATA

ENGINE, BUSH AND SHAFT DIAMETERS

(All Dimensions in Inches, after Reaming or Grinding).

	D1	C10, C11	B31, B32	M33 B33, B34	M20, M21	A7 Up to Engine No. ZA7 11192	A7 On and After Engine No. AA7 101	A10
Overhead Rocker Arm	— —	.569 .567 C10 only	.562 .563	.562 .563	— —	.4995 .5005	.4995 .5005	.4995 .5005
Inlet Valve Guide	— —	.313 .314	.313 .314	.3525 .3515	.3525 .3515	.313 .314	.313 .314	.313 .314
Exhaust Valve Guide	— —	.313 .314	.352 .353	.3785 .3795	.3525 .3535	.313 .314	.313 .314	.313 .314
Inlet Tappet Guide	— —	.3125 .3135 C10 only	.3745 .3755	.3745 .3755	.3745 .3755	.3125 .3135	— —	— —
Exhaust Tappet Guide	— —	.3125 .3135 C10 only	.3745 .3755	.3745 .3755	.3745 .3755	.3125 .3135	— —	— —
Cam Pinion Bush	— —	— —	.6255 .6245	.6255 .6245	.6255 .6245	— —	— —	— —
Cam Shaft Bush	— —	.687 .688	— —	— —	— —	.7485 .7495	.7485 .7495	.7485 .7495
Idler Pinion Shaft Bush	— —	— —	— —	— —	— —	.7485 .7495	.7485 .7495	.7485 .7495
Idler Pinion Bush	— —	— —	.7505 .7495	.7505 .7495	.7505 .7495	.7485 .7495	.7485 .7495	.7485 .7495
Cam Shaft Bush T/Cover	— —	1.0005 .9995	— —	— —	— —	— —	— —	— —
Crankshaft Bush G/S	— —	.983 .982	— —	— —	— —	1.375 1.3745	1.375 1.3745	1.375 1.3745
Conrod Big End	— —	— —	1.7704 1.7702	1.7704 1.7702	1.7704 1.7702	1.4495 1.4500	1.4495 1.4500	1.4495 1.4500
Gudgeon Pin Bush	.4697 .4692	.6255 .625	.7506 .7503	.7506 .7503	.7506 .7503	.6881 .6878	.6881 .6878	.7506 .7503

B.S.A. Service Sheet No. 702 (Contd.).

GEARBOX—BUSH DIAMETERS

(All Dimensions in Inches, after Reaming or Grinding)

	D Group	C Group	B Group 1945/48	M Group 1945/48	A Group	B & M 1949 on
Pinion Sleeve Bush	.4975 / .4965	—	.7505 / .7495	.8755 / .8745	.812 / .813	.8755 / .8745
Layshaft Bush (Shell)	.501 / .500	—	.687 / .688	.687 / .688	.687 / .688	.687 / .688
Mainshaft Bush (I/Cover)	—	.751 / .752	.687 / .688	—	—	—
Layshaft Bush (K/S Quadrant)	—	—	—	.687 / .688	.7495 / .7505	.687 / .688
Layshaft 1st Gear Bush	—	—	.8125 / .8135	.8765 / .8755	.7495 / .7505	.8765 / .8755
Layshaft Pinion/s Bush	—	.562 / .563	—	—	—	—
M/Shaft 3rd L/Shaft 2nd Gear Bush	—	—	.9375 / .9385	1.0005 / 1.0015	—	1.0005 / 1.0015
K/S Quadrant Bush I/Cover	—	.9995 / 1.0005	1.1245 / 1.1255	—	.561 / .563	—
K/S Quadrant Bush O/Cover	—	.812 / .813	.812 / .813	1.187 / 1.188	.7495 / .7505	1.187 / 1.188
Control Shaft Bush (Shell)	—	—	.562 / .563	.562 / .563	—	.562 / .563
Control Shaft Bush (I/Cover)	—	.689 / .688	—	.562 / .563	—	.562 / .563
Control Quadrant Bush (I/Cover)	—	—	—	.562 / .563	—	.562 / .563
Pedal Spindle Bush (I/Cover)	—	.7495 / .7505	.6245 / .6255	.6245 / .6255	.467 / .468	.6245 / .6255
Pedal Spindle Bush (O/Cover)	—	.7495 / .7505	.8745 / .8755	.8745 / .8755	.6245 / .6255	.8745 / .8755
Speedo Spindle Small Bush	—	—	.218 / .219	—	.218 / .219	.218 / .219
Speedo Spindle Long Bush	—	—	.281 / .282	—	.281 / .282	.281 / .282
Clutch Push Rod Bush	—	.257 / .258	—	—	—	—

B.S.A. MOTOR CYCLES LTD., Service Dept., Waverley Works, Birmingham, 10.   *Printed in England.*

BSA SERVICE SHEET No. 703

Revised Dec. 1958.

All Models
WORKSHOP DATA (BEARINGS) 1956

B.S.A. Part No.	Hoffman No.	Skefko No.	Ransome & Marles No.	British Timkin No.	Fischer No.
24–722	RM.9L	CFM7/C2	MRJA.$\frac{7}{8}$	—	RFM.9
24–724	R.325L	402454.B	MRJA.25	—	MFM.25
24–732	325	6305	MJ.25	—	6305
24–4065	135	6207	LJ.35	—	6207
24–4217	LS.8	RLS.6	LJ$\frac{3}{4}$	—	LS.8
24–6860	—	2K.1178X 2K.1130N1	—	1178X 1130.N1	—
27–261	MS.9	RM.S7	MJ.$\frac{7}{8}$	—	MS.9
27–4027	LS.11	RL.S9	LJ.$1\frac{1}{8}$	—	—
29–3857	130	6206	LJ.30	—	6206
29–6211	MS.7	RM.S5	MJ.$\frac{5}{8}$	—	MS.7
42–5819	120	—	—	—	—
65–1388	RMS.11	CRM.9	MRJ.$1\frac{1}{8}$	—	RMS.11
65–2045	125	6205	LJ.25	—	6205
65–5883	LS.9	RLS.7	LJ.$\frac{7}{8}$	—	LS.9
67–670	R.130L	NFL.30	LRJA.30	—	NFL.30
89–3022	LS.10	RLS.8	LJ.1	—	LS.10
89–3023	LS.8	RLS.6	LJ.$\frac{3}{4}$	—	LS.8
90–10	117	6203	LJ.17	—	6203
90–11	LS.7	RLS.5	LJ.$\frac{5}{8}$	—	LS.7
90–12	S.9	EE.8J	KLNJ.$\frac{7}{8}$	—	EE.8
90–5525	112	6201	LJ.12	—	6201
90–5559	—	—	—	A.2126	—
90–6063	115	6202	LJ.15	—	6202

B.S.A. SERVICE SHEET No. 703 (continued)

LOCATION OF BEARINGS

Model	Crankcase Roller Bearing Driveside	Crankcase Ball Bearing Driveside	Crankcase Roller Bearing Gearside	Crankcase Ball Bearing Gearside	Crankcase Ball Bearing (Small)	Crankcase Ball Bearing (Large)	Gearbox Pinion Sleeve Ball Bearing	Gearbox Mainshaft Ball Bearing	Front Hub Ball Bearing	Rear Hub Ball Bearing	Rear Hub Brake Drum and C/Wheel Ball Bearing
Dandy	—	—	—	—	90-6063	24-4217	90-6063 (Output shaft)	90-6063 (Input shaft)	—		
D1, D3 & D5					90-10	24-4217	90-12	90-11	90-5525	90-6063	
D1, D3 (Comp.)									90-5559		
C10L	—	24-732					29-3857	90-11		90-6063	
C12		24-732					29-3857	90-11	65-5383	90-11 O/S 29-6211 N/S	
C15		24-782					29-3857		90-10	90-10 O/S 42-5819 N/S	
B31 S/A	24-724	65-2045	24-722				24-4065	24-4217	89-3022	89-3022	89-3022
B31 S/A (1958)									42-5819	42-5819	89-3022
B32 Comp. Rigid	24-724	65-2045	24-722				24-4065	24-4217	65-5883	65-5883	65-5883
B32/34 Gold Star	65-1338	65-2045	24-722				24-4065	24-4217	65-5883	65-5883	65-5883
B33 S/A	24-724	65-2045	24-722				24-4065	24-4217	89-3022	89-3022	89-3022
B33 S/A (1958)									42-5819	42-5819	89-3022
B34 Comp. Rigid	24-724	65-2045	24-722				24-4065	24-4217	65-5883	65-5883	65-5883
M21 Rigid	24-724	65-2045	24-722	27-261			24-4065	24-4217	65-5883	24-6860 (Tapered Roller)	
M21 Plunger	24-724	65-2045	24-722	27-261			24-4065	24-4217	65-5883	65-5883	89-3022
M33	24-724	65-2045	24-722				24-4065	24-4217	65-5883	65-5883	89-3022
A7 and Shooting Star	67-670						24-4065	24-4217	89-3022	89-3022	89-3022
A7 & S/S (1958)									42-5819	42-5819	89-3022
A10 S/A	67-670						24-4065	24-4217	89-3022	89-3022	89-3022
A10 S/A (1958)									42-5819	42-5819	89-3022
A10 Plunger	67-670						24-4065	24-4217	65-5883	65-5883	89-3022
A10 Road Rocket	67-670						24-4065	24-4217	65-5883	89-3022	89-3022
A10 Super Rocket	67-670						24-4065	24-4217	42-5819	42-5819	89-3022

Printed in England   B.S.A. MOTOR CYCLES LTD., Service Dept., Birmingham 11.

BSA SERVICE SHEET No. 704

ALL MODELS
PISTON CLEARANCES

To avoid the possibility of seizure or piston tap, pistons must be fitted with adequate but not excessive clearance.

The following are the recommended total clearances between the bottom of the piston and the cylinder wall.

		MODEL	Tolerances
Dandy 70		7.25 : 1	.003—.004"
D1			.0027—.0045"
D3, C15			.0025—.004"
D5, D7			.003—.005"
C10, C10L			.0045—.0065"
C11, C11G, C12			.0035—.0055"
C15	(Star Group)	6.4 : 1 to 10 : 1	.0017—.0033"
B31			.004—.0055"
B31	(Split skirt)		.0005—.0016"
B32A			.002—.004"
BB32	Gold Star	8 : 1	.003—.0045"
		6.5 : 1	.004—.0055"
		7.5 : 1	.002—.004"
		9 : 1	.003—.0045"
CB32	Gold Star	6.5 : 1	.002—.004"
		8 : 1	.003—.0045"
		8.5 : 1	.003—.0045"
		9 : 1	.003—.0045"
		12.25 : 1	.004—.0055"
		13 : 1	.004—.0055"
DB32	Gold Star	7.25 : 1	.0025—.004"
		8 : 1	.003—.0045"
		9 : 1	.003—.0045"
B40	(Star Group)	7.0 : 1 to 8.7 : 1	.0015—.003"
B33			.0045—.0065"
B33	(Split skirt)		.0006—.00275"
B34A			.0045—.0065"
BB34	Gold Star	7.5 : 1 Standard	.0045—.0065"
		8 : 1	.0025—.0045"
		9 : 1	.0025—.0045"
		6.8 : 1	.0045—.0065"
		11.1	.0025—.0045"
CB34	Gold Star	7.25 : 1	.003—.0045"
		8 : 1	.003—.0045"
		9 : 1	.003—.0045"
DB34	Gold Star }	8 : 1	.003—.0045"
DBD34	Gold Star }	8.75 : 1	.003—.0045"

B.S.A. Service Sheet No. 704 (contd.)

MODEL			Tolerances
M20			.004—.006″
M21			.004—.006″
M33			.0045—.0065″
M33	(Split skirt)		.0006—.00275″
A7		6.7 : 1	.002—.004″
	(Split skirt)	6.7 : 1	.0011—.0031″
		7.25 : 1	.002—.004″
	(Split skirt)		.0011—.0031″
A7	(Star Twin)		.002—.004″
A7	(Split skirt)	(Star Twin and Shooting Star)	.001—.0031″
A7	(Shooting Star)	8 : 1 (after Engine No. CA7SS-4501)	.0035—.005″
A50	(Star Twin)	8.0 : 1 to 9.0 : 1	.0011—.0025″
A10	(Golden Flash)	6.5 : 1	.003—.0045″
	(Split skirt)	6.5 : 1	.0025—.0045″
	(Split skirt)	7.25 : 1	.0025—.0045″
A10	(Super Flash and Road Rocket)	8 : 1	.003—.0045″
A10	(Golden Flash)	7.5 : 1 (after Engine No. DA10-651)	.0035—.005″
A10	(Super Rocket)	8.5:1 (after Engine No. CA10R-6001)	.004—.0055″
A10	(Rocket Gold Star)	8.75 : 1	.001—.0025″
A65	(Star Twin)	7.5 : 1 to 9.0 : 1	.0012—.0027″

B.S.A. MOTOR CYCLES LTD., Service Department, Armoury Road, Birmingham 11

B.S.A. PRESS

BSA SERVICE SHEET No. 708

ALL MODELS

CARBURATION. Monobloc and Seperate Float Chamber Type

How the Carburetter Works

The function of the carburetter is to atomise the petrol and proportion it correctly with the air drawn in through the intake on the induction stroke. The action of the float and needle in the float chamber maintains the level of fuel at the needle jet, and when the engine is stopped and no further fuel is being used the needle valve cuts off the supply.

The twist-grip controls, by means of a cable, the position of the throttle slide and the throttle needle and so governs the volume of mixture supplied to the engine.

The mixture is correct at all throttle openings, if the carburetter is correctly tuned.

The opening of the throttle brings first into action the mixture supply from the pilot jet, then as it progressively opens, via the pilot by-pass the mixture is augmented from the needle jet. Up to three-quarter throttle this action is controlled by the tapered needle in the needle jet, and from three-quarters onwards the mixture is controlled by the main jet.

The pilot jet (J), which in the older type of carburetter is embodied in the jet block, has been replaced in the Monobloc carburetter by a detachable jet (9) Fig. X5, assembled in the carburetter body and sealed by a cover nut.

The main jet does not spray directly into the mixing chamber, but discharges through the needle jet into the primary air chamber and goes from there as a rich petrol/air mixture through the primary air choke into the main air choke.

Although the maintenance and tuning instruction contained in this Service Sheet apply equally well to the Monobloc and separate float chamber types of carburetter, the new instrument has been designed with a view to giving improved performance, and certain constructional changes have been made.

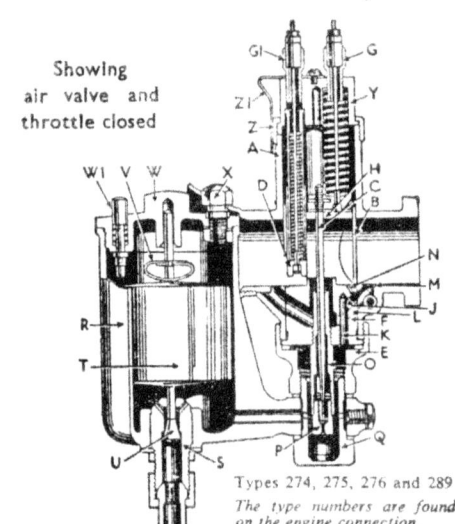

Showing air valve and throttle closed

Types 274, 275, 276 and 289
The type numbers are found on the engine connection.

- A. Mixing Chamber.
- B. Throttle Valve.
- C. Jet Needle and Clip above.
- D. Air Valve.
- E. Mixing Chamber Union Nut.
- F. Jet Block.
- G/G1. Cable Adjusters.
- H. Jet Block Barrel.
- J. Pilot Jet.
- K. Passage to Pilot.
- L. Pilot Air Passage.
- M. Pilot Mixture Outlet.
- N. Pilot by-pass.
- O. Needle Jet.
- P. Main Jet.
- Q. Float Chamber Holding Bolt.
- R. Float Chamber.
- S. Needle Valve Seating.
- T. Float.
- U. Float Needle Valve.
- V. Float Needle Clip.
- W. Float Chamber Cover.
- W1. Tickler.
- X. Float Chamber Lock Screw.
- Y. Mixing Chamber Top Cap.
- Z. Mixing Chamber Lock Ring.
- Z1. Mixing Chamber Security Spring.

Fig. X4. *A sectioned illustration of Needle Jet Carburetter.*

B.S.A. Service Sheet No. 708 (contd.)

The float chamber is a drum-shaped reservoir, die cast in one piece with the mixing chamber. The material used being zinc-alloy. The float is designed to pivot instead of rising and falling, as in the separate float chamber type, and as it does so, it impinges on a nylon needle controlling the inflow of fuel.

Variations of up to 20° in the angle of the carburetter when fitted, do not affect the working of the float, therefore it lends itself to use for down draught carburation and is not so greatly effected by the degree of lean when cornering. Access to the float (Fig. X6) is gained by removing a plate held in place by three screws.

Compensation for over-rich mixture which results from snap throttle openings, is provided by bleed holes in the needle jet (Fig. X5). A compensatory air bleed is provided, this is the larger of the two holes at the mouth of the air intake, which leads to the space around the needle jet (Fig. X5).

The pilot intake is the smaller of the two holes, and operates in conjunction with the detachable pilot jet (Fig. X5). This pilot mixture is adjusted as before, by an adjusting screw (Fig. 8a).

Hints and Tips—Starting from Cold
Flood the carburetter by depressing the tickler and close the air control, set the ignition say, half-retarded. Then open the throttle about ⅛ in., then kick-start. If the throttle is too far open, starting will be difficult.

Starting—Engine Hot
Do not flood the carburetter, but it may be found necessary with some engines to close the air lever, set the ignition to half-retarded, the throttle to ⅛ in. open and kick-start. If the carburetter has been flooded and won't start because the mixture is too rich—open the throttle wide and give the engine several turns to clear the richness, then start again with the throttle ⅛ in. open, and air valve wide open. Generally speaking it is not advisable to flood at all when an engine is hot.

Starting—General
By experiment, find out if and when it is necessary to flood, also note the best position for the air lever and the throttle for the easiest starting. Excessive flooding, particularly when the engine is hot, will make starting more difficult. It is necessary only to raise the level of petrol in the float chamber, by depressing the tickler.

Starting—Single Lever Carburetters
Open the throttle very slightly from the idling position and flood the carburetter more or less according to the engine being cold or hot respectively.

B.S.A. Service Sheet No. 708 (contd.)

SECTIONAL ILLUSTRATIONS OF CARBURETTERS. Types 375, 376 and 389

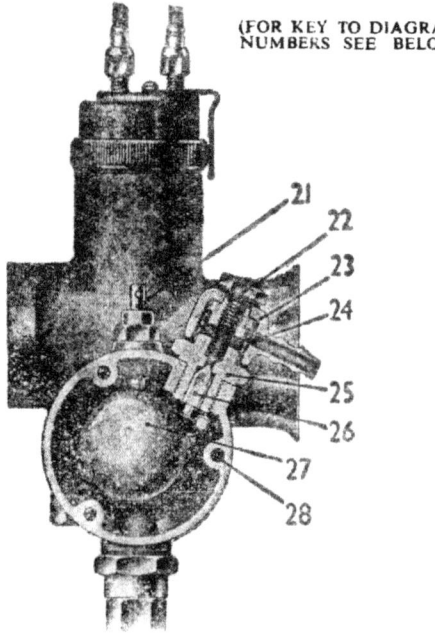

(MONOBLOC)
Fig. X6. *Section through Float Chamber.*

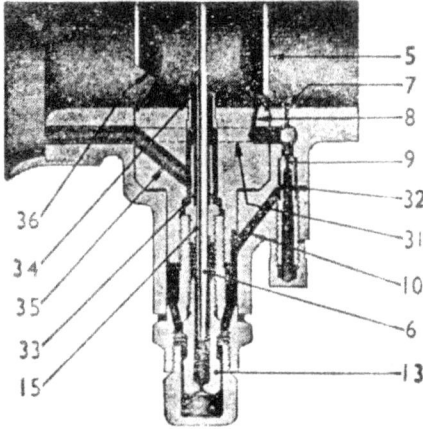

(FOR KEY TO DIAGRAM NUMBERS SEE BELOW)

Diagrammatic section of Carburetter showing only the lower half of the throttle chamber with the throttle a little open—and the internal primary air passages to the main jet and pilot system.

FOR KEY TO DIAGRAM NUMBERS SEE BELOW
Fig. X5.

1. Mixing Chamber Top.
2. Mixing Chamber Cap.
3. Carburetter Body.
4. Jet Needle Clip.
5. Throttle Valve.
6. Jet Needle.
7. Pilot outlet.
8. Pilot by-pass.
9. Pilot Jet.
10. Petrol Feed to Pilot Jet.
11. Pilot Jet Cover Nut.
12. Main Jet Cover.
13. Main Jet.
14. Jet Holder.
15. Needle Jet.
16. Jet Block.
17. Air Valve
18. Mixing Chamber Cap Spring.
19. Cable Adjuster (air).
20. Cable Adjuster (throttle).
21. Tickler.
22. Banjo Bolt.
23. Banjo.
24. Filter Gauze.
25. Needle Seating.
26. Needle.
27. Float.
28. Side Cover Screws.
31. Air to Pilot Jet.
32. Feed Holes in Pilot Jet.
33. Bleed Holes in Needle Jet.
34. Primary Air Choke.
35. Primary Air Passage.
36. Throttle Valve Cut-away

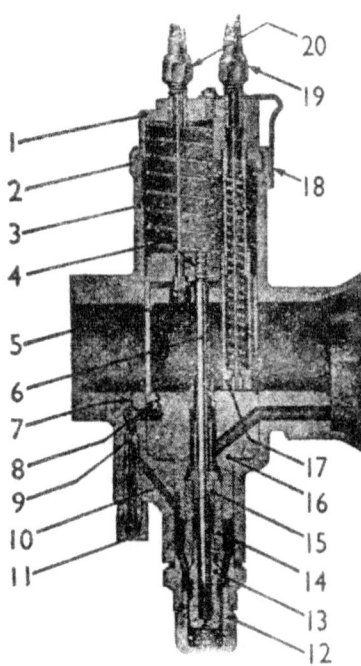

Fig. 7. *Section through Mixing Chamber, showing Air Valve and Throttle closed.*

29. PILOT AIR ADJUSTING SCREW
This screw regulates the strength of the mixture for "idling" and for the initial opening of the throttle. The screw controls the depression on the pilot jet by metering the amount of air that mixes with the petrol.

30. THROTTLE ADJUSTING SCREW
Set this screw to hold the throttle open sufficiently to keep the engine running when the twist-grip is shut off.

B.S.A. Service Sheet No. 708 (contd.)

Cable Controls

See that there is a minimum of backlash when the controls are set back and that any movement of the handlebar does not cause the throttle to open; this is done by the adjusters on the top of the carburetter. See that the throttle shuts down freely.

Petrol Feed

Verification. Detach petrol pipe union at the float chamber end; turn on petrol tap momentarily and see that fuel gushes out. Avoid petrol pipes with vertical loops as they cause air-locks. Flooding may be due to a worn or bent needle or a leaky float, but nearly all flooding with new machines is due to impurities (grit, fluff, etc.) in the tank—so clean out the float chamber periodically till the trouble ceases. If the trouble persists the tank might be drained, swilled out, etc. Note that if the carburetter, either vertical or horizontal, is flooding with the engine stopped, the overflow from the main jet will not run into the engine but out of the carburetter through a hole at the base of the mixing chamber.

Fixing Carburetter and Air Leaks

Erratic slow running is often caused by air leaks, so verify there are none at the point of attachment to the cylinder or inlet pipe—check by means of oil placed around the joint, if there are leaks the oil will be sucked in, and eliminate by new washers and the equal tightening up of the flange nuts. Also in old machines look out for air leaks caused by a worn throttle or worn inlet valve guides.

Explosions in Exhaust

May be caused by too weak a pilot mixture when the throttle is closed or nearly closed—also, it may be caused by too rich a pilot mixture and an air leak in the exhaust system; the reason in either case is that the mixture has not fired in the cylinder and has fired in the hot silencer. If the explosion occurs when the throttle is fairly wide open the trouble will be ignition—not carburation.

Excessive Petrol Consumption

On a new machine may be due to flooding, caused by impurities from the petrol tank lodging on the float needle seat and so preventing its valve from closing. If the machine has had several years use, flooding may be caused by a worn float needle valve. Also excessive petrol consumption will be apparent if the throttle needle jet (o) Fig. X4. or (15) Fig. X5, has worn; it may be remedied or improved by lowering the needle in the throttle, but if it cannot be, then the only remedy is to get a new needle jet.

Air Filters

These may affect the jet setting, so if one is fitted afterwards to the carburetter the main jet may have to be smaller If a carburetter is set with an air filter and the engine is run without it, take care not to overheat the engine due to too weak a mixture; testing with the air control will indicate if a larger main jet and higher needle position are required.

B.S.A. Service Sheet No. 708 (contd.)

Faults

The trouble may not be carburation; if the trouble cannot be remedied by making mixtures richer or weaker with the air control, and you know the petrol feed is good and the carburetter is not flooding, the trouble is elsewhere.

Fault Finding

There are only *two* possible faults in carburation, either *richness* of mixture or *weakness* of mixture, so in case of trouble decide which is the cause, by:—

1. Examining the petrol feed ...
   - Verify jets and passages are clear.
   - Verify ample flow.
   - Verify there is no flooding.

2. Looking for air leaks ...
   - At the connection to the engine.
   - Or due to leaky inlet valve stems.

3. Defective or worn parts ...
   - As a slack throttle-worn needle jet.
   - The mixing chamber union nut not tightened up, or loose jets.

4. *Testing with the air control* to see if by richening the mixture the results are better or worse.

Indications of

Richness:	Weakness:
Black smoke in exhaust.	Spitting in carburetter.
Petrol spraying out of carburetter.	Erratic slow running.
Four strokes, eight-stroking	Overheating.
Two strokes, four-stroking.	Acceleration poor.
Heavy, lumpy running.	Engine goes better if:—
Heavy petrol consumption.	Throttle not wide open, or air control is partially closed.
? If the jet block (F) is not tightened up by washer and nut (E) richness will be caused through leakage of petrol.	? Has air cleaner been removed.
? Air cleaner choked up.	? Jets partially choked up
? Needle jet worn large.	Removing the silencer or running with a racing silencer requires a richer setting and large main jet.
Sparking plug sooty.	

Note

Verify correctness of fuel feed, stop air leaks, check over ignition and valve operation and timing. *Decide by test whether richness or weakness is the trouble and at what throttle position.* See throttle opening diagrams, Fig. X6.

B.S.A. Service Sheet No. 708 (contd.)

Procedure

If at a particular throttle opening you partially close the air control, and the engine goes better, weakness is indicated; or on the other hand the running is worse, richness is indicated. *Then you proceed to adjust the appropriate part as indicated for that position.*

Fault at Throttle Positions indicated on Fig. X9

To Cure Richness:		To Cure Weakness:
Fit smaller main jet.	1st	Fit larger main jet.
Screw out pilot air screw.	2nd	Screw pilot air screw in.
Fit a throttle with larger cut-away.	3rd	Fit a throttle with smaller cut-away.
Lower needle one or two grooves.	4th	Raise needle one or two grooves.

Notes

It is not correct to cure a rich mixture at half-throttle by fitting a smaller main jet because the main jet may be correct for power at full throttle: the proper thing to do is to lower the needle.

Information on throttle slides and needle position is given in paragraphs (*f*) and (*e*) respectively in the next section entitled "Tuning".

Changing from Standard Petrols to Special Fuels.

Such as alcohol mixtures will, with the same setting in the carburetter, certainly cause weakness of mixture and possible damage from overheating.

TUNING

(*a*) Figs. X8 and 8a are two diagrammatic sections of the carburetter to show:
1. The throttle stop screw.
2. The pilot air screw.

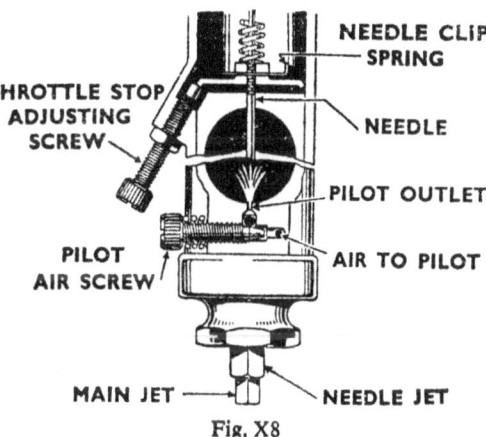

Fig. X8

(*b*) **Throttle Stop Screw**

Set this screw to prop the throttle open sufficiently to keep the engine running when the twist-grip is shut off.

(*c*) **Pilot Air Screw**

This screw regulates the strength of the mixture for "idling" and for the initial opening of the throttle. The screw controls the suction on the pilot petrol jet by metering the amount of air that mixes with the petrol.

NOTE:—The air for the pilot jet may be admitted internally or externally according to one or other of the designs, but there is no difference in tuning.

(*d*) **Main Jet**

The main jet controls the petrol supply when the throttle is more than three-quarters open, but at smaller throttle openings although the supply of fuel goes through the main jet, the amount is diminished by the metering effect of the needle in the needle jet.

Each jet is calibrated and numbered so that its exact discharge is known and two jets of the same number are alike.

B.S.A. Service Sheet No. 708 (contd.)

Never reamer a Jet out, get another of the right size
The bigger the number the bigger the jet. Spare jets *are sealed*.

To get at the main jet, undo the float chamber holding bolt (Q) Fig. X4, or main jet cover number 12 (Fig. X7). The jet is screwed into the needle jet so if the jet is tight, hold the needle jet also carefully with a spanner whilst unscrewing the main jet.

(e) Needle and Needle Jet

The needle is attached to the throttle and being tapered either allows more or less petrol to pass through the needle jets as the throttle is opened or closed throughout the range, except when idling or nearly full throttle. The needle jet is of a defined size and is only altered from standard when using alcohol fuels.

The taper needle position in relation to the throttle opening can be set according to the mixture required by fixing it to the throttle with the needle clip spring in a certain groove (see illustration above), thus either raising or lowering it. Raising the needle richens the mixture and lowering it weakens the mixture at throttle openings from quarter to three-quarter open (see illustration, Fig. X9).

(f) Throttle Valve Cut-away

The atmospheric side of the throttle is cut away to influence the depression on the main fuel supply and thus gives a means of tuning between the pilot and needle jet range of throttle opening. The amount of cut-away is recorded by a number marked on the throttle, viz.: 6/3 means throttle type 6 with number 3 cut-away; larger cut-aways, say 4 and 5, give weaker mixtures, and 2 and 1 richer mixtures.

(g) Air Valve

Is used only for starting and running when cold, and for experimenting with, otherwise run with it wide open.

(h) Tickler

A small plunger located in the float chamber lid. When pressed down on the float, the neddle valve is pushed off its seat and so "flooding" is achieved. Flooding temporarily enriches the mixture until the level of the petrol subsides to normal.

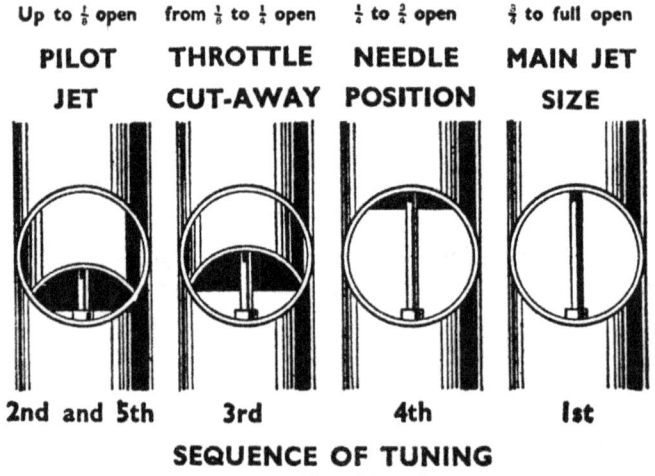

Phases of Amal Needle Jet Carburettor Throttle Openings

Up to $\frac{1}{8}$ open	from $\frac{1}{8}$ to $\frac{1}{4}$ open	$\frac{1}{4}$ to $\frac{3}{4}$ open	$\frac{3}{4}$ to full open
PILOT JET	THROTTLE CUT-AWAY	NEEDLE POSITION	MAIN JET SIZE
2nd and 5th	3rd	4th	1st

SEQUENCE OF TUNING
Fig. X9

B.S.A. Service Sheet No. 708 (contd.)

Sequence of Tuning
Tune up. In the following order only, by so doing you will not upset good results obtained.

NOTE.—The carburetter is automatic throughout the throttle range—the air control should always be wide open except when used for starting or until the engine has warmed up. We assume normal petrols are used.

Read remarks on "Fault Finding" and "Tuning" for each tuning device and get the motor going perfectly on a quiet road with a slight up gradient so that on test the engine is pulling.

1st Main Jet with Throttle in position
Test the engine for full throttle; if when at full throttle, the power seems better with the throttle less than wide open or with the air valve closed slightly the main jet is too small. If the engine runs "heavily" the main jet is too large. If testing for speed work note the jet size is rich enough to keep engine cool, and to verify this, examine the sparking plug by taking a fast run, declutching and stopping engine quickly. If the plug body at the end has a bright black appearance, the mixture is correct; if sooty, the mixture is rich; or if a dry grey colour, the mixture is too weak and a larger jet is necessary.

2nd Pilot Jet with Throttle in positions 2 and 5
With engine idling too fast with the twist-grip shut off and the throttle shut down on to the throttle stop screw, and ignition set for best slow running: (1) Loosen stop screw nut and screw down until engine runs slower and begins to falter, then screw the pilot air screw in or out to make engine run regularly and faster. (2) Now gently lower the throttle stop screw until the engine runs slower and just begins to falter, then lock the nut lightly and begin again to adjust the pilot air screw to get best slow running; if this second adjustment makes engine run too fast, go over the job again a third time. Finally, lock up tight the throttle stop screw nut without disturbing the screw's position.

3rd Throttle Cut-away with Throttle in position
If, as you take off from the idling position, there is objectionable spitting from the carburetter, slightly richen the pilot mixture by screwing the air screw in about half a turn, but if this is not effective, screw it back again and fit a throttle with a smaller cut-away. If the engine jerks under load at this throttle position and there is no spitting, either the throttle needle is much too high or a larger throttle cut-away is required to cure richness.

4th Needle with Throttle in position 4
The needle controls a wide range of throttle opening and also the acceleration. Try the needle in as low a position as possible, viz., with the clip in a groove as near the end as possible; if acceleration is poor and with air valve partially closed the results are better, raise the needle by two grooves; if very much better try lowering needle by one groove and leave it where it is best.

NOTE:—If mixture is still too rich with clip in groove number 1 nearest the end—the needle jet probably wants replacement because of wear. The needle itself never wears out.

5th Finally go over the idling again for final touches.

B.S.A. MOTOR CYCLES LTD., Service Department, Armoury Road, Birmingham 11.
Printed in England
B.S.A. Press.

BSA SERVICE SHEET No. 708B

ALL MODELS

CARBURATION AT HIGH ALTITUDES

The carburetter settings of all B.S.A. motor cycles are designed to give the best all round performance at altitudes of a few thousand feet.

At greater altitudes the air becomes rarefied with the result that the mixture is incorrect.

To overcome this difficulty it is necessary to reduce the size of the main jet, the reduction depending on the altitude at which the machine is mainly used.

The table below shows the percentage of reduction at given altitudes, but it must be emphasised that while the alteration to jet size will correct the mixture, it will not replace the lost power. This can only be corrected by "blowing" or super-charging.

It may also be advisable to re-tune the carburetter for smaller throttle openings this should be done in accordance with Service Sheet 708.

Altitude.	Percentage of reduction in jet size.
3,000 feet	5%
6,000 feet	9%
9,000 feet	13%
12,000 feet	17%

B.S.A. MOTOR CYCLES LTD., Service Dept., Armoury Road, Birmingham 11.

B.S.A. Press.

BSA SERVICE SHEET No. 708C

CARBURATION

"D" Group Models

A CARBURETTOR WITH NEEDLE CONTROLLED SINGLE JET

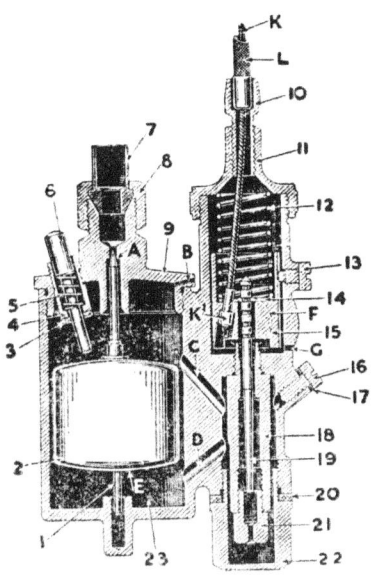

FIG. X13.

This sectioned diagram is taken through the centre of the mixing chamber and float chamber, showing the float and jet and throttle mechanism. The float and needle are shown as one piece as for types 259 and 261, but in type 223 the float needle (1) is separate from the float (2), but is attached thereto by a spring bow fastened to the float at the placed marked (E). The cable (K) and its anchoring (K1) are diagrammatic as in practice the cable anchoring is in front of the jet.

HOW IT WORKS

This carburettor is designed to suit small engines and to eliminate any difficulty arising out of the use of very small jets. The control is automatic, the hand lever on the bar operating the throttle (15), which in its turn controls the mixture according to the engine speed.

The full power control of the mixture is by the main jet (21) feeding the engine through a needle jet (18), in which there is a needle (19). The taper on the needle controls the mixture at lesser throttle openings, and the position of the taper in the needle jet, providing a means for richening or weakening the mixture at various throttle positions. The needle is located in the throttle (19) by a circular spring clip (14) held down by the throttle spring (12) and the needle itself is positioned by the particular groove that the clip (14) is fixed to.

For idling, the fuel supply is controlled by the parallel portion of the needle (19) entering the bore of the needle jet (18), the difference in diameter being the jet orifice, which is small—although in case of obstruction or gumming up due to the petrol and oil system, it can be instantly cleared by opening the throttle.

The petrol feed is into the top of the float chamber (7) where constant levels are maintained, and the petrol at these levels flows to the main jet (21) through a passage (D), and air locks are liberated through the passage (C), back into the float chamber at the top.

The jets (18 and 21) can be got at by undoing jet plug (22). The throttle (15) and adjustable needle (19) can be removed by unscrewing the mixing chamber top (11). The throttle is guided by screw (13) working in a groove in the throttle, and the slot in the throttle enables the cable (K) to be quickly detached.

The intake of the carburettor may have an air strainer and a strangler for closing off the air only for starting when cold.

CARBURETTOR WITH NEEDLE CONTROLLED SINGLE JET

Names of Parts:
1. Float needle.
2. Float.
3. Tickler cotter.
4. Tickler bush.
5. Tickler spring.
6. Tickler.
7. Petrol pipe union nipple.
8. Petrol pipe union nut.
9. Float chamber cover.
10. Cable adjuster.
11. Mixing chamber top.
12. Throttle spring.
13. Throttle valve location screw.
14. Jet needle clip.
15. Throttle valve.
16. Feed hole screw.
17. Feed hole washer.
18. Needle jet.
19. Jet needle.
20. Jet plug washer.
21. Main jet.
22. Jet plug.
23. Float chamber.

A. Petrol feed needle seat.
B. Air vent hole in float chamber cover.
C. Air release passage from 1st chamber into float chamber.
D. Petrol feed passage from float chamber to main jet (21).
E. The illustration shows the float and needle as one piece, but if the needle is separate, the float has a spring bow at this point to hold the needle in a groove.
F. The choke bore of the carburettor, the size of which is specified according to engine size and maximum revs.
G. Drain hole from mixing chamber to liberate any excess petrol due to flooding.
H. Guide groove in the throttle to prevent incorrect assembly.
J. Cutaway of the throttle. There are various cutaways, which are numbered and marked on the bottom of the throttle. The cutaway affects the mixture up to half-throttle position.
K. Throttle cable.
K1. Throttle cable nipple.
L. Throttle cable outer cover.

GENERAL MAINTENANCE INSTRUCTIONS

Keep the float chamber free from impurities, which are the commonest cause of flooding. Otherwise, if flooding takes place, remove the petrol pipe connection from the lid and clean out all the passages. See that the float needle is not bent, nor the petrol float clogged. If the needle seating is at fault, rub the needle lightly in by twisting it between the finger and thumb. (Never use any grinding compound). If the needle itself has a deep groove in it on the taper end, a new needle and float may be necessary. When replacing the float chamber lid, first see that the blunt end of the float needle is in the guide hole at the bottom of the float chamber, and then guide the lid over the taper end of the needle before screwing down. Also see that the tickler works freely and springs back, and that the air hole in the rim of the lid is clear.

If the carburettor is ever removed from the induction pipe, see that it is pushed right home on to the pipe before locking the ring clip. Never fit the carburettor to a pipe on which it is slack, nor ever drive it in to a tight one. A carburettor should be a good push-fit on to the inlet pipe, and should be pushed on true with a screwing motion after having put a little oil on the pipe.

Keep the air intake or gauze free from obstruction and see that the air strangler, if of the knife type fitted into the intake of a carburettor, remains firmly open when opened. If it is inclined to be slack, bend it slightly to stiffen the movement.

If the throttle should become slack after years of use, it should be replaced, otherwise the slow-running may be interfered with. Also, if a throttle has become badly worn, it may be advisable also to replace the needle jet, as this might wear slightly large in diameter through the movement of the needle in the same, thus causing a richer mixture than necessary.

Also bad petrol consumption will be apparent if the throttle needle jet (18) has worn; it may be remedied or improved by lowering the needle in the throttle, but if it cannot be—then the only remedy is to get a new needle jet.

TRACING FAULTS   ASSUMING ENGINE IN GOOD ORDER AND EXHAUST SYSTEM NOT CHOKED

1. Assure yourself of ample petrol supply, good compression, clean sparking plug and good spark at the points. Also rectify if flooding and verify complete closing and opening of throttle and air strangler, and that the air intake gauze or filter are clean.

2. Verify carburettor to be clean internally and that jet and passages are clear and that there is no air leak at the fitting of the carburettor to the engine. Also verify that main jet and needle jet are screwed up firmly.

3. When the above points are in order, there are only two possible faults in carburation—either the mixture is RICH or WEAK, and **you must determine which of the two is causing inefficient running, and at what throttle opening,** so that the carburettor can be tuned correctly. Indications are as follows:—

For Richness:
Black sooty smoke in exhaust.
Petrol spraying out of carburettor.
Two-stroke engine "four-stroking".
Heavy petrol consumption.
Sparking plug sooty.
Heavy lumpy running.
Four-stroke engines "eight-stroking".

For Weakness:
"Spitting" in the carburettor.
Erratic slow-running.
Poor acceleration.
Engine runs better at less than full throttle opening.
Overheating.
Sparking plug dry grey colour around the points.

4. Some causes for above producing:—

Richness:
Punctured float or bent float needle.
Tickler stuck down.
Needle (19) raised too much.
Main jet (21) too large or not screwed up.
In old machines, needle jet (18) worn.
Air filter choked.

Weakness:
Air leaks.
Petrol supply or jet partially choked.
Too small main jet (21).
Needle (19) in too low position.
Air gauze or filter been removed.
Using petrol with water in it.

5. If engine "idles" better after tickling the float and gives better power with air shutter partially closed, the mixture is weak.
   Idling with petrol turned off temporarily and no suspicion of spitting when opening throttle quickly when engine is cold—the mixture is rich.

6. Trouble at half to full throttle is most likely to be connected with the main jet (21) supply. Trouble at quarter to three-quarters throttle opening will be due to needle position. If the power is good, at full throttle, very poor acceleration is the effect of too low a needle position, which can be remedied. Bad, slow-running will probably be due to air leaks.

HOW TO TUNE UP—(READ PARTS TO TUNE UP WITH)

1. Generally speaking: for power at full throttle the main jet is selected and at other lower throttle positions, the needle is either raised or lowered to richen or weaken the mixture.

2. To tune up precisely throughout the throttle range imagine four throttle positions:—
   (a) Throttle slightly open as for idling.
   (b) Throttle about quarter open as for running light.
   (c) Throttle from one-quarter to three-quarters open as for general running.
   (d) Throttle three-quarter to wide open as for full power.

3. From the preceding paragraph start tuning in this order, having read "PARTS TO TUNE UP WITH" and with the engine warmed up:—
   1st (d) use the smallest main jet (21) that will give full power when running under load on the level. If the engine runs slightly better with the throttle not quite wide open, the jet is either just right for economy or on the small side.
   2nd (c) set the needle (19) position as low as possible in relation to good acceleration and running at half throttle—"spitting" in the carburettor on acceleration means the needle is too low, so try a groove higher.
   3rd (a and b) if the idling mixture at (a) and the take off at (b) are weak—the engine spitting and fading out—use a smaller cutaway throttle, or if the engine runs lumpily on a rich mixture use a higher cutaway.
   4th Finally, if any alteration has been made to the throttle cutaway it may be necessary to alter the needle position again: putting in a throttle of a smaller cutaway may require the needle lowering by a groove and alternatively a larger cutaway may necessitate raising the needle.

PARTS TO TUNE UP WITH

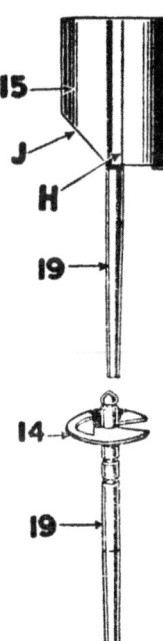

FIG. X15

Main Jet (21) with seal. This jet does not control the slow-running mixture, but it controls the maximum supply of petrol from half to full throttle positions. This jet is interchangeable with other larger Amal carburettors except for the number stamped on it, which indicates the amount of petrol that will flow through. The bigger the number the bigger the jet, and numbers go up and down in fives. Example, 20, 25, 30, etc. These jets should never be reamed out—the seal on the jet you may purchase is a guarantee of its size.

Throttle (15). This part is controlled from the handlebar, and from the shut-off to full-open position progressively increases the amount of gas taken into the engine. The slope at (J) is called the cutaway, and its number is stamped on the bottom. Throttles can be had with different cutaways—the bigger the cutaway and number the weaker the mixture for idling and up to half throttle positions and vice versa. The throttle holds the needle of the needle jet.

Needle (19) for Needle Jet (18). This works up and down with the throttle and the taper end goes into the needle jet, so controlling the amount of petrol at different throttle openings. Its position in the throttle and of its taper in the needle jet is therefore affected by which groove the clip (14) is fixed in: the extreme end groove is (1), giving the lowest position and the weakest mixture and vice versa, raising the needle richens the mixture. The spring clip (14) can be sprung off and on. (The illustration shows clip 14 in position 2.)

Needle Jet (18), see section. The standard jet is not marked in any way, but can be had in other sized bores on request, which are marked accordingly. If the mixture gets rich at half-throttle when the machine is old this needle jet has probably worn large and should be replaced. (Extreme weakness when idling may be corrected by a larger bore needle jet, which can be obtained on special application.)

FIG. X14.

For Tuning with Engine Running, but Cycle Stationary

Air Shutter on the intake of the carburettor. This is closed only for starting from cold to reduce the amount of air and to increase the suction on the jet. When tuning, however, the shutter might be used experimentally to indicate if richening the mixture improves matters.

Tickler (6), see section. This is for pressing down the float needle off its seat to allow more petrol to come into the float chamber and so raise the petrol level, and consequently richening the mixture.

NOTE:—For idling, if excessive richness cannot be cured by a larger cutaway nor will the throttle opening range allow a lower needle position—then change the needle jet for a new one, as the old one may be worn. If weakness prevents idling and cannot be cured by a smaller cutaway throttle and a raised needle position, use a larger bore needle jet, which will have its bore marked on it.

GENERAL HINTS AND TIPS

Starting from Cold. Flood the carburettor by depressing the tickler momentarily three or four times and close the air strangler; set the ignition, say half-retarded, then shut the throttle and open it a little, about one-eighth open; then kick-start.

When started, gradually open the throttle to make the engine run faster and when the engine is warmed up, close down again and open the strangler. Should the engine falter either tickle the float chamber again or partially close the strangler until the engine is warm enough to stand the strangler being opened fully.

Starting with Engine Hot. Do not flood the carburettor nor close the air strangler; set the ignition and close the throttle, then, open it again one-eighth of its movement and kick-start. If the engine does not start at once, flood slightly or close the strangler and try again. After starting, open the strangler but if this should cause the engine to falter and not respond to opening the throttle, flood the carburettor momentarily.

Starting Generally. Find out by experiment if and how much it is necessary to flood and also the best position for the air strangler on the carburettor intake.

Usually for easy starting a small throttle opening is desirable and the best position is accompanied by a sucking noise when the engine is being turned over. If this noise cannot be heard, the throttle is probably too wide open and there is, consequently, insufficient "pull" on the starting system.

Given a good engine and a fat spark at the plug, if the engine will not start, the mixture is either too rich or too weak.

Over-richness of the mixture, especially with petroil lubrication, may be caused by over-flooding or by the machine being left with the petrol tap turned on and the float chamber flooding. To clear this over-richness open the throttle wide, also the strangler, and turn the engine over several times, then close the throttle and start again. If the engine does not start at once, the sparking plug points may have become damp or oiled up, so remove the plug and dry the points, and whilst it is out, swing the engine over several times before replacing it; then try again without flooding and with strangler open.

Cable Control. See that there is a minimum of backlash when the control is set back and that any movement of the handlebar does not cause the throttle to open; this is done by the adjuster on the top of the carburettor. See that the throttle shuts down freely.

Petrol Feed, verification. Detach petrol pipe union at the float chamber end; turn on petrol tap momentarily and see that fuel gushes out. Avoid petrol pipes with vertical loops as they cause air locks. Flooding may be due to a worn or bent needle or a leaky float, but nearly all flooding with new machines is due to impurities (grit, fluff, etc.) in the tank—so clean out the float chamber periodically till the trouble ceases. If the trouble persists, the tank might be drained, swilled out, etc.

Fixing Carburettor and Air Leaks. Erratic slow-running is often caused by air leaks, so verify there are none at the point of attachment to the cylinder or inlet pipe—check by means of an oil can and eliminate. Also in old machines look out for leaks caused by a worn throttle (or worn inlet valve guides if a four-stroke engine).

Bad Petrol Consumption of a new machine may be due to flooding caused by impurities from the petrol tank lodging on the float needle seat and so prevent its valve from closing. If the machine has had several years use, flooding may be caused by a worn float needle valve.

Faults. Read "Tracing Faults". The trouble may not be carburation; if the trouble cannot be remedied by making mixture richer or weaker and you know the petrol feed is good and the carburettor is not flooding, the trouble is elsewhere.

B.S.A. MOTOR CYCLES LTD., Service Department, Armoury Road, Birmingham 11

PRINTED IN ENGLAND AT THE B.S.A. PRESS

BSA SERVICE SHEET No. 709

ALL MODELS
FAULT FINDING

No adjustments should be made, or any part tampered with, until the cause of the trouble is known. Otherwise adjustments which are correct may be deranged.

Engine Stops Suddenly:
   Petrol shortage in tank, or choked petrol supply pipe or tap.
   Choked main jet, or water in float chamber.
   Oiled up or fouled sparking plug.
   Water on high-tension pick-up or on sparking plug.

Engine Fails to Start, or is difficult to start:
   Lack of fuel, or insufficient flooding if cold.
   Excessive flooding, allowing neat petrol to enter the cylinder.
   Oil sparking plug, or stuck-up valve or valve stem sticky.
   Weak valve spring, or valve not seating properly.
   Throttle opening too large, or pilot jet choked.
   Contact points dirty, or gap incorrect.
   Flat battery, if coil ignition, or faulty electrical connections in ignition circuit.

Loss of Power:
   Valve, or valves, not seating properly.
   Weak valve spring or springs, or sticking valve.
   No tappet clearance, or excessive clearance.
   Lack of oil in tank.
   Brakes adjusted too closely.
   Badly fitting or broken piston rings.
   Punctured carburettor float.
   Incorrect ignition timing.

Engine Overheats:
   Lack of proper lubrication.
   Weak valve springs, or pitted valve seats.
   Worn piston rings, or late ignition setting.
   Carburettor setting too weak, or partly choked petrol pipe.

Engine Misses Fire:
   Weak valve spring.
   Defective or oiled sparking plug, or oil on contact points.
   Incorrectly adjusted contact points or tappets.
   Faulty condenser.
   Defective sparking plug or high-tension cable.
   Loose sparking plug terminal.
   Carburettor flooding, due to stuck or defective float.
   Partly choked main jet.
   Choked vent hole in petrol tank filler cap.

Excessive Oil Consumption:
   Stoppage, or partial stoppage, in pipe returning oil from engine to tank.
   Clogged, or partially clogged, filter in sump, or oil tank.
   Badly worn or stuck-up piston rings, causing high pressure in engine crankcase.
   High crankcase pressure, caused by release valve (breather) action.
   Air leak in dry sump oiling system.
   Non-return valve in system not seating.
   Ball valve in oil pump stuck on its seat.

B.S.A. MOTOR CYCLES LTD., Service Department, Armoury Road, Birmingham 11
B.S.A. PRESS

BSA SERVICE SHEET No. 710

ALL MODELS
CHAIN ALTERATIONS AND REPAIRS

A chain rarely breaks if it is kept properly lubricated and adjusted. Usually it is worn out long before it reaches breaking point. The rear chain is the most heavily stressed and is therefore the one most likely to give trouble. Spare parts should be carried to enable the rider to carry out a repair on the road with the aid of a chain rivet extractor (see Fig. X7). The front chain will probably be worn out before it requires shortening.

How to use the Chain Rivet Extractor
First press down lever (A) Fig. X7 to open the two jaws (B). Insert the link to be removed so that the jaws grip the roller and support the uppermost inner side plate. The punch (C) is then screwed on to the rivet head until the rivet is forced through the outer plate.

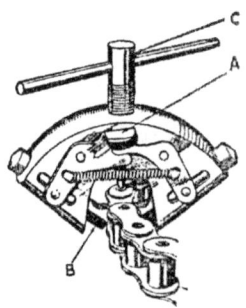

Fig. X7.

To shorten a worn Rear Chain
After a big mileage, the rear chain may have stretched so that no further adjustment is possible by the usual method. In this case it is possible to shorten the chain by one link or pitch, so increasing its useful life. First remove the single connecting spring link (A) securing the two ends of the chain, Fig. X8. If the chain terminates in two ordinary links as in Fig. X8 (in which case the chain will be an even number of pitches) extract the third and fourth rivets (B) from the end and replace the detached three pitches by a single connecting link (C). The connection is made with an additional spring link (D). If one end of the chain has a double cranked link, Fig. X9—in which case the chain will have an odd

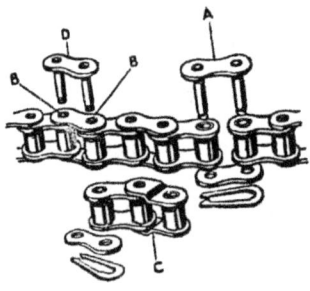

Fig. X8.

Printed in England

B.S.A. Service Sheet No. 710 (contd.)

number of pitches—extract the second and third rivets (A), releasing the cranked link unit complete, which can be retained for further use. Replace with one inner link (B) and again connect up with an additional single connecting link (C).

To repair a damaged Chain

If a roller or link has been damaged (X) Fig. X9, remove rivets (D), take out the damaged link and replace with one inner link, secured by two single connecting links.

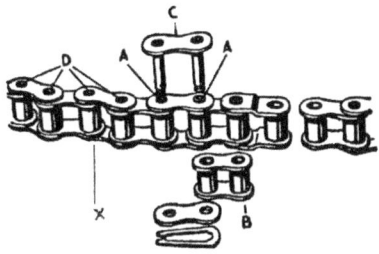

Fig. X9.

It is important that the spring clip fastener should always be put on so that the *closed* end faces the direction of travel of the chain—i.e. when clip is on top run of chain, closed end is toward front of machine—when clip is on bottom run, closed end is towards rear of machine.

It should be noted that once a rivet has been extracted it must not be used again, so that it is important to check that the correct rivet is being removed before actually removing it. In the case of double cranked links, the complete unit comprises an inner link and the cranked outer link—three rollers in all—and these must never be separated.

Fitting Rear Chain

To fit a new rear chain, turn wheel until the spring link of the old chain is located on rear sprocket. Disconnect, and allow the lower run to drop down. Join the top run of the old chain to the new chain by means of the connecting link, and then by pulling on the bottom run of the old chain the new one will be carried round the gearbox sprocket. Then the old chain can be disconnected and the ends of the new one joined together.

When the rear chain breaks and falls from its sprockets, the new or repaired chain can be replaced without taking off the chainguards. One end of the chain must be fed (from the rear) under the front end of the rear top chainguard on to the gearbox sprocket A long bladed screwdriver or a piece of stiff wire may assist this operation When the chain has located on the sprocket teeth, engage a gear and gently turn gearbox over with the kickstarter This will feed chain round gearbox sprocket When sufficient length of chain is hanging below sprocket, disengage gear and chain can then be pulled round until both runs can be fed inside rear chainguard and engaged on rear wheel sprocket.

B.S.A. MOTOR CYCLES LTD., Service Department, Armoury Road, Birmingham 11.

SERVICE SHEET No. 710x

MARCH, 1969

FRAME REPAIRS

ALL MODELS

Frame repairs must not be attempted unless adequate workshop facilities are available.

The information given in this sheet is intended for the use of Dealers who are unable to take advantage of the B.S.A. repair service and who have frame repair facilities.

Spotting points to enable frame trueing to be carried out can be determined by making use of the dimensions given.

B.S.A. Motor Cycles Ltd., Armoury Road Birmingham 11.
PRINTED IN ENGLAND

IT IS DIFFICULT TO UNDERSTAND WHY B.S.A. ISSUED THE FOLLOWING FRAME DRAWINGS IN VARYING SCALES AND AT SUCH SMALL SIZES - MAKING SOME OF THE DIMENSIONS ALMOST IMPOSSIBLE TO READ. HOWEVER, THEY ARE INCLUDED FOR THE SAKE OF COMPLETENESS

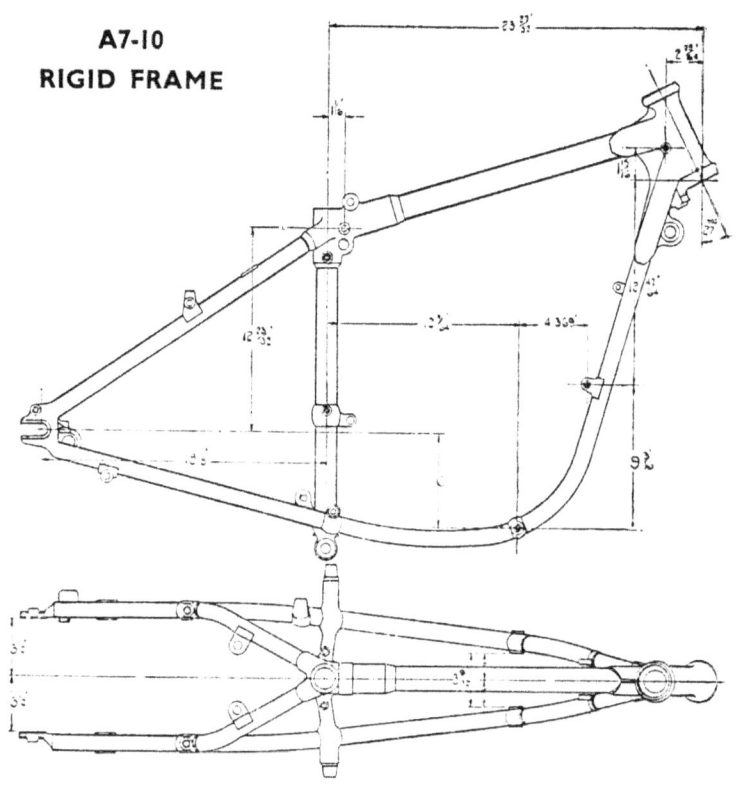

A7-10 RIGID FRAME

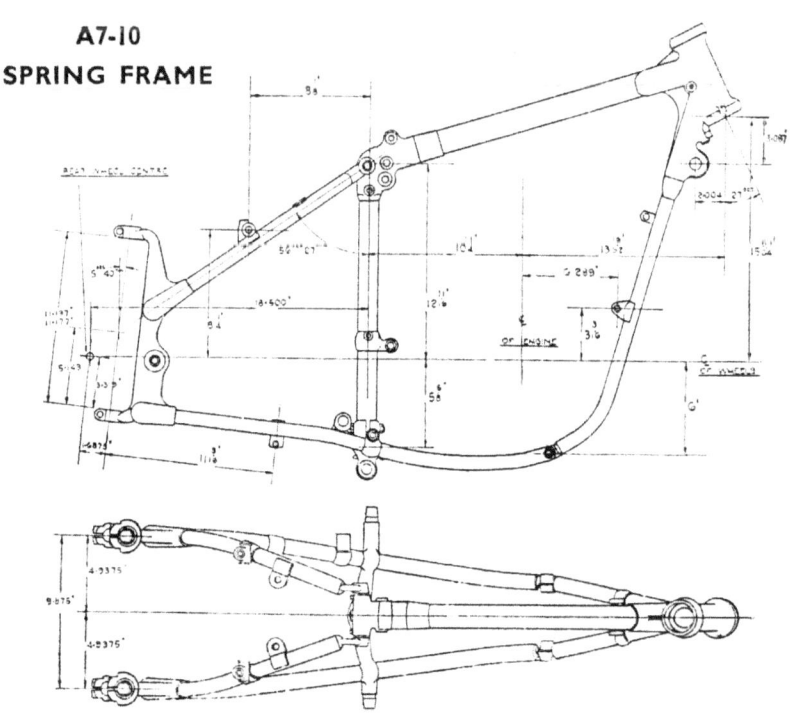

A7-10 SPRING FRAME

1953 SUPER FLASH SPRING FRAME

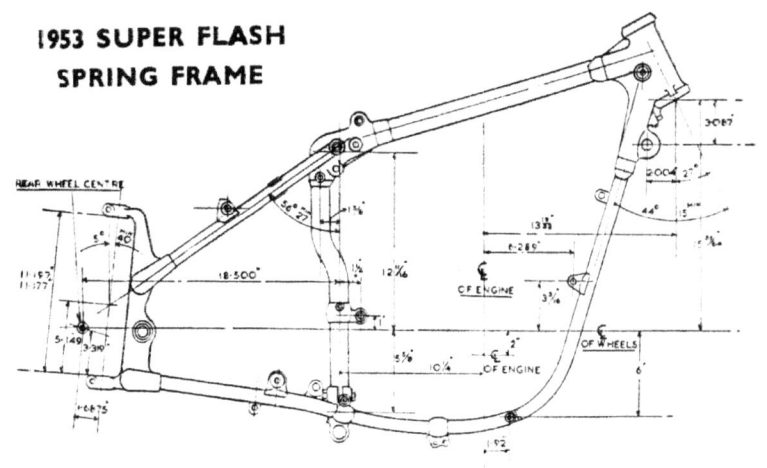

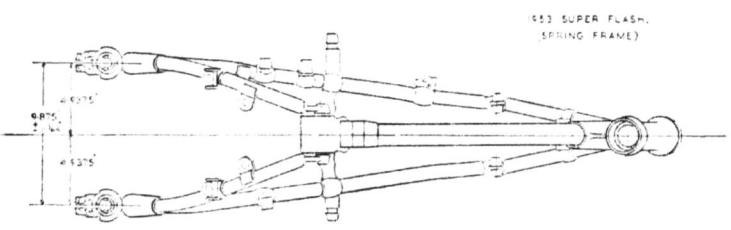

M20, M21 and M33 RIGID FRAME 1945 - 1948

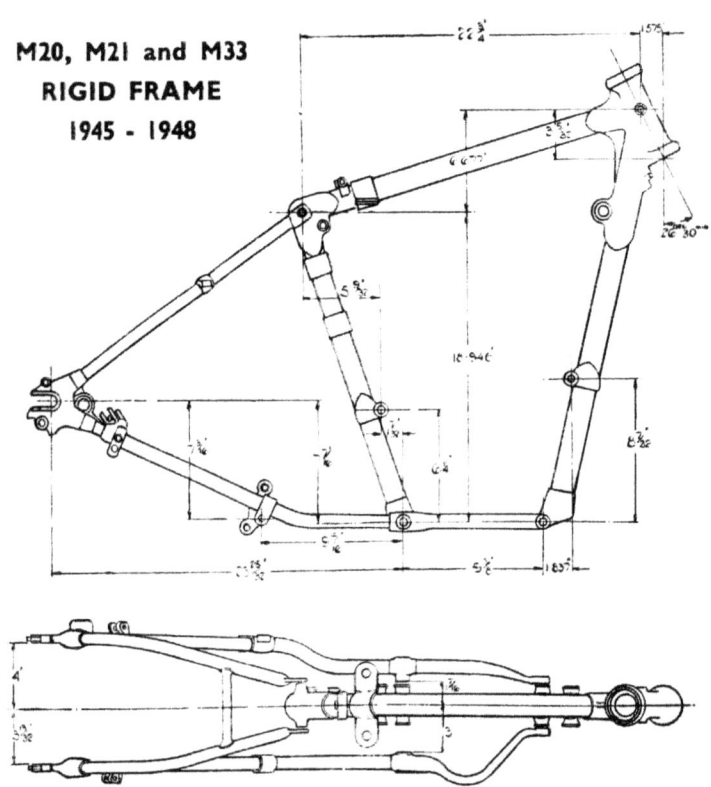

M20, M21 and M33 RIGID FRAME
1949 onwards

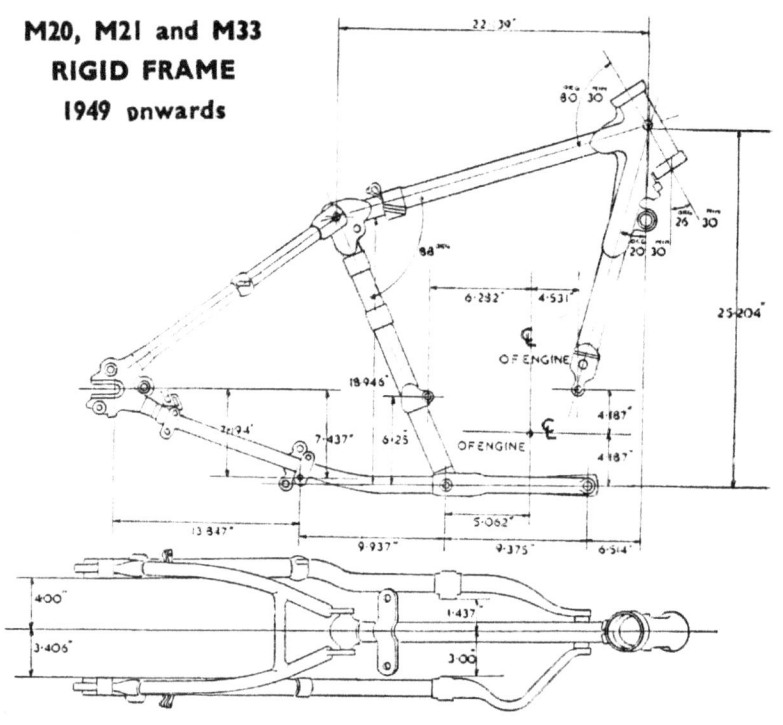

M20, M21 and M33 SPRING FRAME

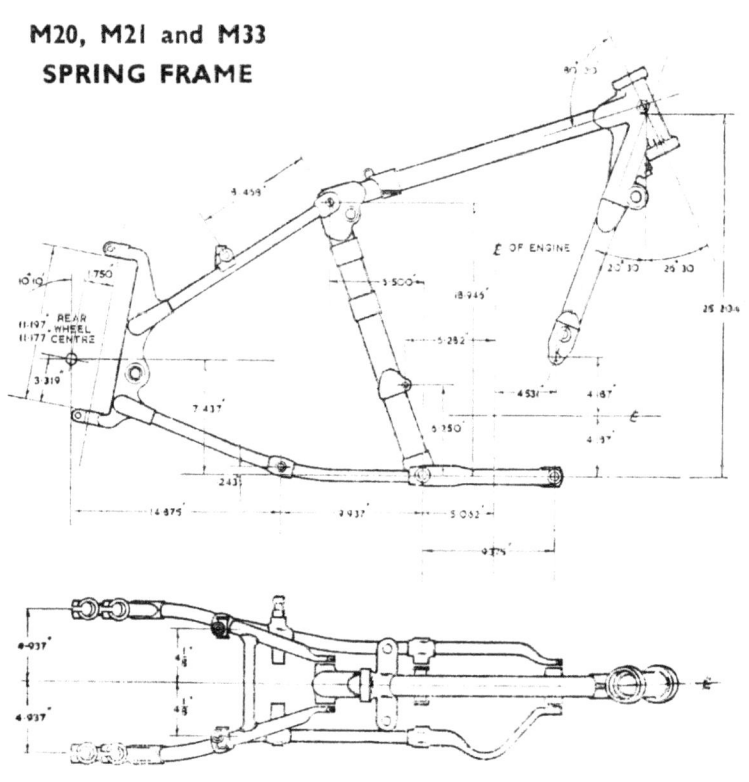

B31-32-33-34 RIGID FRAME

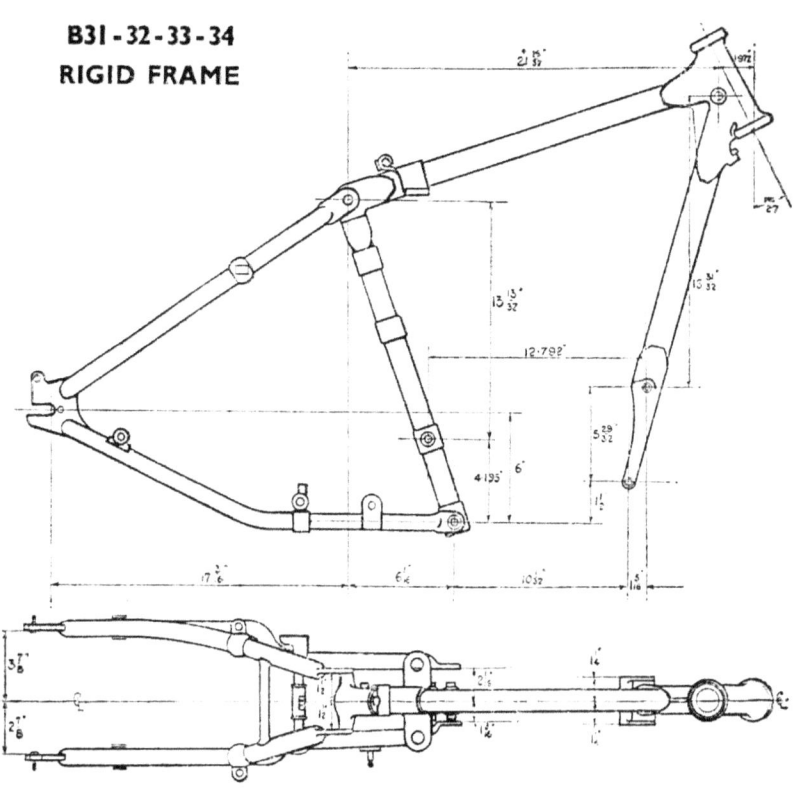

B31-32-33-34 SPRING FRAME

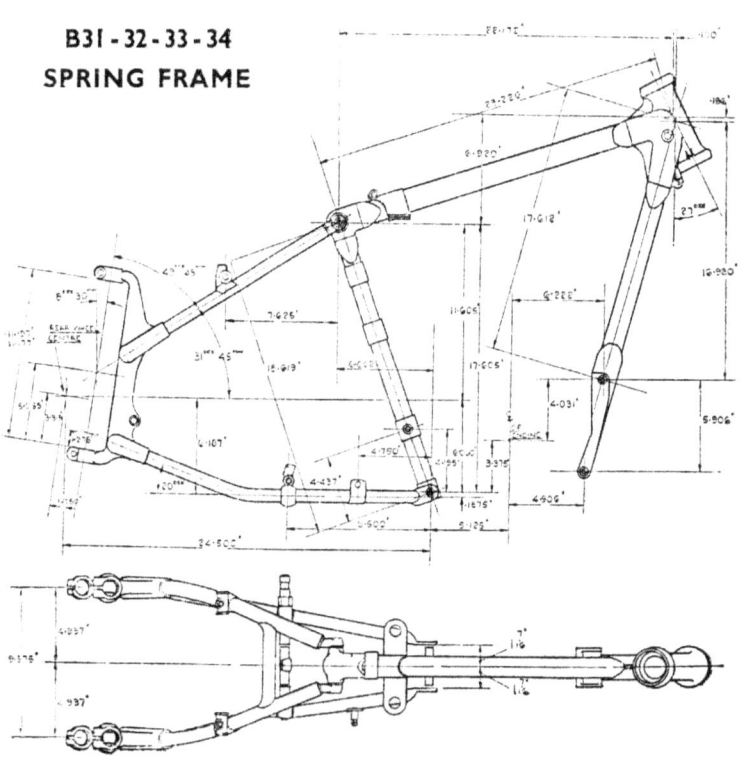

D1 and D3 RIGID FRAME

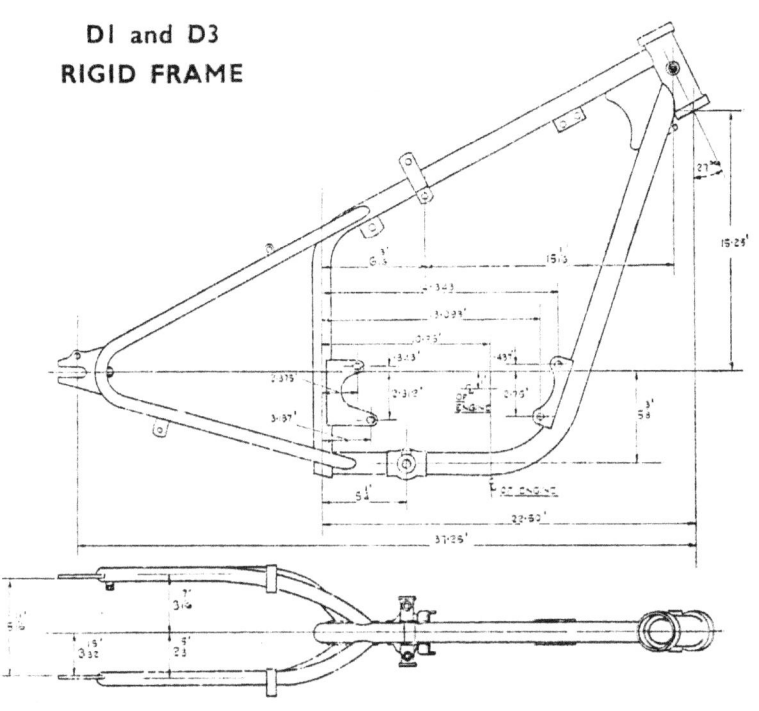

D1 and D3 SPRING FRAME

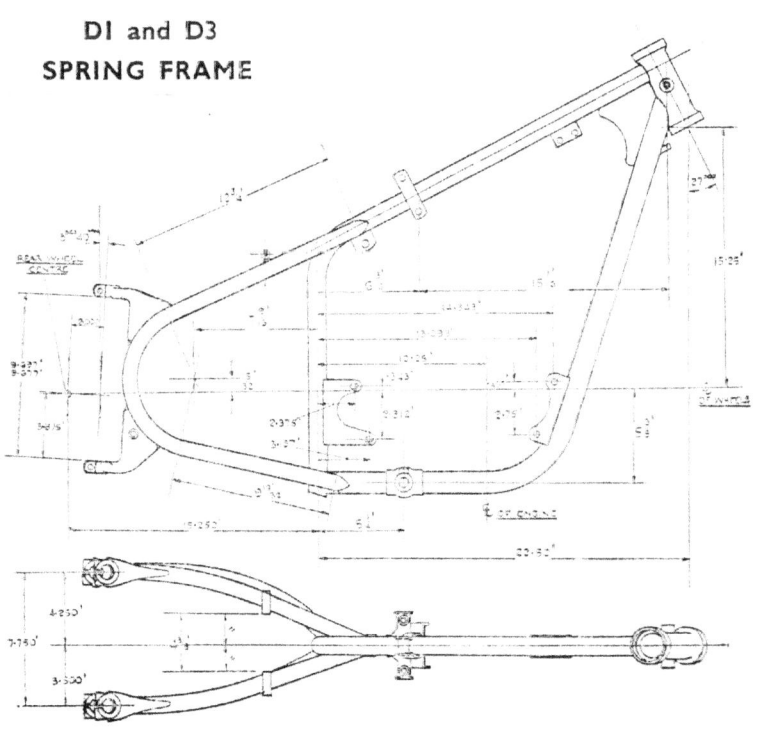

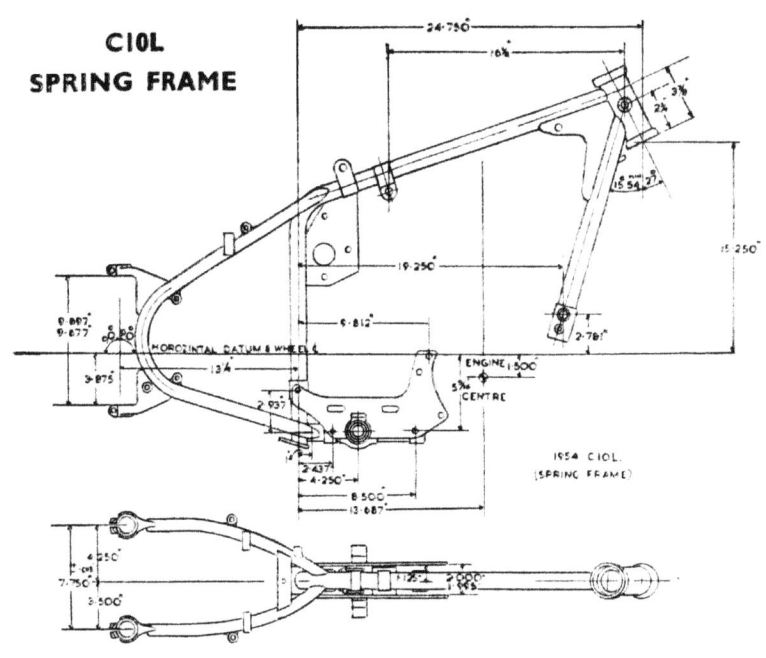
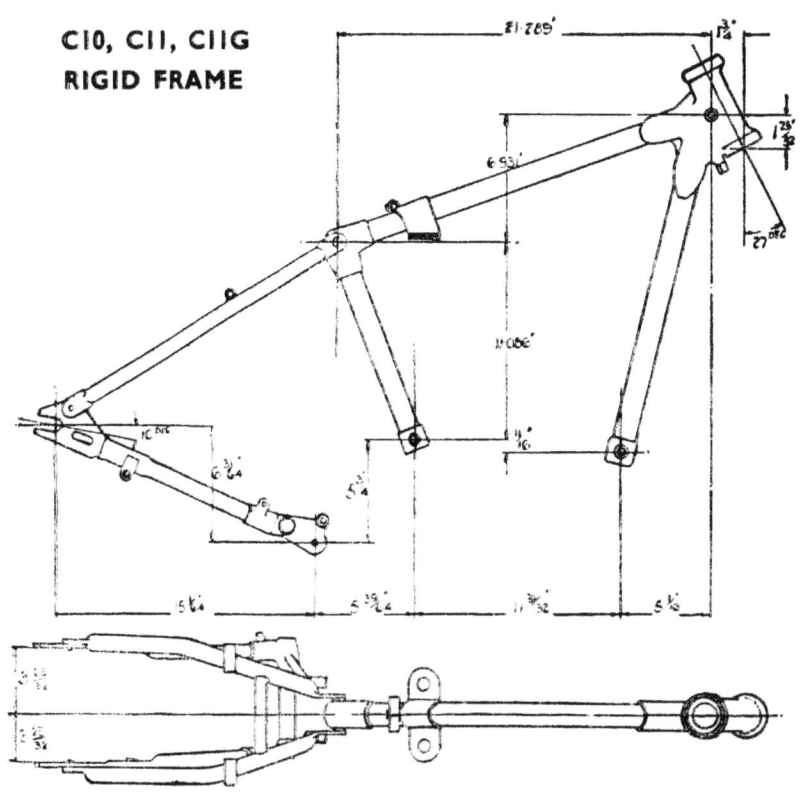

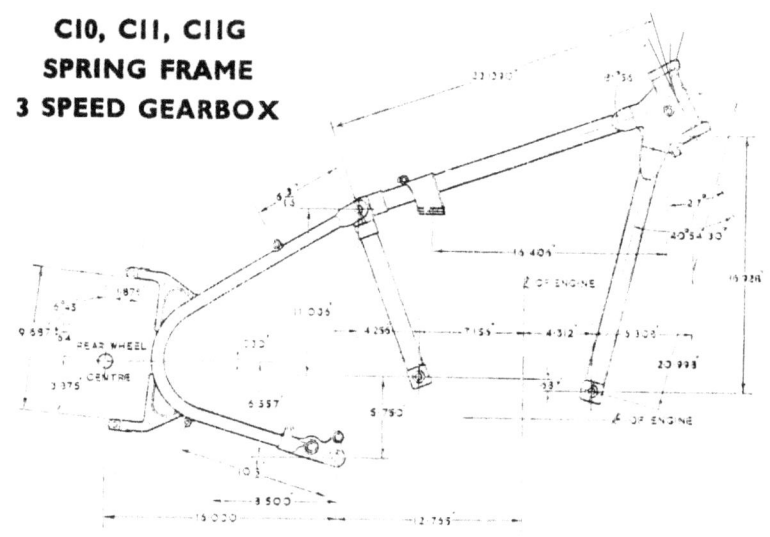
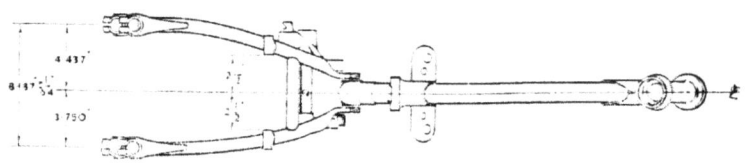
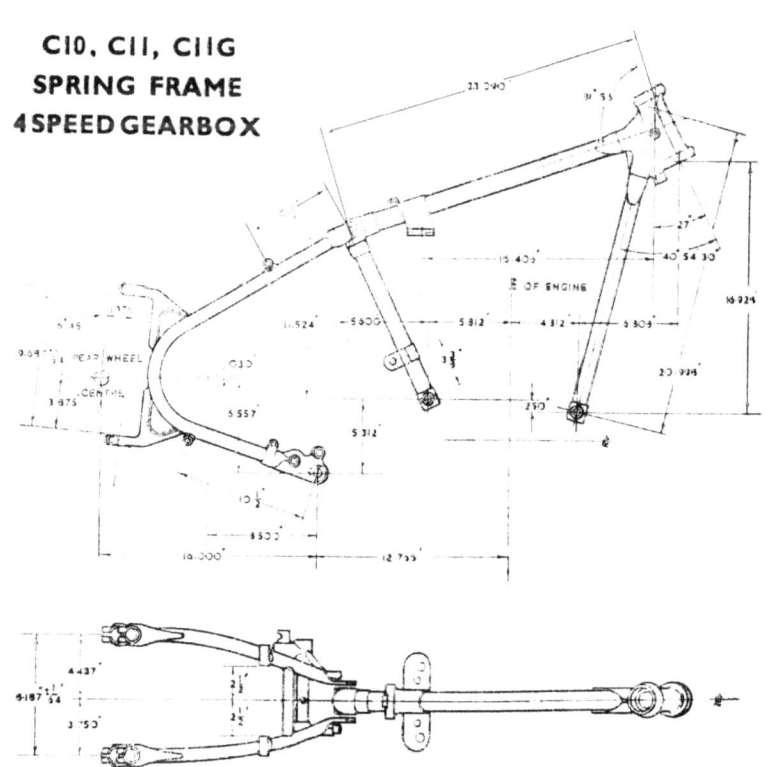

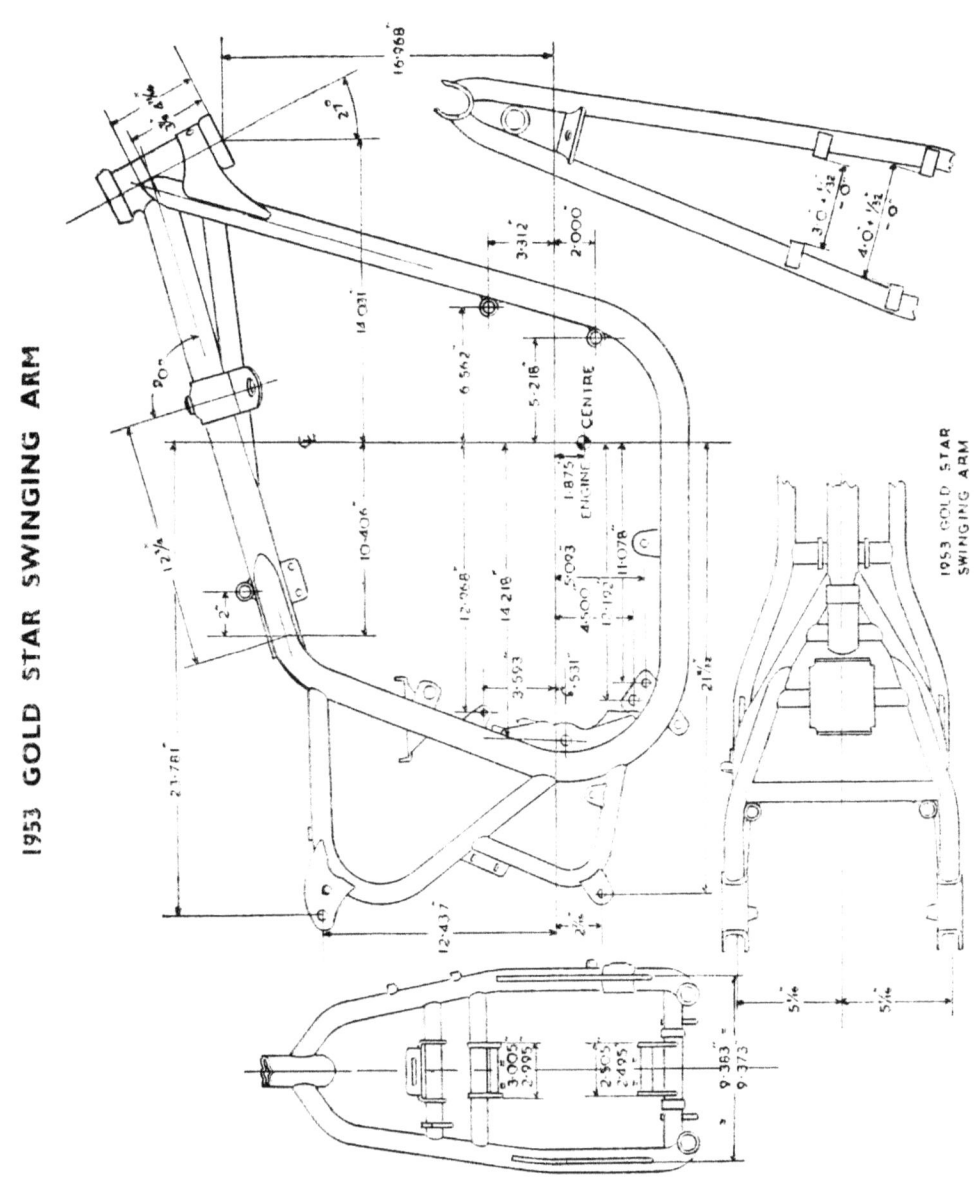

A GROUP, B GROUP and GOLD STAR 1954 SWINGING ARM

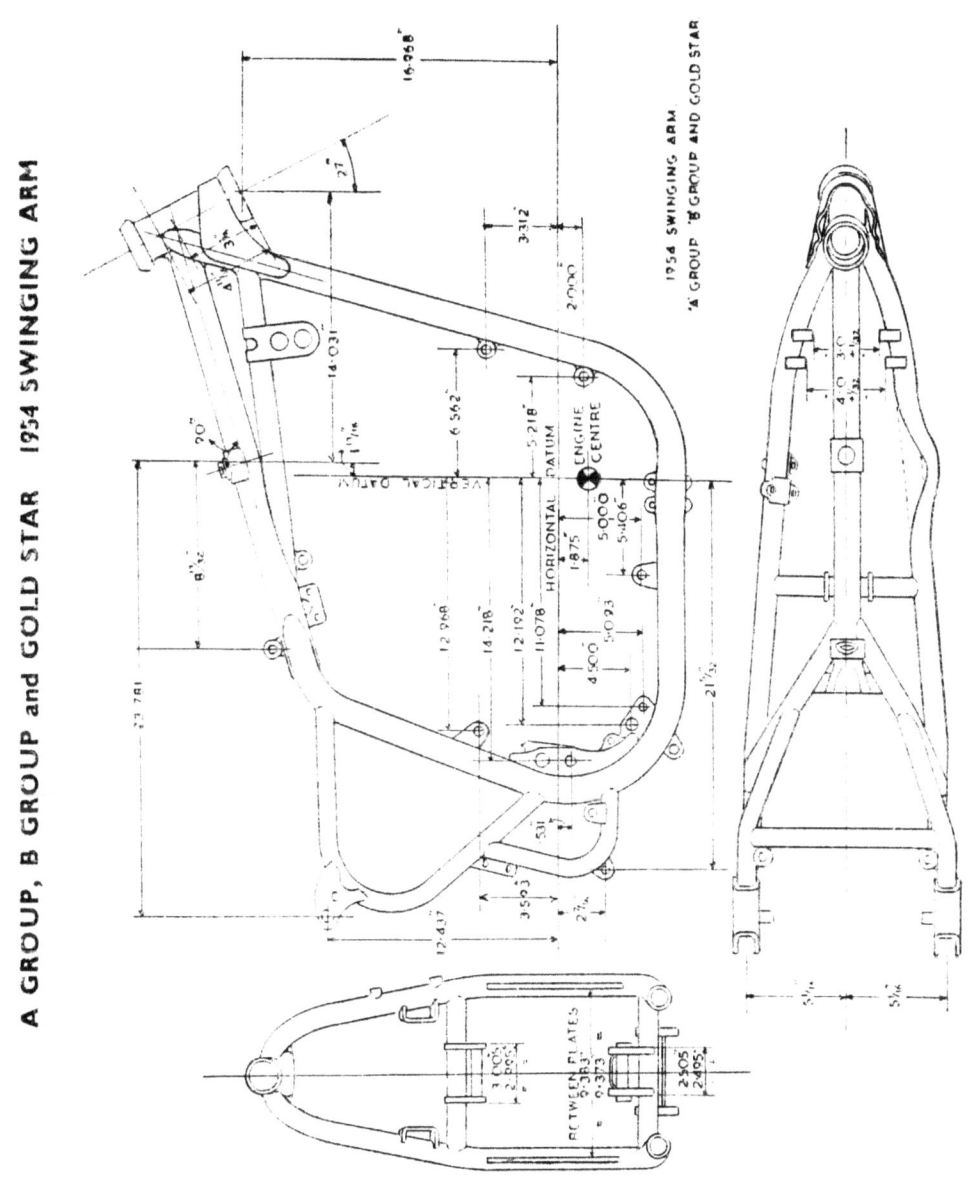

B32 and B34
1954 RIGID FRAME

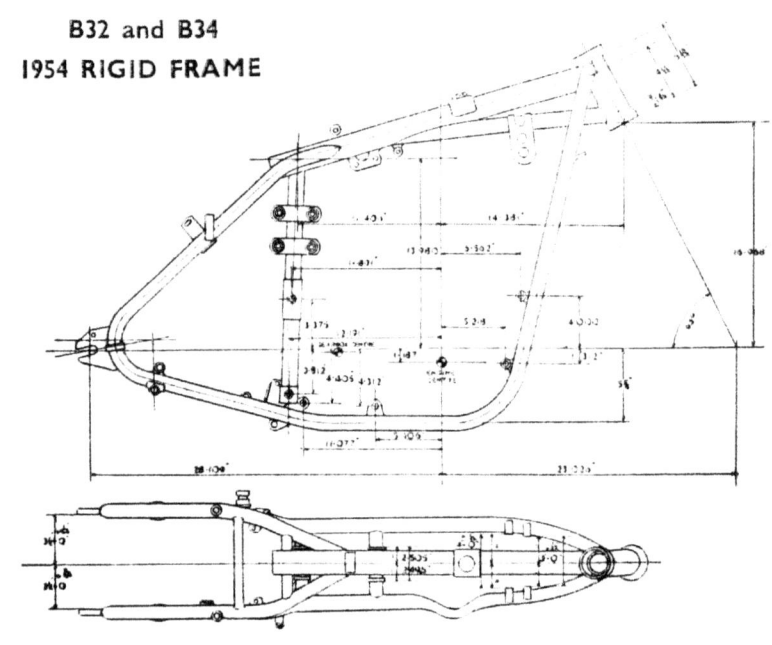

D3 SWINGING ARM

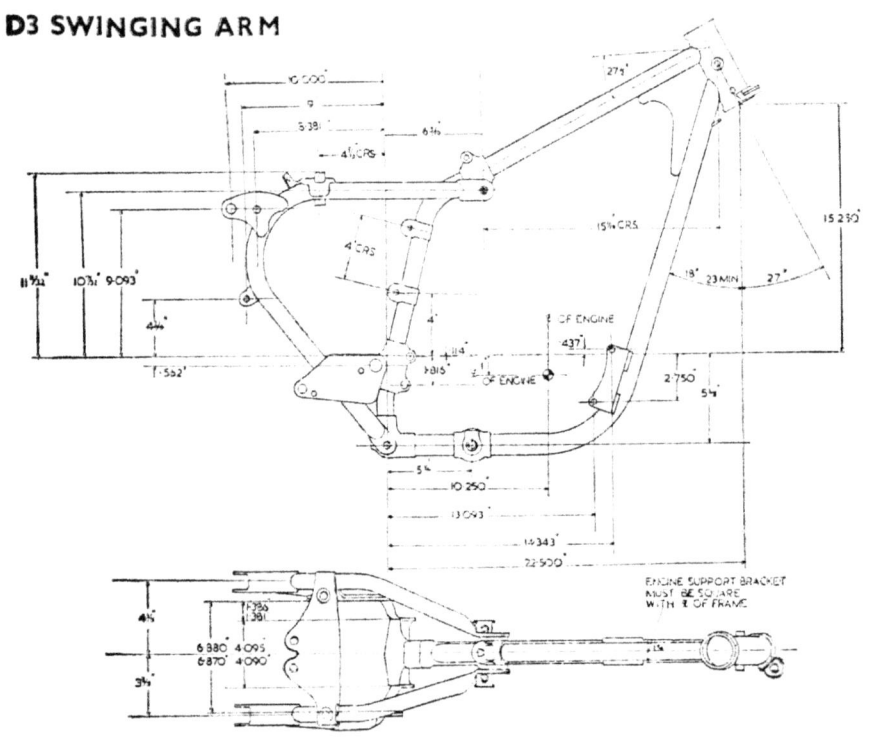

C12 SWINGING ARM

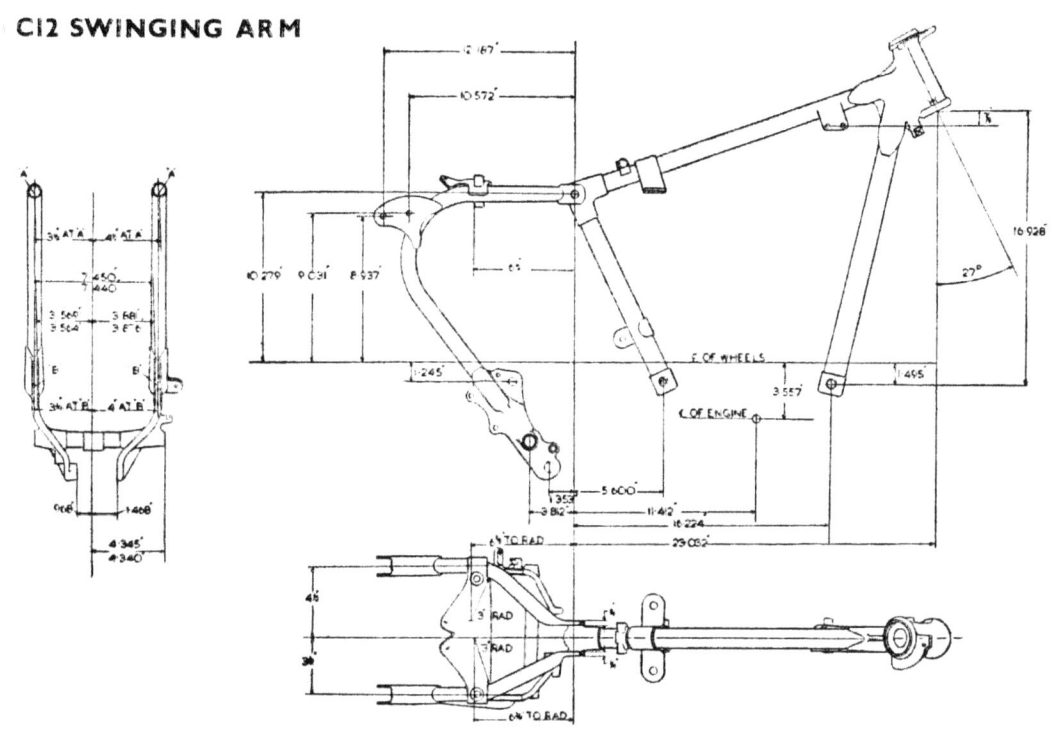

D5 SWINGING ARM

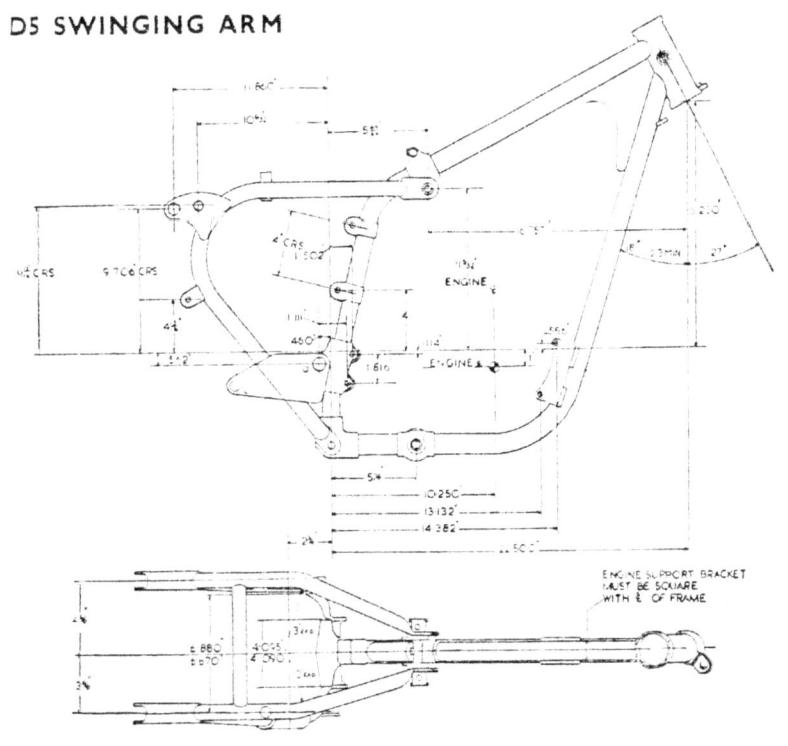

D7 SWINGING ARM

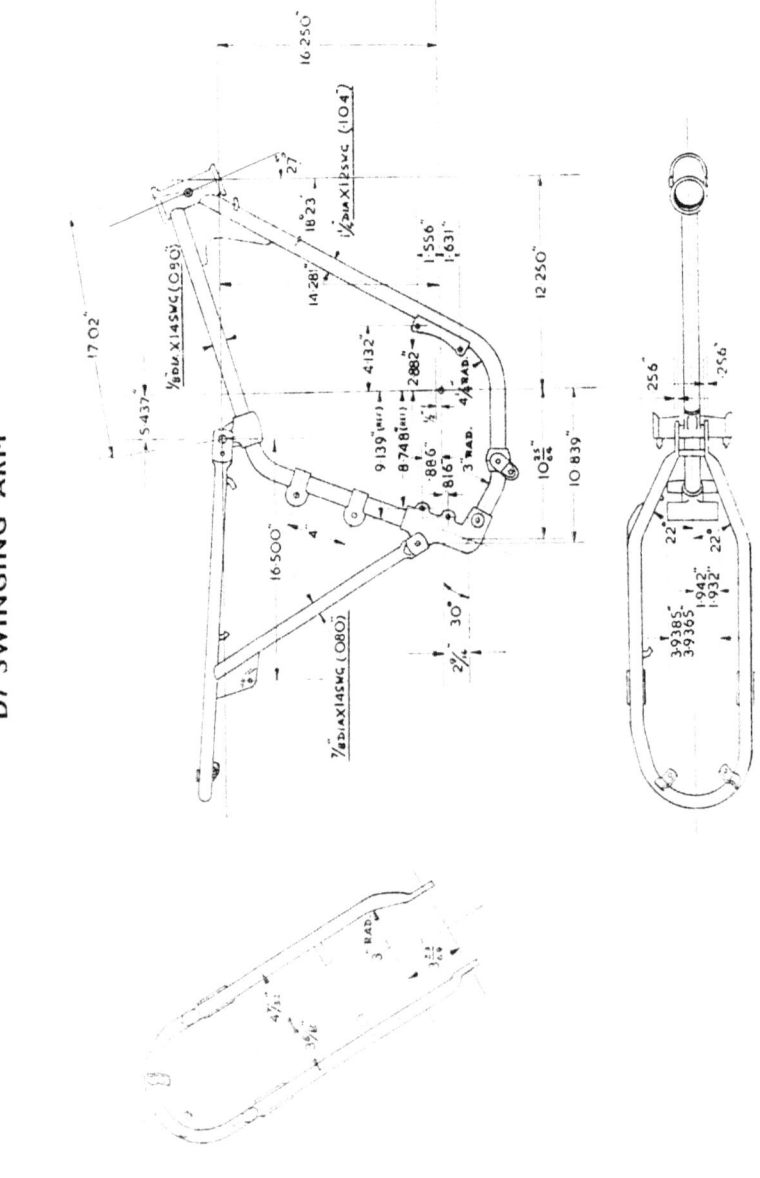

C15 STAR AND C15 SPORTS STAR

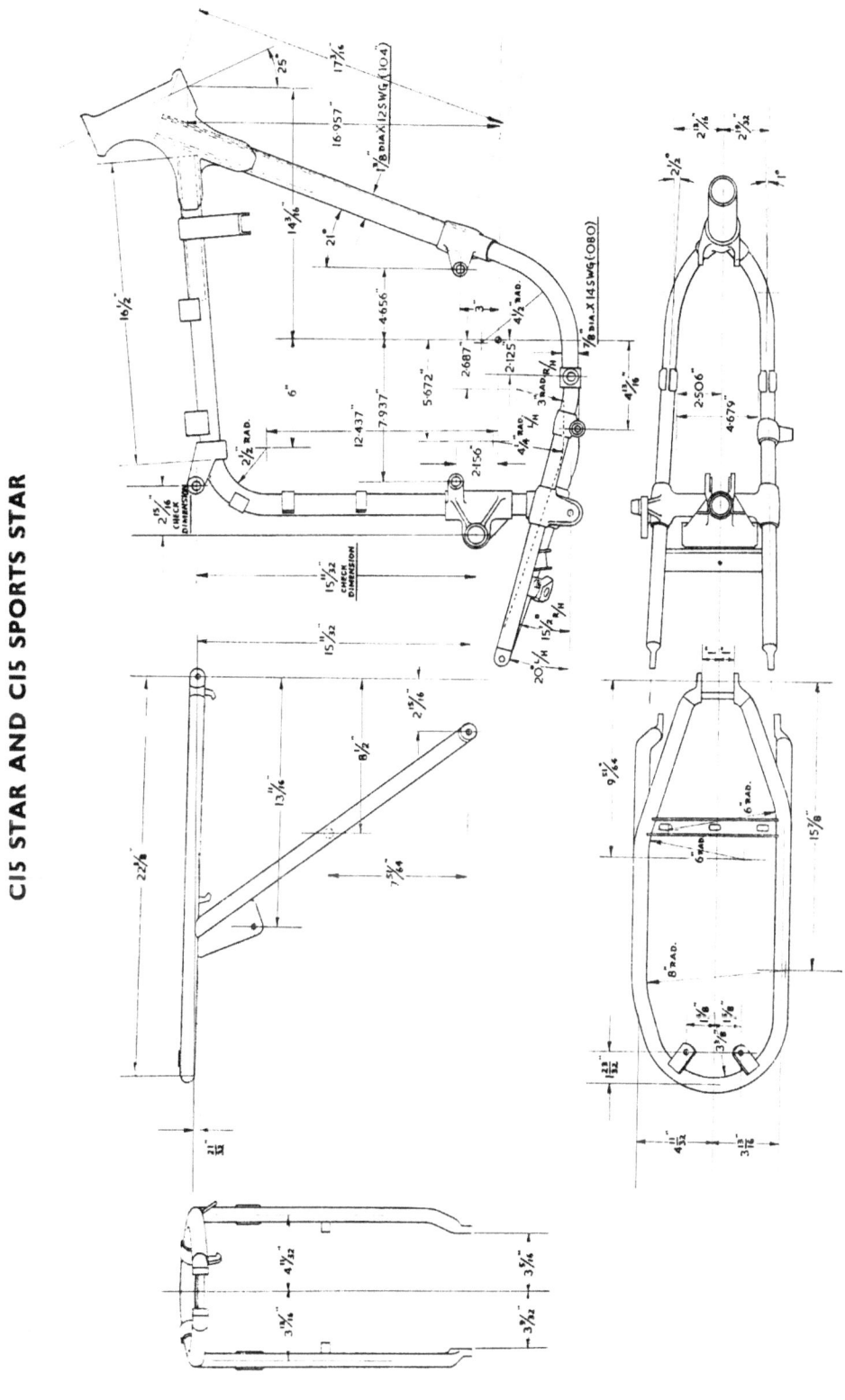

C15 TRIALS AND C15 SCRAMBLES

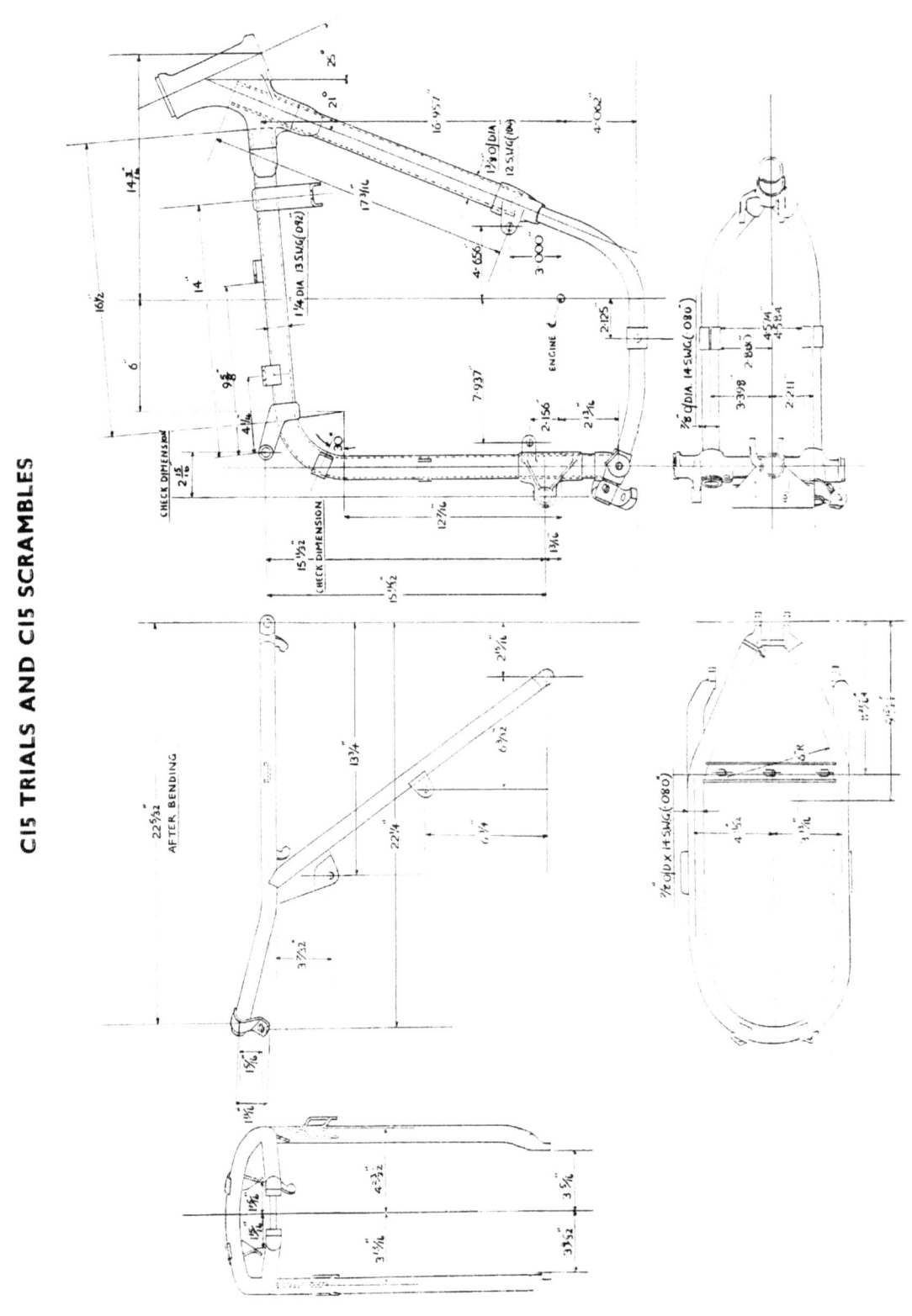

B40 STAR

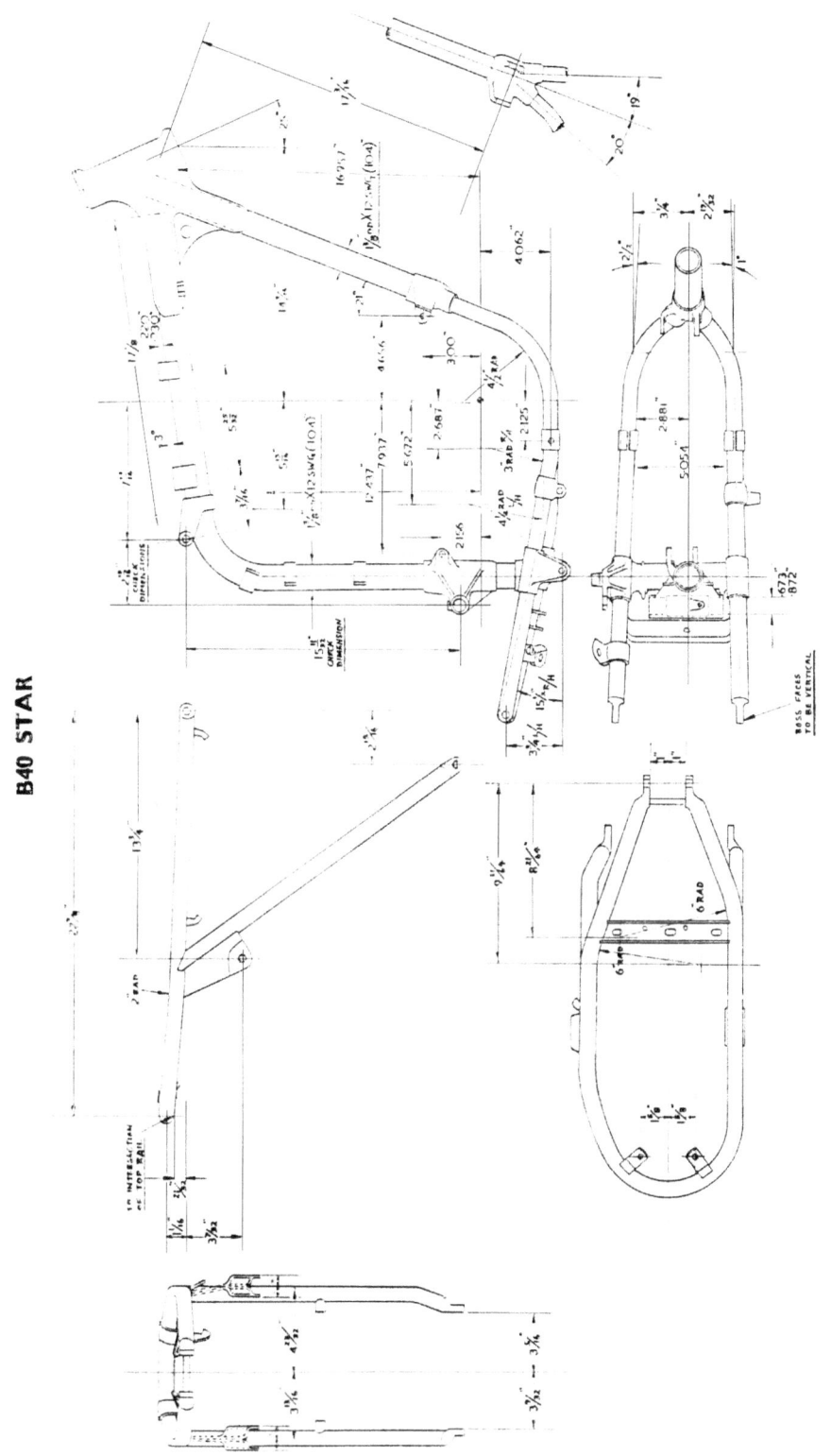

500 c.c. STAR AND 650 c.c. STAR MODELS A50 AND A65

B.S.A. Service Sheet No. 711

Revised Sept. 1958.

SERVICE TOOLS

for all

MOTOR CYCLES

1946 to 1958 Inclusive

Use in conjunction with
Service Sheet No. 711A
For Details of Models and Prices.

BSA SERVICE SHEET No. 711

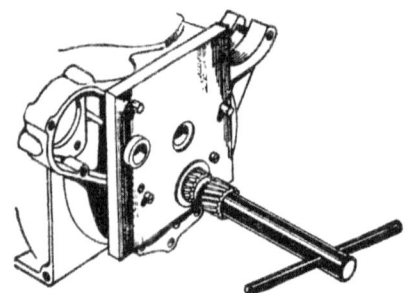

61-3281 Reaming Jig (mainshaft and camshaft gear bushes)
61-3275 Reaming Jig (mainshaft and camshaft gear bushes)

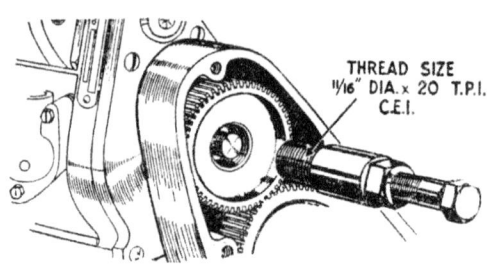

61-1903 Magdyno Driving Pinion Extractor Tool complete.
For Models fitted with Magdyno Lighting Equipment.

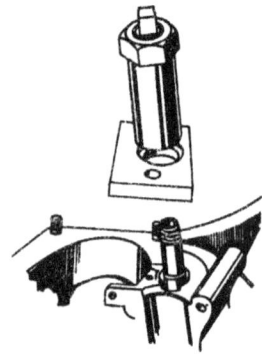

61-3069 Inlet Tappet Guide Extractor

61-3284 Mainshaft Bush Reamer
61-3285 Pilot for Jigs 61-3275
61-3286 Pilot for Jigs 61-3281
61-3287 Shell Reamer Holder
61-3288 Tommy Bar for 61-3287

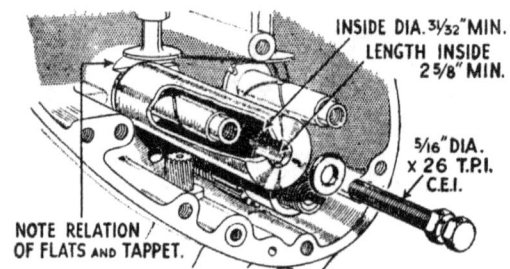

61-691 Cam Pinion Post Extractor

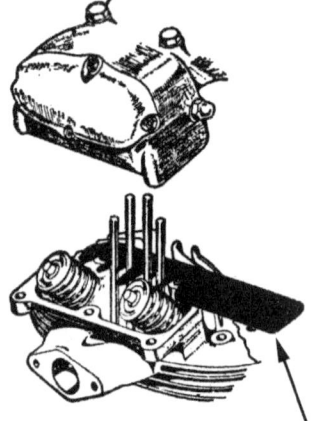

67-9114 Push Rod Assembly Tool

61-3167 Reamer for use with 61-3162 61-3281 and 61-3275

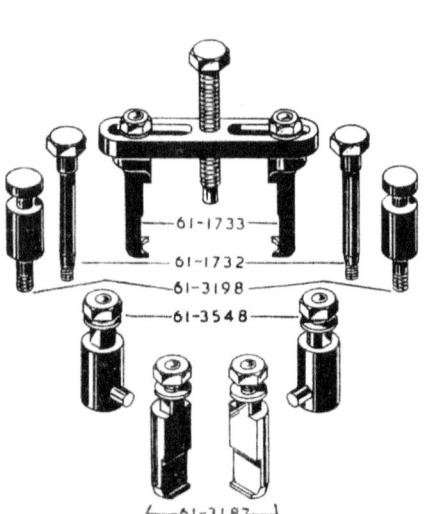

61-3256 Extractor Set Complete

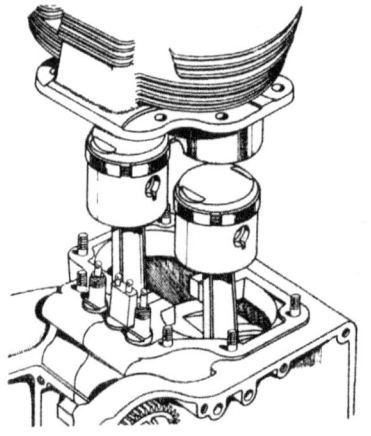

61-3061 Piston Ring Slipper
61-3334 Piston Ring Slipper,
61-3262 Piston Ring Slipper.
(2 per set)

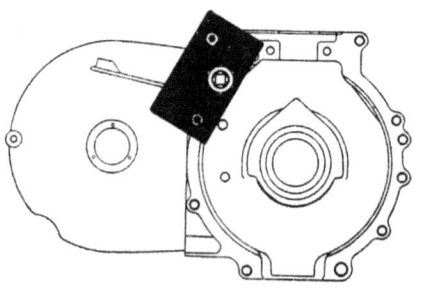

61-3159 Camshaft Bush Extractor

B.S.A. SERVICE SHEET No. 711—continued

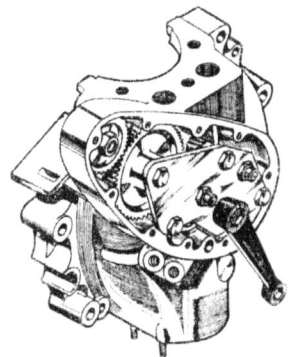

15-832 Mainshaft Nut Spanner

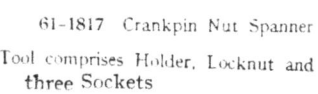

61-1817 Crankpin Nut Spanner

Tool comprises Holder, Locknut and three Sockets

Sockets for 61-1817
61-1754
61-1755
61-3228

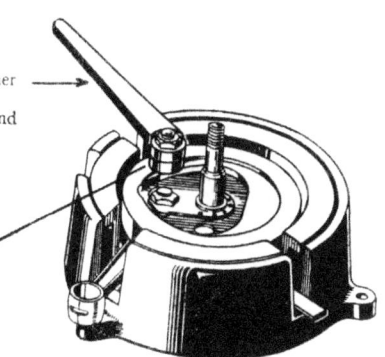

61-1751 Flywheel Bolster
61-1750 " " Gauge Rod
61-1747 " " Ring
61-1749 " " "

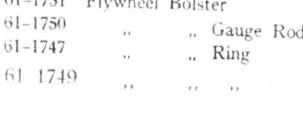

61-658 Gudgeon Pin Bush Extractor comprising Spindle with various size bushes.

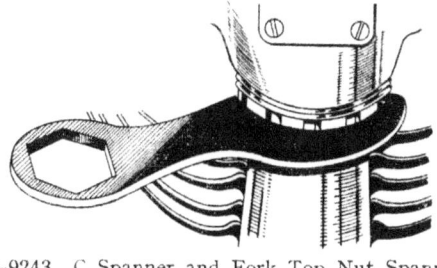

65-9243 C Spanner and Fork Top Nut Spanner

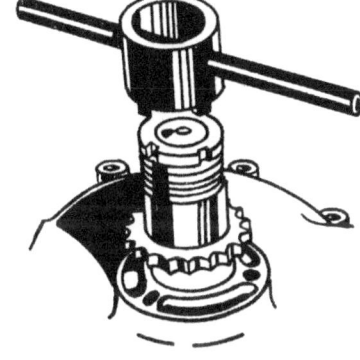

61-3220 Cush Drive Nut Tube Spanner

61-3305 Valve Seating Tool complete

Comprising Tommy Bar 61-3291
Holder 61-3290

Cutters
61-3298 .. 1 1/16" × 45° × 20°
61-3299 .. 1 1/2" × 45° × 20°
61-3300 .. 1 5/8" × 45° × 20°
61-3301 .. 1 3/4" × 45° × 20°
61-3302 .. 1 7/8" × 45° × 20°

Pilots
61-3293 .. 5/16"
61-3294 .. .350"
61-3295 .. 3/8"

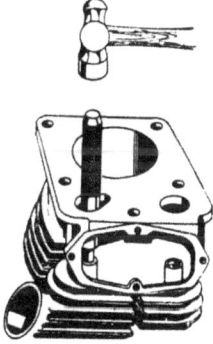

61-3263 61-3264 61-3265 61-3267 61-3268
Valve Guide fitting and extracting punches

61-699 1/4" C.E.I. Stud Boxes
61-317 5/16"   "   "   "
61-545 3/8"   "   "   "

65-9240 Valve Grinding Tool

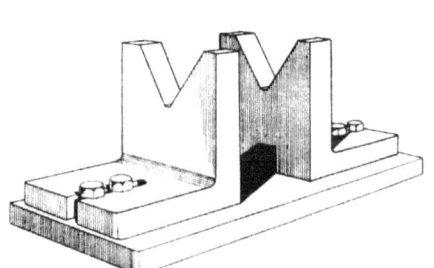

61-692 Vee Block and Base Plate

B.S.A. SERVICE SHEET No. 711—continued

61-3049 Cylinder Head Spanner

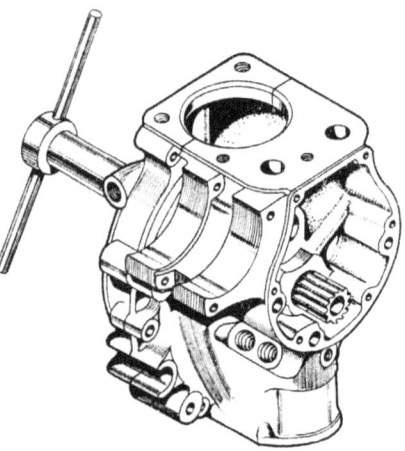

61-1932 Reamer and Holder complete (mainshaft bush)
61-1922 Reamer for 61-1932

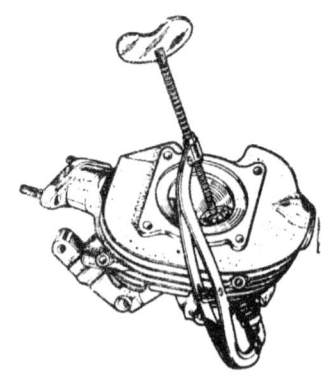

61-3340 Valve Spring Compressor with Adaptor
Models M33
"B" Group, "A" Group, and Sunbeam

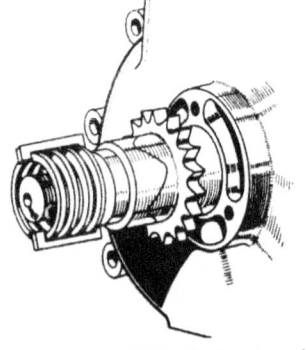

61-1822 Cush Drive Spring Assembly Tool
For holding Spring compressed whilst fitting Lockring.
(2 per set)

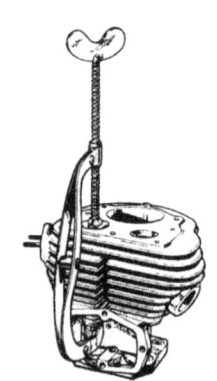

61-3340 Valve Spring Compressor
Models C10, C11, M20, M21
(Use without adaptor)

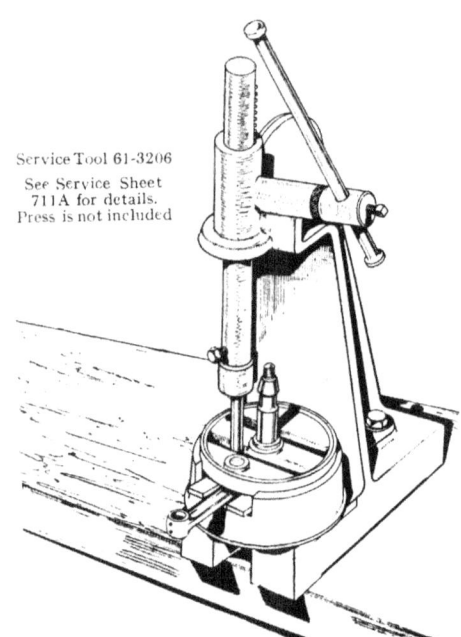

Service Tool 61-3206
See Service Sheet 711A for details.
Press is not included

61-3052 Cylinder Base Nut Spanner

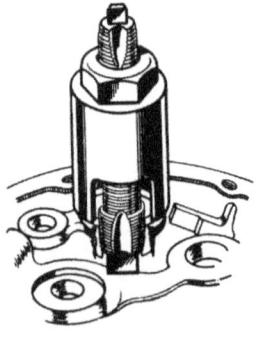

61-3257 Gearbox Sprocket Locknut Spanner.
61-3258 Gearbox Sprocket Locknut Spanner.

61-3185 Bush Extractor

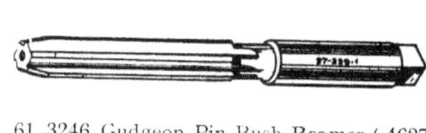

61-3246 Gudgeon Pin Bush Reamer (.4687″)
61-3367 Gudgeon Pin Bush Reamer (.625″)
61-3556 Gudgeon Pin Bush Reamer (.6875″)
61-3366 Gudgeon Pin Bush Reamer (.750″)
61-3580 Gudgeon Pin Bush Reamer (.4375″)
61-3581 Gudgeon Pin Bush Reamer (.5625″)

B.S.A. SERVICE SHEET No. 711—continued

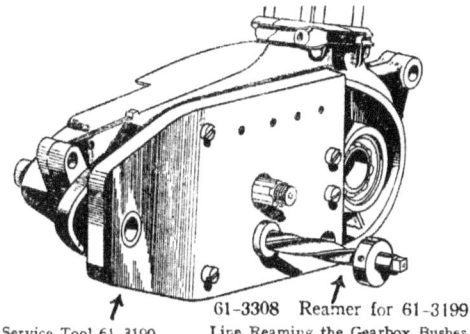

Service Tool 61-3199.   61-3308 Reamer for 61-3199
Line Reaming the Gearbox Bushes

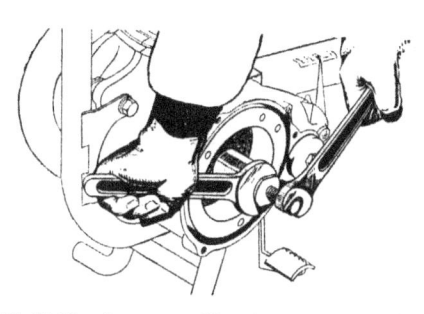

61-3188 Generator Flywheel Removal Tool (Wico Pacy)
90-297 Generator Flywheel Removal Tool (Lucas)

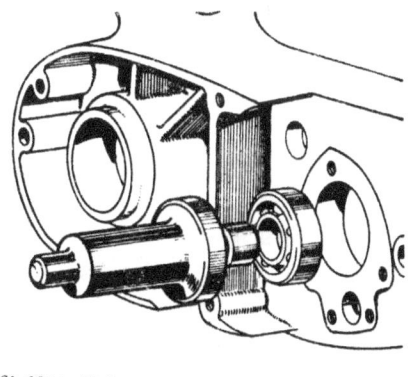

61-3214 Ballrace Pilot (gearbox pinion bearing)
61-3215 Ballrace Pilot (gearbox mainshaft bearing)

61-3064 Pinion Sleeve Extractor

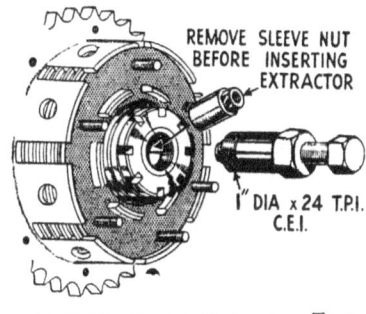

61-1912 Clutch Extractor Tool

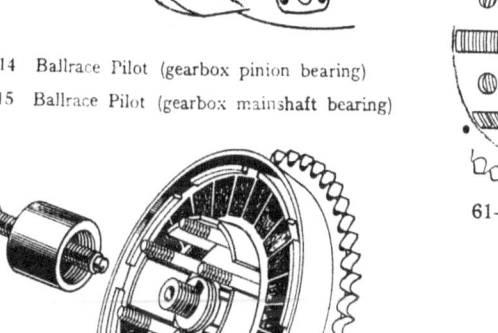

61-3362 Clutch Extractor Tool

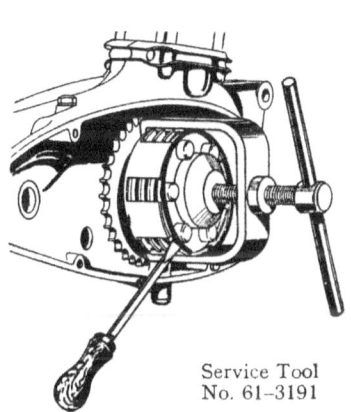

Service Tool No. 61-3191
Removing the Clutch Plate Circlip

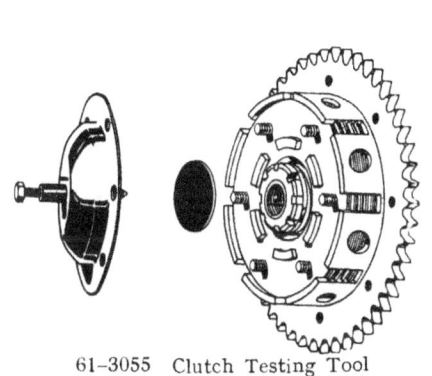

61-3055 Clutch Testing Tool

61-3212 Ballrace Pilot for large engine bearing
61-3213 Ballrace Pilot for small engine bearing

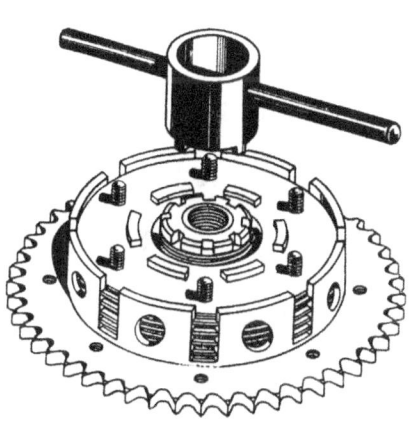

61-1915 Clutch Spring Nut Tube Spanner.

B.S.A. SERVICE SHEET No. 711—continued

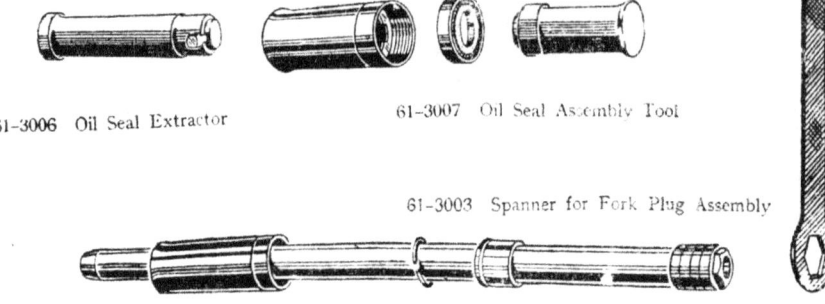

61-3006 Oil Seal Extractor
61-3007 Oil Seal Assembly Tool
61-3003 Spanner for Fork Plug Assembly

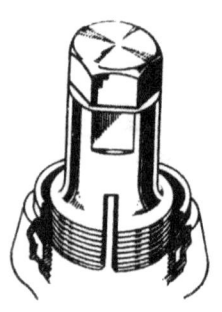

61-3060 Ballrace Extractor (steering head) for all 3/16" balls

61-3063 Ballrace Extractor (steering head) for all 1/4" balls

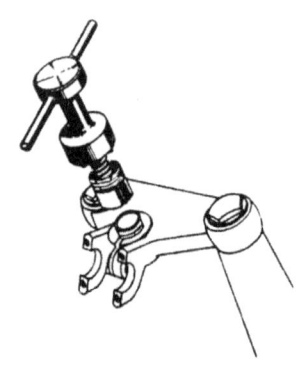

61-3002 Assembly Tool for Adjuster Sleeve
61-3008 Assembly Tool for Adjuster Sleeve

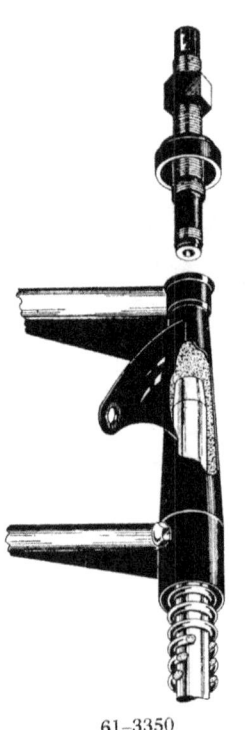

61-3350 Fork Shaft Dismantling and Assembly Tool

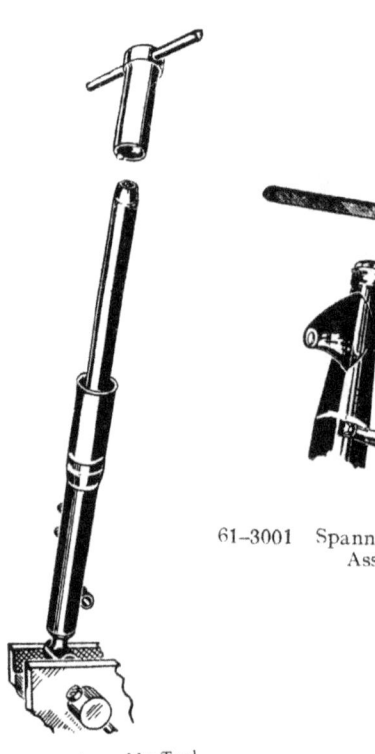

61-3005 Assembly Tool for Oil Seal Holder

61-3001 Spanner for Fork Top Nut Assembly

61-3222 Rear Suspension Strip and Assembly Tool

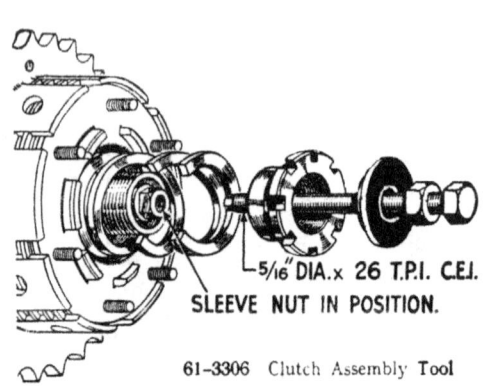

5/16" DIA. x 26 T.P.I. C.E.I. SLEEVE NUT IN POSITION.

61-3306 Clutch Assembly Tool

B.S.A. SERVICE SHEET No. 711—continued

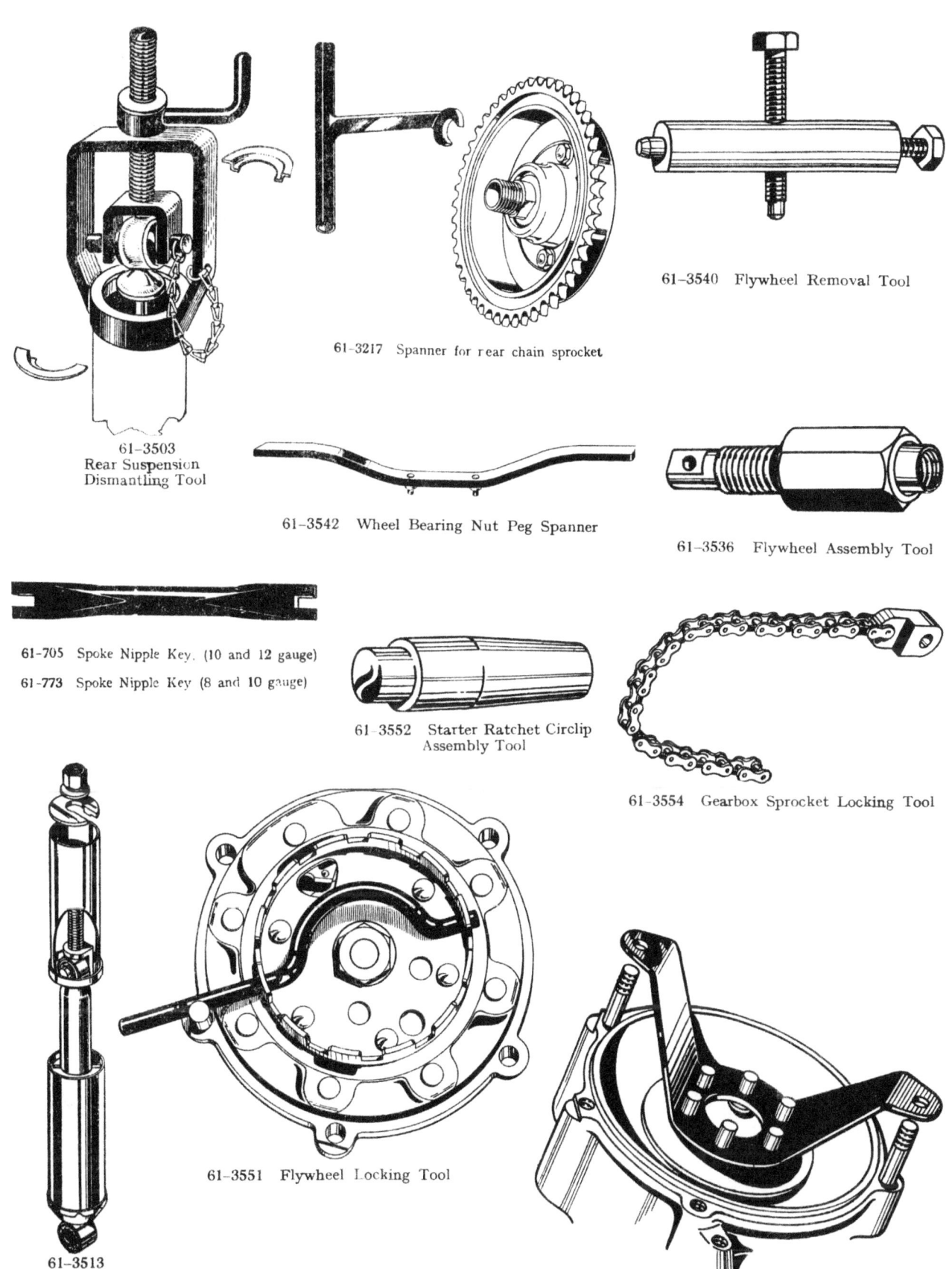

61-3503 Rear Suspension Dismantling Tool

61-3217 Spanner for rear chain sprocket

61-3540 Flywheel Removal Tool

61-3542 Wheel Bearing Nut Peg Spanner

61-3536 Flywheel Assembly Tool

61-705 Spoke Nipple Key (10 and 12 gauge)
61-773 Spoke Nipple Key (8 and 10 gauge)

61-3552 Starter Ratchet Circlip Assembly Tool

61-3554 Gearbox Sprocket Locking Tool

61-3513 Rear Suspension Dismantling Tool

61-3551 Flywheel Locking Tool

61-3553 Clutch Back Plate Locking Tool

B.S.A. SERVICE SHEET No. 711—continued

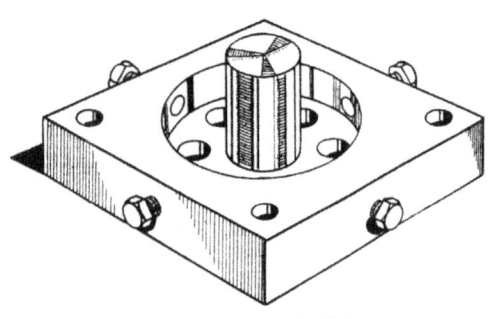

61-3499 Bench Die Holder

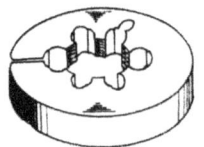

61-3483 Die

Die Nut

Tap

Part No.	Description	For
61-3574	Tap and Die Set in wooden case comprising tools listed below except 61-3483 ...	General Workshop use
61-3575	Tap and Die Set in wooden case comprising all tools listed below	General Workshop use

TAPS.

Part No.	Taps.		For
61-3461	3/8" x 19 TPI B.S.P.	(R/H)	Petrol Tap Hole.
61-3462	3/8" x 20 TPI B.S.F.	(L/H)	Sunbeam Dynamo.
61-3463	7/16" x 20 TPI C.E.I.	(R/H)	General.
61-3464	1/2" x 20 TPI C.E.I.	(R/H)	General.
61-3502	9/16" x 20 TPI C.E.I.	(R/H)	General.
61-3465	9/16" x 20 TPI C.E.I.	(L/H)	Front Fork Spindle Hole.
61-3466	5/8" x 20 TPI C.E.I.	(R/H)	General.
61-3467	3/4" x 20 TPI C.E.I.	(R/H)	General.
65-3468	3/4" x 20 TPI B.S.W.	(R/H)	General.
61-3469	3/4" x 12 TPI B.S.F.	(L/H)	Sunbeam Rear Spindle Hole.
61-3470	7/8" x 20 TPI B.S.W.	(R/H)	Rear Suspension Shaft.
61-3471	1-1/16" x 20 TPI C.E.I.	(R/H)	Fork Shaft Top.
61-3472	1 1/8" x 28 TPI B.S.W.	(R/H)	Fork Shaft Bottom.
61-3473	1 1/4" x 20 TPI B.S.W.	(R/H)	Filler Caps.
61-3531	14 mm. x 1.25 mm.	(R/H)	14 mm. Spark Plug Hole
61-3533	1.250" x 20 TPI B.S.W.	(R/H)	Bantam Fork Tube (90-5021)

DIES.

Part No.	Dies.		For
61-3474	7/16" x 20 TPI C.E.I.	(R/H)	General.
61-3475	1/2" x 20 TPI C.E.I.	(R/H)	General.
61-3476	9/16" x 20 TPI C.E.I.	(R/H)	Gearbox Mainshaft.
61-3477	9/16" x 20 TPI C.E.I.	(L/H)	"A" Group Mainshaft.
61-3478	5/8" x 20 TPI C.E.I.	(R/H)	General.
61-3479	3/4" x 20 TPI C.E.I.	(R/H)	General.
61-3480	3/4" x 12 TPI B.S.F.	(L/H)	Sunbeam Rear Spindle.
61-3481	1" x 24 TPI C.E.I.	(R/H)	Fork Stem.
61-3482	1.120" x 24 TPI C.E.I.	(R/H)	Fork Stem.
61-3483	1 7/8" x 28 TPI WHIT.	(R/H)	Fork Sliding Tube Top.
61-3499	Bench Die Holder (for use with 61-3483)		

B.S.A. MOTOR CYCLES LTD.
Service Dept., Birmingham 11
Printed in England

B.S.A. Service Sheet No. 711A

Revised Sept., 1958

PRICE LIST

for

SERVICE TOOLS

1946 to 1958 Inclusive

Use in conjunction with Service Sheet No. 711

Part No.	Description	Used on Model	Retail Price Per Unit £ s. d.
15–832	Rear Hub Nut Spanner	A, B, C and M	4 5
61–317	Stud Box 5/16″ c.e.i.	General	3 0
61–545	Stud Box 3/8″ c.e.i.	General	3 0
61–658	Gudgeon Pin Bush Extractor	All Models	10 6
61–691	Cam Pinion Post Extractor	B and M	4 6
61–692	Flywheel "V" Blocks (used with 61-1821)	B, C and M	2 5 4
61–696	Socket Nut (used with 61-1817)	B, C and M	1 5
61–698	Crankpin Nut Spanner only (used with 61-1817)	B, C and M	1 1 0
61–699	Stud Box 1/4″ c.e.i.	General	3 0
61–705	Nipple Key (10 and 12 gauge)	General	3 10
61–773	Nipple Key (8 and 10 gauge)	General	3 10
61–1747	Flywheel Bolster Ring	C Group	4 1 3
61–1749	Flywheel Bolster Ring	B and M 500 c.c.	4 1 3
61–1750	Flywheel Bolster Gauge Rod (2 per set)	B, C and M	7 7
61–1751	Flywheel Bolster	B, C and M	3 11 9
61–1754	Crankpin Nut Socket (used with 61-1817)	C Group	8 0
61–1755	Crankpin Nut Socket (used with 61-1817)	B and M	8 0
61–1817	Crankpin Nut Spanner complete	B, C and M	2 7 6
	Comprising:—		
	61–696 Socket Nut		1 5
	61–698 Spanner		1 1 0
	61–1754 Socket	C Group	8 0
	61–1755 Socket	B and M	8 0
	61–3228 Socket	Gold Star	9 1

BSA SERVICE TOOLS

Part No.	Description	Used on Model	Per Unit Retail Price £ s. d.
61-1821	"V" Block Base Plate (used with 61-692)	B, C and M	1 10 3
61-1822	Cush Drive Spring Assembly Tool (2 per set)	A, B, C and M	4 6
61-1903	Magdyno Drive Pinion Extractor	B and M	3 0
61-1912	Clutch Extractor	M to 1948	6 0
61-1915	Clutch Spring Nut Tube Spanner	M to 1948	4 6
61-1922	Reamer (used with 61-1932) (mainshaft bush)	C Group	3 5 0
61-1932	Reamer and Holder complete (used with 61-1922)	C Group	4 4 9
61-3001	Fork Top Nut Spanner (front fork)	A, B, C and M	13 6
61-3002	Adjuster Sleeve Assembly Tool (steering head)	B, C and M	12 1
61-3003	Fork Plug Spanner (front fork)	A, B, C and M	13 6
61-3005	Oil Seal Holder Assembly Tool (front fork)	A, B, C and M	1 1 2
61-3006	Oil Seal Extractor (front fork)	A, B, C and M	15 1
61-3007	Oil Seal Assembly Tool (front fork)	A, B, C and M	6 0
61-3008	Adjuster Sleeve Assembly Tool (steering head)	A7/10, S7/8	12 1
61-3049	Cylinder Head Spanner	M20/21	10 6
61-3052	Cylinder Base Nut Spanner	M20/21	1 1 2
61-3055	Clutch Testing Tool	M to 1948	15 1
61-3060	Steering Head Ballrace Extractor	For 3/16" Balls	8 3
61-3061	Piston Ring Slipper (2 per set)	A7 to 1950	7 6
61-3063	Steering Head Ballrace Extractor	For 1/4" Balls	8 3
61-3064	Pinion Sleeve Extractor	B, C and M	2 11 5
61-3069	Inlet Tappet Guide Extractor	A7 to 1950	7 7
61-3159	Camshaft Bush Extractor	A7, A10	12 8
61-3167	Camshaft Bush Reamer (used with 61-3275/81)	A Group	3 0 6
61-3185	Gearbox Bush Extractor	M Group	15 9
61-3188	Flywheel Magneto Removal Tool (Wico Pacy)	D1, D3 and D5	6 8
61-3191	Clutch Plate Circlip Removal Tool	D1, D3 and D5	1 10 3
61-3199	Gearbox Bush Line Reaming Plate (used with 61-3205)	D1, D3 and D5	2 1 6
61-3205	Layshaft Bush Reamer only (used with 61-3199)	D1, D3 and D5	2 1 11
61-3206	Flywheel Dismantling and Assembly Tool	D1, D3 and D5	3 15 6

Comprising:—
  61-3207   Jig Body
  61-3208(2)   Dismantling Bar
  61-3209   Dismantling Punch
  61-3210   Assembly Bridge
(*Note:*— Press as illustrated is not included).

Part No.	Description	Used on Model	Per Unit Retail Price £ s. d.
61-3212	Ballrace Pilot for large engine bearing	D1, D3 and D5	7 7
61-3213	Ballrace Pilot for small engine bearing	D1, D3 and D5	6 8
61-3214	Ballrace Pilot for gearbox pinion bearing	D1, D3 and D5	7 7
61-3215	Ballrace Pilot for gearbox mainshaft bearing	D1, D3 and D5	6 8
61-3217	Spanner for rear wheel sprocket	A7, A10	11 3
61-3220	Tube Spanner for cush drive nut	A, B, C and M	3 6
61-3222	Rear Suspension Strip and Assembly Tool	A, B and M	13 6
61-3228	Crankpin Nut Socket (used with 61-1817)	B32/4 G/S	9 1
61-3246	Reamer Gudgeon Pin Bush	D1, D3	14 6
61-3256	Extractor Set complete	All Models	1 12 7

Comprising:—
  61-351(1)   Plate
  61-776(1)   Bolt
  61-1732(2)   Extractor Leg (A Group cam pinion)
  61-1733(2)   Extractor Leg (engine pinion B, C and M).
  61-3187(2)   Extractor Leg (crankshaft pinion A7/10).
  61-3198(2)   Extractor Leg (engine sprocket etc., D, C and A).
  61-3548(2)   Extractor Leg (Dandy flywheel)

BSA SERVICE TOOLS

Part No.	Description	Used on Model	Retail Price Per Unit £ s. d.
61-3257	Gearbox Sprocket Locknut Spanner	A, B and M	15 1
61-3258	Gearbox Sprocket Locknut Spanner	C	15 1
61-3262	Piston Ring Slipper (2 per set)	A10	6 0
61-3263	Valve Guide Punch (used on B33/34, exhaust and G/Stars with .374 dia. valve stems).		3 0
61-3264	Valve Guide Punch (comprising 61-3265/66 and 61-3307)	C10 In. and Ex.	12 8
61-3265	Valve Guide Punch (B31/32 inlet, A7/10, C11, C12 inlet and exhaust and G/Stars with .310" dia. valve stems)		6 0
61-3267	Valve Guide Punch (comprising 61-3268/9/70)	M20, M21 In. and Ex.	8 3
61-3268	Valve Guide Punch (B31/32 exhaust, B33/34 inlet and G/Stars with .348" dia. valve stems)		6 0
61-3275	Mainshaft and Camshaft Bush Reaming Jig	A7 to 1950	2 12 11
61-3281	Mainshaft and Camshaft Bush Reaming Jig	A10, AA7 onwards	2 12 11
61-3284	Reamer (mainshaft used with 61-3275/81)	A7, A10	4 6 2
61-3285	Pilot for 61-3275	A7 to 1950	15 1
61-3286	Pilot for 61-3281	A10, AA7 onwards	15 1
61-3287	Reamer Holder (used with 61-3284)	A7, A10	9 1
61-3290	Valve Seat Cutter Holder	A, B, C and M	5 3
61-3293	Valve Seat Cutter Pilot ($\frac{5}{16}$")	A, B and C	6 8
61-3294	Valve Seat Cutter Pilot (.350")	B and M	6 8
61-3295	Valve Seat Cutter Pilot (.375")	B, and M33	6 8
61-3298	Valve Seat Cutter ($1\frac{7}{16}$" dia. x 45° x 20°)	A7 and C	2 6 2
61-3299	Valve Seat Cutter ($1\frac{1}{2}$" dia. x 45° x 20°)	A10 and C	2 6 2
61-3300	Valve Seat Cutter ($1\frac{5}{8}$" dia. x 45° x 20°)	B	2 6 2
61-3301	Valve Seat Cutter ($1\frac{3}{4}$" dia. x 45° x 20°)	B and M	2 6 2
61-3302	Valve Seat Cutter ($1\frac{7}{8}$" dia. x 45° x 20°)	B and M	2 6 2
61-3305	Valve Seating Tool complete	A, B, C and M	12 16 2
61-3306	Clutch Assembly Tool	M to 1948	3 0
61-3308	Reamer for 61-3199 (comprising 61-3205 and 61-3309)	D1, and D3	2 8 1
61-3311	Crankshaft Balance Weight (18 ozs., 12 drms.)	A7 1951 onwards	15 1
61-3312	Crankshaft Balance Weight (16 ozs., 14 drms.)	A7 to 1951	15 1
61-3334	Piston Ring Slipper (2 per set)	A7 1951 onwards	6 0
61-3340	Valve Spring Compressor complete	A, B, C and M	1 1 2
61-3350	Front Fork Dismantling and Assembly Tool	A, B, C, M and S7/8	15 1
61-3362	Clutch Extractor Tool	A, B, C and M 1949 onwards	6 8
61-3366	Gudgeon Pin Bush Reamer (.750")	B, M and A10	1 1 10
61-3367	Gudgeon Pin Bush Reamer (.625")	C only	1 2 8
61-3487	Valve Guide Assembly Punch	S7 and S8	15 1
61-3497	Crankshaft Balance Weight (19 ozs. 8 drms.)	A10R/R and S/R	13 9
61-3499	Bench Die Holder (used with 61-3483)	A, B, C and M	2 18 6
61-3503	Rear Suspension Dismantling Tool	A and B S/A	1 17 10
61-3513	Rear Suspension Dismantling Tool	C12 and D3 S/A	1 14 4
61-3536	Flywheel Assembly Tool	Dandy	5 6
61-3540	Flywheel Removal Tool	Dandy	6 3
61-3542	Wheel Bearing Nut Peg Spanner	A and B, S/A	10 4
61-3548	Flywheel Removal Tool (2) (used with 61-3256)	Dandy	4 7
61-3551	Flywheel Locking Tool	Dandy	1 2
61-3552	Starter Ratchet Circlip Assembly Tool	Dandy	5 3
61-3553	Clutch Back Plate Locking Tool	Dandy	9 2
61-3554	Gearbox Sprocket Locking Tool	Dandy	5 5
61-3556	Gudgeon Pin Bush Reamer ($\frac{11}{16}$")	A7	1 17 10
61-3558	Locking Ring Spanner	8" Brake	11 10
61-3580	Gudgeon Pin Bush Reamer ($\frac{7}{16}$")	Dandy	1 0 0
61-3581	Gudgeon Pin Bush Reamer ($\frac{9}{16}$")	D5	1 6 10
65-9240	Valve Grinding Tool	A, B, C and M	1 10
65-9243	Combined "C" and Fork Top Nut spanner	A, B, C and M	1 10
67-9114	Push Rod Assembly Tool	A7/10 1951 onwards	1 5
90-297	Lucas Rotor Removal Tool	D1	1 3

BSA SERVICE TOOLS

Part No.	Description	Used on Models	Retail Price £ s. d.
61-3574	Tap and Die Set in wood case comprising taps and dies listed below except 61-3483	General	23 15 0
61-3575	Tap and Die Set in wood case comprising taps and dies listed below	General	32 7 0

TAPS

Part No.	Taps	Description	Retail Price £ s. d.
61-3461	3/8" x 19 T.P.I. B.S.P. R/H	Petrol Tap Hole	7 7
61-3462	3/8" x 20 T.P.I. B.S.F. L/H	Sunbeam Dynamo	7 7
61-3463	7/16" x 20 T.P.I. C.E.I. R/H	General	13 1
61-3464	1/2" x 20 T.P.I. C.E.I. R/H	General	14 6
61-3502	9/16" x 20 T.P.I. C.E.I. R/H	General	18 7
61-3465	9/16" x 20 T.P.I. C.E.I. L/H	Front Fork Spindle Hole	1 0 0
61-3466	5/8" x 20 T.P.I. C.E.I. R/H	General	17 3
61-3467	3/4" x 20 T.P.I. C.E.I. R/H	General	18 7
61-3468	3/4" x 20 T.P.I. B.S.W. R/H	General	18 7
61-3469	3/4" x 12 T.P.I. B.S.F. L/H	Sunbeam Rear Spindle Hole	1 0 0
61-3470	7/8" x 20 T.P.I. B.S.W. R/H	Rear Suspension Shaft	1 7 6
61-3471	1 1/16" x 20 T.P.I. C.E.I. R/H	Fork Shaft Top	1 5 6
61-3472	1 1/8" x 28 T.P.I. B.S.W. R/H	Fork Shaft	1 14 4
61-3473	1 1/2" x 20 T.P.I. B.S.W. R/H	Filler Cap	2 14 7
61-3531	14 mm. x 1.25 mm. R/H	Spark Plug	1 0 7
61-3533	1.250" x 20 T.P.I. B.S.W. R/H	D1 Fork Tube	1 11 0

DIES

Part No.	Dies	Description	Retail Price £ s. d.
61-3474	7/16" x 20 T.P.I. C.E.I. R/H	General	11 0
61-3475	1/2" x 20 T.P.I. C.E.I. R/H	General	12 4
61-3476	9/16" x 20 T.P.I. C.E.I. R/H	Gearbox Mainshaft	13 9
61-3477	9/16" x 20 T.P.I. C.E.I. L/H	A Group Mainshaft	17 3
61-3478	5/8" x 20 T.P.I. C.E.I. R/H	General	13 9
61-3479	3/4" x 20 T.P.I. C.E.I. R/H	General	18 7
61-3480	3/4" x 12 T.P.I. B.S.F. L/H	Sunbeam Rear Spindle	1 2 0
61-3481	1" x 24 T.P.I. C.E.I. R/H	Fork Stem	1 4 1
61-3482	1.120" x 24 T.P.I. C.E.I. R/H	Fork Stem	1 13 9
61-3483	1 7/8" x 28 T.P.I. Whit. R/H (Used with holder 61-3499)	Fork Sliding Tube Top	9 9 1

B.S.A. Motor Cycles Ltd., Service Department, Birmingham 11

Printed in England. Sept. 1958

B.S.A. Service Sheet No. 711B
Supplement to No. 711 and 711A

July 1960

SERVICE TOOLS

for

MOTOR CYCLES

B.S.A. SERVICE SHEET No. 711B (contd.)

Removing the Clutch Centre with Extractor No. 61-3583 (Model C15).

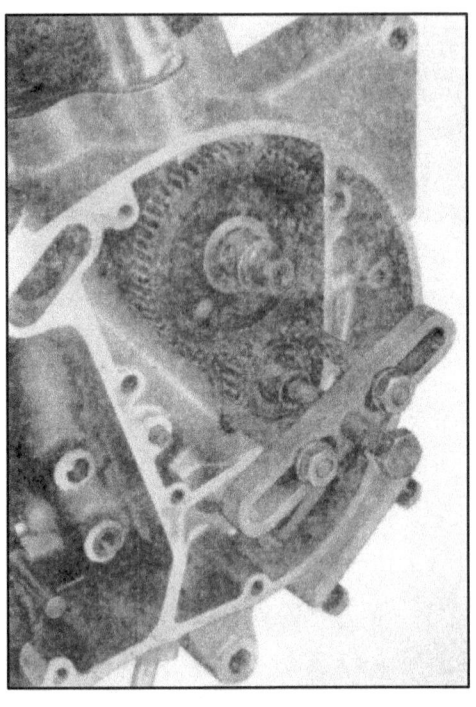

Removing the Crankshaft Pinion with Extractor No. 61-3681 using Legs No. 61-3588 (fitted with Legs 61-3585 for removing the Worm Wheel) (Model C15).

Parting the Flywheels using Bolster 61-3589, Stripping Bars 61-3590 and Punch 61-3601 (Model C15).

Assembling the Crankpin into the Gear Side Flywheel using Locating Gauge No. 61-3597 and Punch No. 61-3601 (Model C15).

B.S.A. SERVICE SHEET No. 711B (contd.)

Assembling the Drive Side Flywheel on to the Gear Side, using Bolster No. 61-3589, Bridge Piece No. 61-3591 and Punch No. 61-3601 (Model C15).

Flywheel Truing Sleeve No. 61-3592 used with Drive Side bearing on "V" blocks No. 61-692 (Model C15).

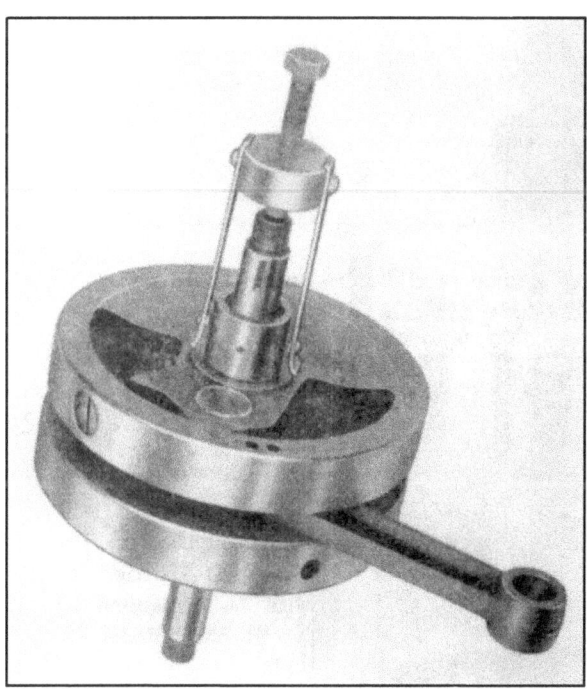

Removing the Gear Side Sleeve with Tool No. 61-3593 (Model C15).

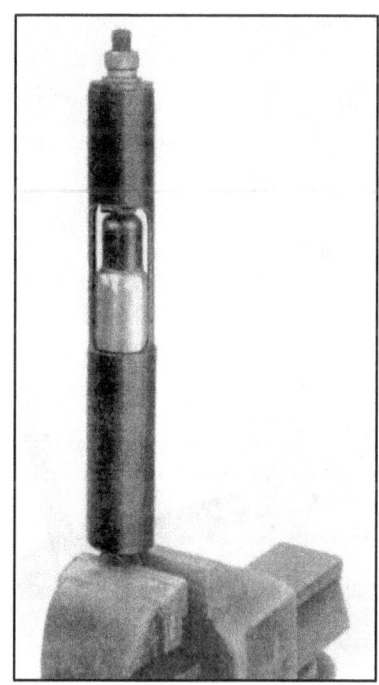

Dismantling the Rear Damper with Tool No. 61-3642 (for Models C15 and D7).

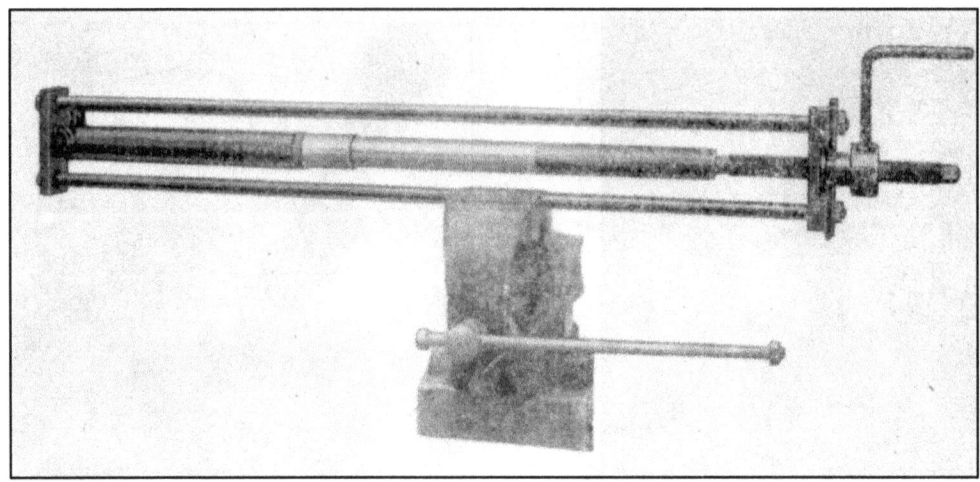

Withdrawing the Fork Main Member and Bushes from the Sliding Member using Tool No. 61-3587.

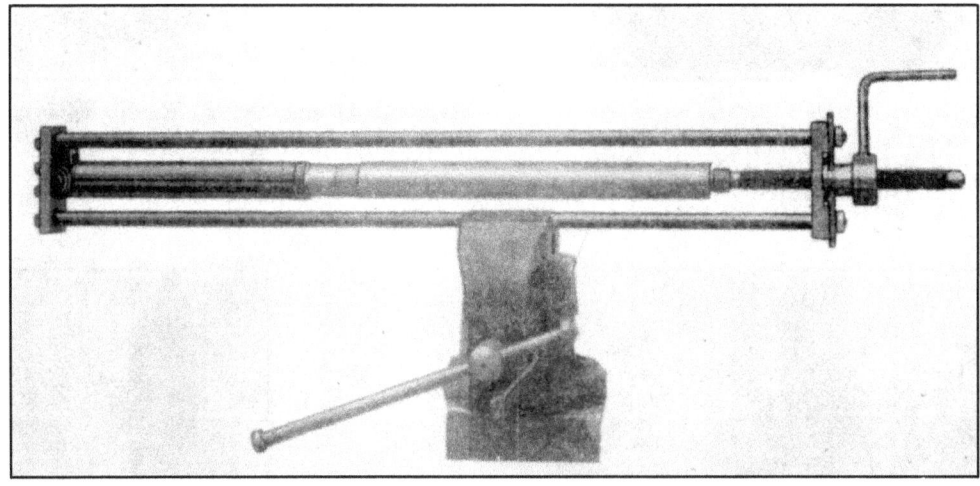

Reassembling the Fork Main Member, Sliding Member and Bushes using Tools No. 61-3587 and 61-3602 (Model C15).

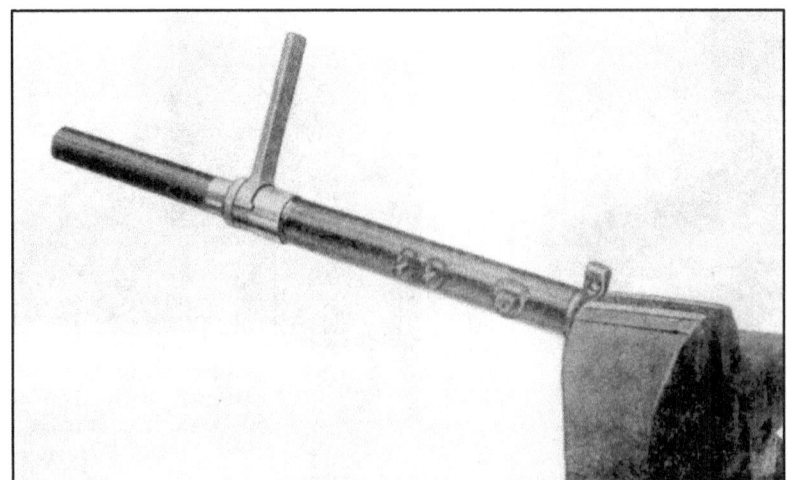

Removing the Fork Oil Seal Holder with "C" Spanner No. 61-3586 (Model C15).

B.S.A. SERVICE SHEET No. 711B (contd.)

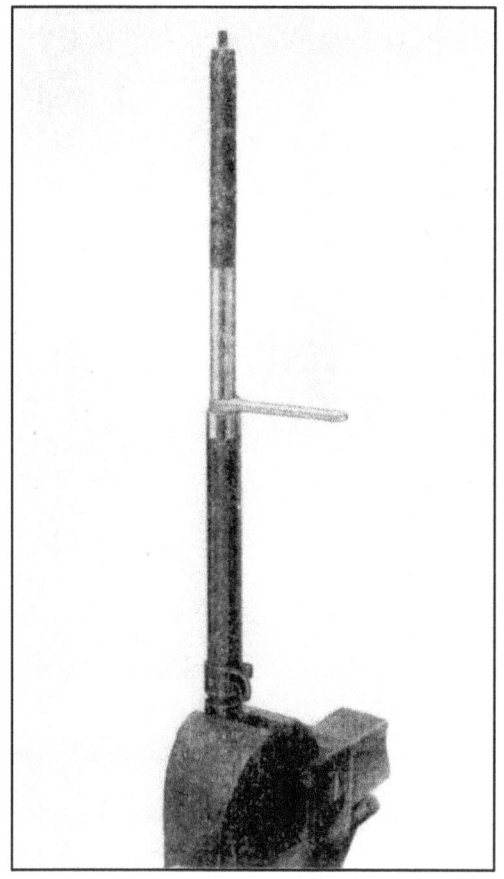

Taking off the Fork Leg Oil Seal Holder with Tool No. 3633 (Model D7).

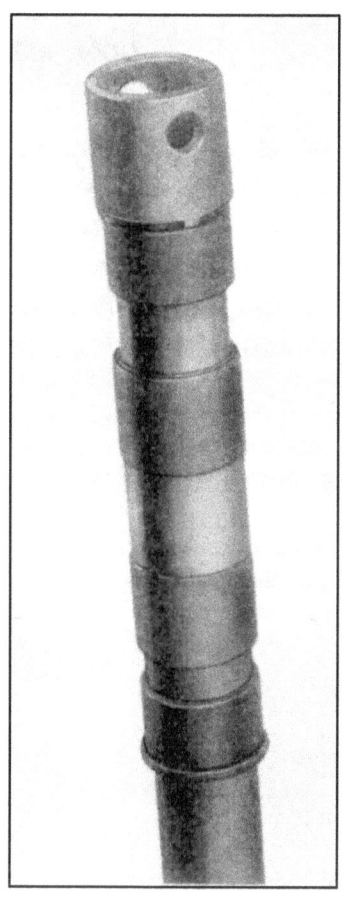

(Model C15). Removing the Fork Leg Bottom Nut with Dog Spanner No. 61-3606 (Tommy Bar not supplied).

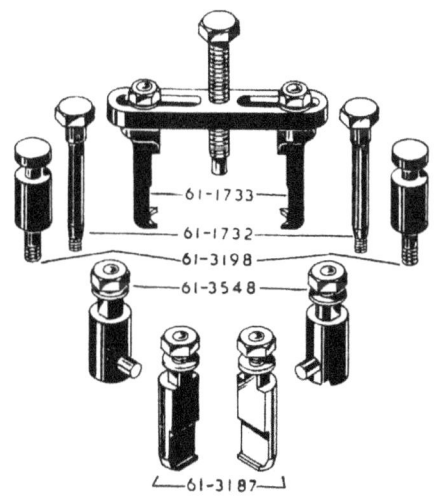

Pinion Extractor showing some of the special Legs.

PINION EXTRACTOR SETS

A Group	Part No. 61-3676
B and M Groups	Part No. 61-3677
C Group (excepting C15)	Part No. 61-3678
C15	Part No. 61-3681
D Group	Part No. 61-3679
Dandy	Part No. 61-3680
Complete Set	Part No. 61-3256

Details of comprising parts and applications are given overleaf.

B.S.A. SERVICE SHEET No. 711B (contd.)

COMPRISING PARTS OF EXTRACTOR SETS

61–3676 = 61–351 Plate, 61–776 Bolt, 61–1732 Leg (2), 61–3187 Leg (2), 61–3198 Leg (2).
61–3677 = 61–351 Plate, 61–776 Bolt, 61–1733 Leg (2).
61–3678 = 61–351 Plate, 61–776 Bolt, 61–1732 Leg (2), 61–1733 Leg (2), 61–3198 Leg (2).
61–3679 = 61–351 Plate, 61–776 Bolt, 61–3198 Leg (2).
61–3680 = 61–351 Plate, 61–776 Bolt, 61–3548 Leg (2).
61–3681 = 61–351 Plate, 61–776 Bolt, 61–3585 Leg (2), 61–3588 Leg (2).

These extractors are extremely useful for the removal of timing, worm or other gears, the legs being specially designed for the particular models.

They can also be used for other jobs of a like nature where a puller is required. All the legs are interchangeable and can be purchased separately if required.

61-358 GUDGEON PIN BUSH EXTRACTOR

is now cancelled and replaced by 61–3672.

This tool is now available for the individual models as detailed below:—

Tool No.	Model	Comprising
61–3651	—	Holder, Rod and Nut only.
61–3652	A7, A10	61–3651, and Bushes 61–3319/20.
61–3653	B Group	61–3651, and Bushes 61–3654/5.
61–3656	C10, C11, C12	61–3651, and Bushes 61–3657/8.
61–3659	C15, A7 (Steel Rod)	61–3651, and Bushes 61–3660/1.
61–3662	D1, D3	61–3651, and Bushes 61–3663/4.
61–3665	D5, D7	61–3651, and Bushes 61–3666/7.
61–3668	M20, M21	61–3651, and Bushes 61–654/5.
61–3669	Dandy	61–3651, and Bushes 61–3670/71.

B.S.A. SERVICE SHEET No. 711B (contd.)

Using a piston Ring Slipper makes replacement easier.

Piston Ring Slippers (Terry).

Now available for the following models:—

61–5004	55–60 mm. Bore	Models D1, D3.
61–5051	60–65 mm. Bore	Models C10L, C11, C12, D5, D7.
61–3682	65–70 mm. Bore	Models A Group, C15.

Additional Tools not illustrated

61–5035 valve grinding tool (Suction type). This tool is similar to 65–9240 shown on Service Sheet No. 711 but is suitable for valves with $\frac{3}{4}$ in. to 1 in. diameter heads.

61–3673 clutch nut screwdriver, designed specially for the moded C15.

BSA SERVICE SHEET No. 714

Printed September, 1956
Revised October, 1957

SPOKE SIZES.

NOTE.—All Models use Forty Spokes per Wheel except "D" Group which have Thirty-six.

YEAR	MODEL	FRONT							REAR						
		RIM SIZE	LEFT			RIGHT			RIM SIZE	LEFT			RIGHT		
			Length	Gauge	Part Number	Length	Gauge	Part Number		Length	Gauge	Part Number	Length	Gauge	Part Number
1947	C10	WM1–19	8 3/4″	10	24–7012	8 3/4″	10	24–7012	WM1–19	8 3/4″	10	24–7012	6 7/8″	10	24–7014
	C11	WM1–20	9 1/4″	10	24–6912	9 3/16″	10	29–5772	WM2–20	9 1/4″	10	24–6912	7 3/8″	10	65–5873
	B31–B33	WM2–19	8 11/16″	10	65–5872	7 1/2″	10	65–5910	WM2–19	8 9/16″	8/10	65–6072	8 3/4″	10	24–7012
	B32–B34	WM1–21	9 11/16″	10	65–5537	8 9/16″	10	90–5584	WM2–19	8 9/16″	8/10	65–6027	8 3/4″	10	24–7012
	M20–M21 Girder Fork	WM3–19	8 3/4″	10	24–7012	6 3/4″	8/10	24–6899	WM3–19	8 5/8″	8/ 3/16	15–7037	8 3/4″	8	26–6824
	A7	WM2–19	7 29/32″	10/12	67–6008	8 1/16″	10/12	67–6007	WM3–19	7 29/32″	10/12	67–6008	8 1/16″	10/12	67–6007
1948	C10	WM1–19	8 3/4″	10	24–7012	8 3/4″	10	24–7012	WM1–19	8 3/4″	10	24–7012	6 7/8″	10	24–7014
	C11	WM1–20	9 1/4″	10	24–6912	9 3/16″	10	29–5772	WM1–20	9 1/4″	10	24–6912	7 3/8″	10	65–5873
	B31	WM2–19	8 11/16″	10	65–5872	7 1/2″	10	65–5910	WM2–19	8 9/16″	8/10	65–6027	8 3/4″	10	24–7012
	B32	WM1–21	9 11/16″	10	65–5537	8 9/16″	10	29–5846	WM2–19	8 9/16″	8/10	65–6027	8 3/4″	10	24–7012
	B33	WM2–19	8 11/16″	10	65–5872	7 1/2″	10	65–5910	WM2–19	8 9/16″	8/10	65–6027	8 3/4″	10	24–7012
	B34	WM1–21	9 11/16″	10	65–5537	8 9/16″	10	90–5584	WM2–19	8 9/16″	8/10	65–6027	8 3/4″	10	24–7012
	M20–M21 Girder Fork	WM3–19	8 3/4″	10	24–7012	6 3/4″	8/10	24–6899	WM3–19	8 5/8″	8/ 3/16	15–7037	8 3/4″	8	26–6824
	M33–G.F.	WM3–19	8 3/4″	10	24–7012	6 3/4″	8/10	24–6899	WM3–19	8 5/8″	8/ 3/16	15–7037	8 3/4″	8	26–6824
	A7	WM2–19	7 29/32″	10/12	67–6008	8 1/16″	10/12	67–6007	WM3–19	7 29/32″	10/12	67–6008	8 1/16″	10/12	67–6007
1949	D1	WM1–19	8 9/16″	10	90–5584	7 1/8″	10	90–5583	WM1–19	8 5/16″	10	15–7072	8 9/16″	10	29–5846
	D1 Comp	WM1–19	8 9/16″	10	90–5584	7 1/8″	10	90–5583	WM2–19	8 5/16″	10	15–7072	8 9/16″	10	29–5846
	C10	WM1–19	8 3/4″	10	24–7012	8 3/4″	10	24–7012	WM1–19	8 3/4″	10	24–7012	6 7/8″	10	24–7014
	C11	WM1–20	9 1/4″	10	24–6912	9 3/16″	10	29–5772	WM1–20	9 1/4″	10	24–6912	7 3/8″	10	65–5873
	B32–B34 G/S Std. & Spg. Frame	WM1–21	9 11/16″	10	65–5537	8 9/16″	10	90–5584	R	8 9/16″	8/10	65–6027	8 3/4″	10	24–7012
									WM2–19S	7 29/32″	10/12	67–6008	7 29/32″	10/12	67–6008
	B31–B32 Std. & Spg Frame	WM2–19	8 11/16″	10	65–5872	7 1/2″	10	65–5910	R	8 9/16″	8/10	65–6027	8 3/4″	10	24–7012
									WM2–19S	7 29/32″	10/12	67–6008	7 29/32″	10/12	67–6008
	M20–M21–M33 Tele. Forks	WM2–19	8 11/16″	10	65–5872	7 1/2″	10	65–5910	WM2–19	8 5/8″	8/ 3/16	15–7037	8 5/8″	8	24–6896
	A7 Star Twin Std. & Spg. Frame	WM2–19	8 11/16″	10	65–5872	7 1/2″	10	65–5910	WM2–19	7 29/32″	10/12	67–6008	7 29/32″	10/12	67–6008

B.S.A. Service Sheet No. 714—continued

SPOKE SIZES—continued.

YEAR	MODEL	FRONT - RIM SIZE	FRONT LEFT Length	FRONT LEFT Gauge	FRONT LEFT Part Number	FRONT RIGHT Length	FRONT RIGHT Gauge	FRONT RIGHT Part Number	REAR - RIM SIZE	REAR LEFT Length	REAR LEFT Gauge	REAR LEFT Part Number	REAR RIGHT Length	REAR RIGHT Gauge	REAR RIGHT Part Number
1950	D1 Std. & Spg. D1 Comp. Spg.	WM1-19	8 7/16"	10	90-5584	7 7/8"	10	90-5583	WM1-19	8 9/16"	10	15-7072	8 9/16"	10	90-5584
	C10	WM1-19	8 3/4"	10	24-7012	8 3/4"	10	24-7012	WM1-19	8 3/4"	10	24-7012	6 7/8"	10	24-7014
	C11	WM1-20	9 1/4"	10	24-6912	9 5/16"	10	29-5772	WM1-20	9 1/4"	10	24-6912	7 7/8"	10	65-5873
	B31-B33 Std. & Spg. Frame	WM2-19	8 11/16"	10	65-5872	7 1/2"	10	65-5910	R WM2-19S	8 3/8"	8/10	65-6027	8 3/4"	10	24-7012
	B32-B34 Comp. Models	WM1-21	9 1/4"	10	65-5537	8 9/16"	10	90-5584	WM2-19	8 9/16"	10	65-6027	7 29/32"	10	65-6302
	350 and 500 Scramble & Grass Track Models	Varies to Spec.	9 1/4"	10	65-5537	8 9/16"	10	90-5584	Varies to Spec.	7 29/32"	10	65-6302	8 3/4"	10	24-7012
	350 & 500 O.H.V. Gold Star, Clubmans and Road Racing	Varies to Spec.	9 9/16"	10	65-5926	6 7/8"	10	24-7014	Varies to Spec.	7 29/32"	10	65-6302	7 29/32"	10	65-6302
	M20-M21-M33	WM2-19	8 11/16"	10	65-5872	7 1/8"	10	65-5910	WM3-19	8 3/8"	8/10	15-7037	8 3/8"	8	24-6896
	A7 Star Twin Rigid & Spg. Frame	WM2-19	8 11/16"	10	65-5872	7 1/2"	10	65-5910	WM2-19	7 29/32"	10	65-6302	7 29/32"	10	65-6302
	A10	WM2-19	8 7/8"	10	67-5545	5 1/8"	10	67-5544	WM3-19	7 29/32"	10	65-6302	7 29/32"	10	65-6302
1951 and 1952 (other models as 1950)	C10 Spring Frame	WM1-19	8 3/8"	10	24-7012	8 3/4"	10	24-7012	WM1-19	8 3/4"	10	24-7012	6 7/8"	10	24-7014
	C11 Spring Frame	WM1-20	9 1/4"	10	24-6912	9 5/16"	10	29-5772	WM1-20	9 1/4"	10	24-6912	7 7/8"	10	65-5873
	M20-M21 M33 Spring Frame	WM1-19	8 11/16"	10	65-5872	7 1/8"	10	65-5910	WM2-19	7 29/32"	10	65-6303	7 29/32"	10	65-6302
1953 (other models as 1950,52)	B33-A7-A10 Rigid	WM2-19	8 7/8"	10	67-5545	5 1/8"	10	67-5544	WM2-19	8 3/4"	10	24-7012	8 9/16"	10	65-6027
	B33-A7-A10 Spring	WM2-19	8 3/4"	10	67-5545	5 1/8"	10	67-5544	WM2-19	7 29/32"	10	65-6303	7 29/32"	10	65-6302
	GOLD STAR Clubmans, Road Racing & Touring	WM1-19	8 3/4"	10	67-5537	5 1/8"	10	67-5544	WM2-19	7 29/32"	10	65-6303	7 29/32"	10	65-6302
	B32 B34 Trials	WM1-21	9 1/4"	10	67-5537	8 9/16"	10	90-5584	WM3-19	7 29/32"	10	65-6303	7 29/32"	10	65-6302
	B32-B34 Scrambles	WM1-21	9 1/4"	8	42-5524	8 7/16"	8	31-6015	WM3-19	7 29/32"	10	65-6303	7 29/32"	10	65-6302

B.S.A. Service Sheet No. 714—continued

SPOKE SIZES—continued

YEAR	MODEL	RIM SIZE	FRONT LEFT Length	FRONT LEFT Gauge	FRONT Part Number	FRONT Length	FRONT RIGHT Gauge	FRONT RIGHT Part Number	RIM SIZE	REAR LEFT Length	REAR LEFT Gauge	REAR Part Number	REAR Length	REAR RIGHT Gauge	REAR RIGHT Part Number
1954 and 1955	D1-D3 Rigid & Spring	WM1-19	8 3/8"	10	90-5584	7 1/8"	10	90-5583	WM1-19	8 5/16"	10	90-6042	8 3/16"	10	90-5584
	D1-D3 Comp.	WM1-19	8 3/8"	10	90-5584	7"	10	29-5940	WM1-19	8 5/16"	10	90-6042	8 3/16"	10	90-5584
	C10L	WM1-19	8 5/8"	10	90-5584	7"	10	29-5940	WM1-19	8 5/16"	10	90-6042	8 3/16"	10	90-5584
	C11G	WM1-19	8 3/4"	10	24-7012	8 3/4"	10	24-7012	WM1-19	6 7/8"	10	24-7014	8 3/4"	10	24-7012
	C11G (1955) Rigid & Spring	WM1-19	8 3/4"	10	24-7012	7 1/2"	10	65-5910	WM1-19	6 7/8"	10	24-7014	8 3/4"	10	24-7012
	B31-B33 Rigid	WM2-19	8 11/16"	10	65-5872	7 1/2"	10	65-5910	WM1-19	8 5/16"	Butted 8/10	65-6027	8 3/4"	10	65-6302
	B31-B33 Spring	WM2-19	8 11/16"	10	65-5872	7 1/4"	10	65-5910	WM2-19	7 22/32"	10	65-6303	7 22/32"	10	65-6302
	B32-B34 Comp. Rigid	WM1-21	9 11/16"	10	65-5537	8 5/8"	10	90-5584	WM3-19	7 22/32"	10	65-6303	7 22/32"	10	65-6302
	B31 Swinging Arm	WM2-19	8 11/16"	10	65-5872	7 1/2"	10	65-5912	WM2-19	7 22/32"	10	65-6303	7 22/32"	10	65-6302
	B32-B34 Swinging Arm	WM1-21	9 11/16"	10	65-5537	8 5/16"	10	90-5584	WM2-19	7 22/32"	10	65-6303	7 22/32"	10	65-6302
	B33 1954 Swinging Arm	WM2-19	8 7/8"	10	67-5545	5 5/16"	10	67-5544	WM2-19	7 22/32"	10	65-6303	7 22/32"	10	65-6302
	B33 1955 Swinging Arm	WM2-19	8 7/8"	Butted 8/10	67-5606	5 5/16"	10	67-5544	WM2-19	7 22/32"	10	65-6303	7 22/32"	10	65-6302
	GOLD STAR Clubmans, Road Racing & Touring	WM1-19	8 11/16"	10	67-5545	5 5/16"	10	67-5544	WM2-18	7 7/8"	10	42-6011	7 7/16"	10	42-6012
	GOLD STAR Trials	WM1-21	9 11/16"	10	65-5537	8 5/16"	10	90-5584	WM3-19	7 22/32"	10	65-6303	7 22/32"	10	65-6302
	GOLD STAR Scrambles	WM1-21	9 11/16"	8	42-5524	8 5/16"	8	31-6015	WM3-19	7 22/32"	10	65-6303	7 22/32"	10	65-6302
	M20-M21-M33 Rigid	WM2-19	8 11/16"	10	65-5872	7 1/2"	10	65-5910	WM2-19	8 5/8"	Butted 8	15-7037	8 3/8"	Butted 8	24-6896
	M20-M21-M33 Spring	WM2-19	8 11/16"	10	65-5872	7 1/4"	10	65-5910	WM2-19	7 22/32"	10	65-6303	7 22/32"	10	65-6302
	"A" GROUP Plunger & Swinging Arm 1954	WM2-19	8 5/8"	10	67-5545	5 11/16"	10	67-5544	WM2-19	7 22/32"	10	65-6303	7 22/32"	10	65-6302
	"A" GROUP Plunger & Swinging Arm 1955	WM2-19	8 7/8"	Butted 8/10	67-5606	5 11/16"	10	67-5544	WM2-19	7 22/32"	10	65-6303	7 22/32"	10	65-6302

B.S.A. Service Sheet No. 714—continued

SPOKE SIZES—continued.

YEAR	MODEL	FRONT							REAR						
		RIM SIZE	LEFT		Part Number	RIGHT		RIM SIZE	LEFT		Part Number	RIGHT	
			Length	Gauge		Length	Gauge		Length	Gauge		Length	Gauge	Part Number
1956/7	D1 Plunger	WM1-19	8 3/16"	10	90-5584	7 7/8"	10	WM1-19	8 3/16"	10	90-6042	8 3/8"	10	90-5584
	D3 Swinging Arm	WM1-19	8 3/16"	10	90-5584	7 7/8"	10	WM1-19	8 3/16"	10	90-6042	8 3/8"	10	90-5584
	C10L	WM1-19	8 3/4"	10	24-7012	8 3/4"	10	WM1-19	8 3/16"	10	90-6042	8 3/8"	10	90-5584
	C12	WM1-19	6 5/8"	10	29-5976	6 5/8"	10	WM1-19	7"	10	29-5940	7"	10	29-5940
	B31 B33	WM2-19	6 1/4"	Butted 8/10	42-5635	6 1/4"	Butted 8/10	WM2-19	6 1/4"	Butted 8/10	42-5635	6 1/4"	Butted 8/10	42-5635
	GOLD STAR Clubmans, Road Racing & Touring	WM1-19	5 1/8"	10	42-5552	5 1/8"	10	WM2-19	7 22/32"	10	65-6303	7 22/32"	10	65-6302
	B32-B34 Comp.	WM1-21	9 11/16"	10	65-5537	8 7/8"	10	WM3-19	7 22/32"	10	65-6303	7 22/32"	10	65-6302
	GOLD STAR Scrambles	WM1-21	9 11/16"	8	42-5524	8 7/16"	8	WM3-19	8 5/8"	Butted 8	15-7037	8 5/8"	Butted 8	24-6896
	M21 Rigid	WM2-19	8 3/4"	Butted 8/10	67-5606	5 11/16"	Butted 8/10	WM3-19	7 22/32"	10	65-6303	7 22/32"	10	65-6302
	M21-M33 Plunger	WM2-19	8 3/4"	Butted 8/10	67-5606	5 11/16"	Butted 8/10	WM2-19	6 1/4"	Butted 8/10	42-5635	6 1/4"	Butted 8/10	42-5635
	A7 and Shooting Star	WM2-19	6 1/4"	Butted 8/10	42-5635	6 1/4"	Butted 8/10	WM2-19	7 22/32"	Butted 8/10	67-6017	7 22/32"	Butted 8/10	67-6016
	A10 Plunger	WM2-19	8 3/4"	Butted 8/10	67-5606	5 11/16"	Butted 8/10	WM2-19	6 1/4"	Butted 8/10	42-5635	6 1/4"	Butted 8/10	42-5635
	A10 and Road Rocket	WM2-19	6 1/4"	Butted 8/10	42-5635	6 1/4"	Butted 8/10	WM2-19	6 1/4"	8/10	42-5635	6 1/4"	Butted 8/10	42-5635
	Dandy 70	WM0-15	5 5/8"	12	64-5505	5 5/8"	12	WM0-15	5 5/8"	Butted 11/12	64-5507	5 5/8"	Butted 11/12	64-5507

BSA SERVICE SHEET No. 805

Reprinted June, 1960

All Models

BATTERY — LEAD-ACID TYPES

The range of Lucas batteries listed here covers those models fitted to B.S.A. motor cycles in recent years.

PU5E and LVW5E Small capacity batteries for lightweight machines.

PU7E .. .. Standard battery for cradle mountting.

GU11E .. .. Larger capacity battery for sidecar machines.

SC7E .. .. Large capacity lightweight battery for machines fitted with starting motors or two-way radio equipment, e.g. police machines.

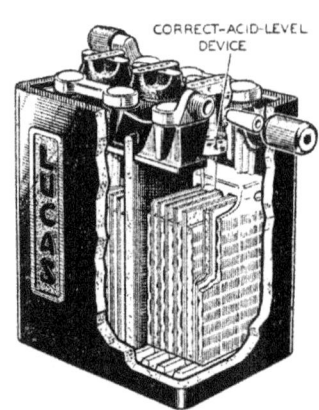

Fig. Y18. Sectioned battery, model PU7E/9

All current Lucas motor cycle batteries are 'dry charged', and do not require initial charging. Except that these batteries have porous rubber separators, they are identical with earlier models supplied wet or uncharged and require the same routine maintenance when in service.

STORAGE

Used batteries must be fully charged before storing. In temperate climates they should be examined fortnightly, or weekly in the case of model LVW5E and all models when stored in the tropics. If necessary, give them a short refreshing charge.

After a long period of storage, the condition of the battery will often improve if it is put through a 'cycle', as described on page 4.

MAINTENANCE

Every fortnight, or more frequently in hot climates, examine the condition of the battery. Examine five-plate batteries every week.

Never use a naked light when examining the condition of the cells, as there is a **danger** of igniting the gas coming from the active materials.

Cleaning

Remove the battery cover and clean the cell tops. Examine the connections. If they are loose or dirty, remove them and scrape the contact surfaces clean. Coat them with petroleum jelly before replacing.

Remove the filler plugs and check that the vent holes are clear and that the rubber washer fitted under some plugs is in good condition.

Topping-up

During charging, water is lost by gassing and evaporation. Examine the electrolyte level in each cell and, if necessary, add distilled water to raise the electrolyte level with the top edges of the separators.

SC7E batteries have a woven glass pad fitted in each cell to reduce splashing when the battery is gassing during charging. When 'topping-up' this type of battery it is useful to note that the correct electrolyte level is reached when moisture appears through the porous glass pad.

B.S.A. Service Sheet No. 805 (continued)

The Lucas Battery Filler

The use of a Lucas motor cycle Battery Filler will be found helpful in this 'topping-up' process, as it ensures that the correct electrolyte level is automatically attained and also prevents distilled water from being spilled over the battery top.

Correct-Acid-Level-Devices

The correct-acid-level-device fitted to some Lucas batteries consists of a central tube with a perforated flange which rests on a ledge in the filling orifice.

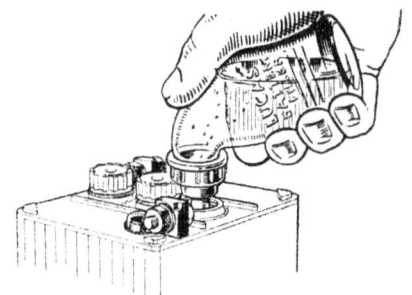

Fig Y19. The Lucas battery filler

When 'topping-up' a battery fitted with these devices, pour distilled water round the flange (not down the tube) until no more drains through into the cell. This will happen when the electrolyte level reaches the bottom of the central tube and prevents further escape of air displaced by the 'topping-up' water. Lift the tube slightly to allow the small amount of water in the flange to drain into the cell. The electrolyte level will then be correct.

If a battery requires 'topping-up' too frequently, the voltage regulator (on machines fitted with d.c. generators) may be out of adjustment, i.e. set too high, and should be checked. Conversely, a persistently low state of charge may be due to a regulator being set too low.

If one cell in particular needs 'topping-up' more than another, it is likely the container is cracked, in which event replace the battery and clean the carrier, using a solution of ammonia or bi-carbonate of soda in water. After cleaning and drying, paint the battery carrier and other surfaces affected by the electrolyte with anti-sulphuric paint.

TABLES OF SPECIFIC GRAVITIES AND CHARGING RATES

Battery	Plates per cell	Amp. Hr. Capacity		Electrolyte to fill one two-volt cell		Home Trade and Climates Ordinarily below 90°F. (32°C.) Specific Gravity of Acid (corrected to 60°F.)		Climates frequently over 90°F. (32°C.) Specific Gravity of Acid (corrected to 60°F.)		Initial Charge Current	Re-charge Current
		At 10 hour rate	At 20 hour rate	Pint	c.c.	Filling	Fully Charged	Filling	Fully Charged	Amp.	Amp.
1	2	3		4		5	6	7	8	9	10
LVW5E	5	5	5.7	1/8	71	1.270	1.270–1.290	1.210	1.210–1.230	0.3	0.5
PU5E	5	8	9	1/6	94	1.270	1.270–1.290	1.210	1.210–1.230	0.6	1.0
PU7E	7	12	13.5	1/5	113	1.270	1.270–1.290	1.210	1.210–1.230	0.8	1.5
GU11E	11	20	22.8	1/3	189	1.270	1.270–1.290	1.210	1.210–1.230	1.3	2.2
SC7E	7	22.5	26	—	250	1.270	1.270–1.290	1.210	1.210–1.230	1.5	2.5

The maximum permissible electrolyte temperature during charging is given below. Should the temperature of the electrolyte exceed this value interrupt the charge and allow the battery temperature to fall at least 10°F. (5.5°C.) before charging is resumed.

Climates normally below 80°F. (27°C.)	Climates between 80°–100°F. (27°–38°C.)	Climates frequently above 100°F. (38°C.)
100°F. (38°C.)	110°F. (43°C.)	120°F. (49°C.)

The specific gravity of the electrolyte varies with temperature. For convenience in comparing specific gravities, they are always corrected to 60°F., which is adopted as the reference temperature. The method of correction is as follows:

For every 5°F. *below* 60°F., *deduct* 0.002 from the observed reading to obtain the true specific gravity at 60°F. For every 5°F. *above* 60°F., *add* 0.002 to the observed reading to obtain the true specific gravity at 60°F.

The temperature must be that indicated by a thermometer having its bulb actually immersed in the electrolyte, and not the ambient temperature.

B.S.A. Service Sheet No. 805 (continued)

SERVICING
Battery Persists in Low State of Charge
First consider the conditions under which the battery is used. If the battery is subject to continuous discharge, e.g. long periods of night parking with lights on without suitable opportunities for recharging, a low state of charge is inevitable.

A fault in the dynamo or regulator, or neglect during a period out of commission, may also be responsible.

Vent Plugs
See that the ventilating holes in each vent plug are clear, and that the rubber washer fitted under the plug is in good condition.

Level of Electrolyte
The surface of the electrolyte should be level with the tops of the separators. If necessary, top-up with distilled water. Any loss of acid from spilling or spraying (as opposed to normal loss of *water* by evaporation) should be made good by dilute acid of the same specific gravity as that already in the cell.

Cleanliness
See that the top of the battery is free from dirt or moisture which might provide a discharge path. Check that the battery connections are clean and tight.

Hydrometer Tests
The space between each separator is not wide enough to permit the nozzle of an hydrometer to be inserted. Before taking a sample, tilt the battery to bring sufficient electrolyte above the separators. If the level of the electrolyte is so low that an hydrometer reading cannot be taken, no attempt should be made to take a reading after adding distilled water until the battery has been on charge for at least 30 minutes.

Measure the specific gravity of the acid in each cell in turn. The reading given by each cell should be approximately the same; if one cell differs appreciably from the others, an internal fault in that cell is indicated.

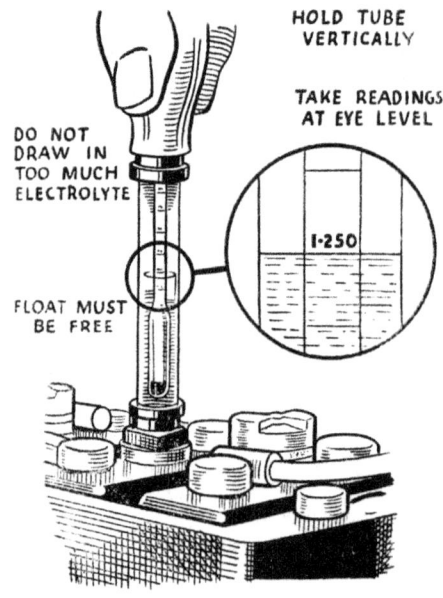

Fig Y20. Taking hydrometer readings

Specific gravity readings and their indications are as follows:

Climates under 90°F.			Climates over 90°F.
1.270—1.290	..	Cell fully charged ..	1.210—1.230
1.190—1.210	..	Cell about half discharged ..	1.130—1.150
1.110—1.130	..	Cell fully discharged ..	1.050—1.070

The appearance of the electrolyte drawn into the hydrometer when taking a reading gives a useful indication of the state of the plates: if it is very dirty, or contains small particles in suspension, it is possible that the plates are in a bad condition.

Discharge Test
Motor-cycle batteries must *not* be subjected to the heavy discharge test, as recommended for motor-car and commercial vehicle batteries.

RECHARGING FROM AN EXTERNAL SUPPLY
If the hydrometer test indicates that the battery is merely discharged, and is otherwise in a good condition, it should be recharged, either on the motor-cycle by a period of daytime running, or on the bench from an external supply.

B.S.A. Service Sheet No. 805 (continued)

If the latter, the battery should be charged at the rate given in the table until the specific gravity and voltage show no increase over three successive hourly readings. During the charge the electrolyte must be kept level with the tops of the separators by the addition of distilled water.

A battery that shows a general falling-off in efficiency, common to all cells, will often respond to the process known as 'cycling'. This process consists of fully charging the battery by passing through it from an external source the appropriate re-charge current given in the table. The battery is then discharged by connecting to a lamp board, or other load, taking a current equal to the normal re-charge current. The battery should be capable of providing this current for at least 7 hours before it is fully discharged, as indicated by the voltage of each cell falling to 1.8. If the battery discharges in a shorter time, repeat the 'cycle' of charge and discharge.

PREPARING BATTERIES FOR SERVICE

All new batteries are supplied without electrolyte but with the plates in a charged condition. When they are required for service it is only necessary to fill each cell with sulphuric acid of the correct specific gravity. No initial charging is required.

Preparation of Electrolyte

The electrolyte is prepared by mixing together distilled water and concentrated sulphuric acid. The mixing must be carried out either in a lead-lined tank or in suitable glass or earthenware vessels. Slowly add the acid to the water, stirring with a glass rod. *Never add water to acid*, as the resulting chemical reaction causes violent and dangerous spurting of the concentrated acid. The specific gravity of the filling electrolyte depends on the climate in which the battery is to be used.

The approximate proportions of acid and water are indicated in the following table:

To obtain Specific Gravity (corrected to 60°F.) of	Add 1 vol. of acid 1.835 S.G. (corrected to 60°F.) to
1.270	2.8 vols. of water
1.210	4.0 vols. of water

Heat is produced by the mixture of acid and water, and the electrolyte should be allowed to cool before pouring it into the battery.

The total volume of electrolyte required can be estimated from the figures quoted in the table on page 2.

Filling the Battery

Carefully break the seals in the cell filling holes and fill each cell with electrolyte to the top of the separators, *in one operation*. The temperature of the filling room, battery and electrolyte should be maintained between 60°F. and 100°F. If the battery has been stored in a cool place, it should be allowed to warm up to room temperature before filling.

Putting into Use

Batteries filled in this way are 90 per cent charged. If time permits, however, a freshening charge of four hours at the normal recharge rate given in the table would be beneficial.

During the charge the electrolyte must be kept level with the top edge of the separators by the addition of distilled water. Check the specific gravity of the acid at the end of the charge; if 1.270 acid was used to fill the battery, the specific gravity should now be between 1.270 and 1.290; if 1.210, between 1.210 and 1.230.

Maintenance in Service

After filling, the battery needs only the recommended attention.

B.S.A. MOTOR CYCLES LTD.
Service Dept., Waverley Works,
Birmingham, 10.
Printed in England.

JU/B5029

BSA SERVICE SHEET No. 806

Reprinted April, 1960

All Models

LAMPS

LUCAS LIGHTING

Headlamps

Although the headlamps fitted to individual models may vary in detail, they remain similar with regard to the general features described below. All headlamps are fitted with a double filament main bulb and a pilot bulb. One of the double filaments provides the main riding beam while the second, brought into operation by means of the dipper switch, provides the dipped beam.

On some models the headlamp incorporates a panel containing the ammeter and lighting switch but if a cowl is fitted then it carries these components externally to the headlamp shell.

Other headlamps contain wire wound resistances for the purpose of reducing the charging rates under certain conditions and these are described under the appropriate lighting circuit.

Setting and Focusing

The best way of checking the setting of the lamp is to park the motor cycle in front of a light coloured wall at a distance of about 25 feet. If necessary, slacken the bolts securing the headlamp and move the lamp until, with the main driving light switched on, the beam is projected straight ahead and parallel with the ground. With the lamp in this position, the height of the beam centre from the ground should be the same as the height of the centre of the headlamp from the ground.

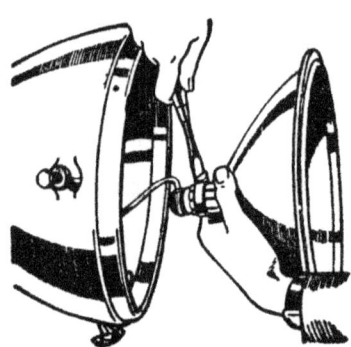

Fig. Y.22 Headlamp Focusing.

The headlamp must be focused so that, when the main driving light is switched on, a uniform beam without any dark centre is given. If the bulb needs adjusting, remove the lamp front and reflector, as described below, and slacken the bulb holder clamping clip at the back of the reflector. Move the bulb holder backwards and forwards until the correct position is obtained, and then tighten the clamping clip.

More sealed beam light units are fitted with the pre-focus type of bulb and therefore no focusing is necessary.

Removal of Front and Reflector, pre-1948 models

Press back the fixing clip at the bottom of the lamp. The front and reflector can now be taken off. The bulb holder is secured to the reflector by means of two fixing springs. When replacing the front, locate the top of the rim first, then press on at the bottom and secure with the fixing clip.

B.S.A. Service Sheet No. 806 (cont.)

1948 Models (Fig. Y.23)

Press back the fixing clip at the bottom of the lamp, and remove the lamp front. The reflector is secured to the lamp body by means of a rubber bead. When refitting the rubber bead, locate its thinner lip between the reflector rim and the edge of the lamp body. To replace the front, locate the metal tongue in the slot at the top of the lamp, press the front on, and secure by means of the fixing catch.

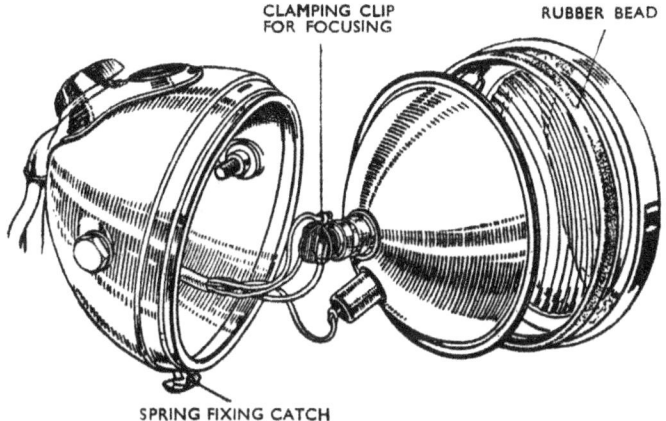

Fig. Y.23.

Sealed Beam Headlamps

Later models are fitted with a sealed light unit having the reflector and glass sealed together. After slackening the securing screw on the top of the headlamp, the rim, complete with light unit, may be removed. To replace, locate the rim on the lip at the bottom of the lamp body, press the light unit assembly and rim into position and tighten the securing screw. The main headlamp bulb in some of these headlamps is of the pre-focus type and is held in position by a cap with bayonet type fitting. In all cases access to the main or pilot bulbs is obtained by removal of the light unit assembly.

Breakage of the headlamp glass with this type of unit involves replacement of the glass and reflector complete. The light unit may be removed from the headlamp rim after prising out the retaining clips.

Replacement of Bulbs

When the replacement of a bulb is necessary, it is important not only that the same size bulb is fitted, but that it has a high efficiency and will focus in the reflector. Cheap and inferior replacement

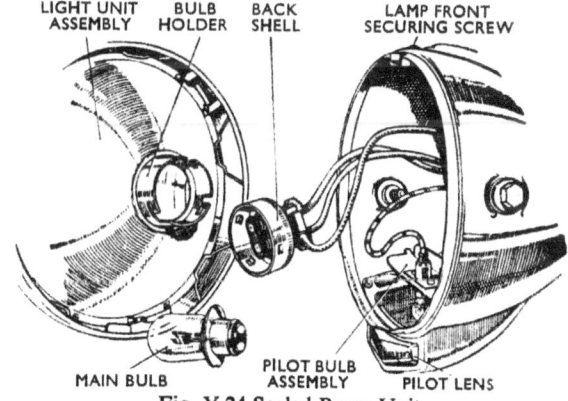

Fig. Y.24 Sealed Beam Unit.

bulbs often have the filament of such a shape that it is impossible to focus correctly; for example, the filament may be to the one side of the axis of the bulb resulting in loss of range and light efficiency.

Lucas Genuine Spare Bulbs are specially tested to check that the filament is in the correct position to give the best results with Lucas lamps. To assist in identification, Lucas bulbs are marked on the metal cap with a number. When fitting a replacement, see that it has the same number as the original bulb.

B.S.A. Service Sheet No. 806 (cont.)

When fitting a main headlamp bulb, care must be taken to insert it the correct way round, i.e. with the dipped beam filament above the centre filament.

The pre-focus type bulb is located by a flange and there is a notch which engages on a raised portion of the bulb holder to ensure correct positioning.

Where the pilot bulb is contained in an underslung cowl, the metal strip on which the bulb is mounted should be pushed to the rear and lifted away in order to provide access to the bulb.

Tail Lamps

Where the tail lamp is of the metal type the body or back should be removed by pushing it in, rotating to the left, and pulling away, thus providing access to the bulb. The moulded plastic type of rear lamp can be dismantled by unscrewing the two screws in the cover.

When a stop lamp is fitted, a two-filament type of bulb is employed with offset bayonet type fixing pins to ensure that it can only be fitted correctly.

MAIN BULBS

Models A7, A10, B31, 32, 33, 34, C12, C15 and M20, M21.

Lucas No. 168, 6v. 24/24w. (with E3H Dynamo). Lucas No. 169, 6v. 30/30w. (with E3L Dynamo). Lucas No. 312, 6v. 30/24w. (Pre-focus type Bulb).

Models C10 and C11.

Lucas No. 180, 6v., 18/18w. (with E3H Dynamo). Lucas No. 168, 6v. 24/24w. (with E3L Dynamo).

Models C11G and D1 (early) Lucas

Lucas No. 312, 6v. 30/24w. (Pre-focus type Bulb).

PILOT

Lucas No. 200, 6v. 3w. Lucas No. 988, 6v. 3w. (with Sealed Beam Light Unit).

TAIL

Lucas No. 205, 6v. 6w.
Lucas No. 384, 6v. 6/18w. (Stop/Tail Lamp).

B.S.A. MOTOR CYCLES LTD.
Service Dept., Waverley Works,
Birmingham, 10
Printed in England.

JU/B4780

BSA SERVICE SHEET No. 807

Reprinted June 1960

All Models

ELECTRIC HORN—HIGH FREQUENCY MODELS

General

Electric horns are adjusted to give their best performance before leaving the Works, and will give long periods of service without any attention.

Servicing

If the horn becomes uncertain in action or does not vibrate, it does not follow that the horn has broken down. The trouble may be due to a discharged battery or a loose or broken connection in the horn wiring.

The performance of the horn may be upset by the fixing bolt working loose, or by the vibration of some part adjacent to the horn. To check this, remove the horn from its mounting, hold it firmly in the hand by its bracket and press the push. If the note is still unsatisfactory, the horn may require adjustment, but this should only be necessary after a very long period of service.

Method of Adjusting

The adjustment of a horn does not alter the characteristics of the note but merely takes up wear of vibrating parts.

If the horn is used repeatedly when badly out of adjustment, due usually to unsuccessful attempts at adjustment, the horn may become damaged, due to the excessive current which it will take. When testing, do not continue to operate the push if the horn does not sound. If, when the push is operated, the horn does not take any current (indicated by an ammeter connected in series with the horn) it is possible that the horn has been adjusted so that its contact breaker is permanently open.

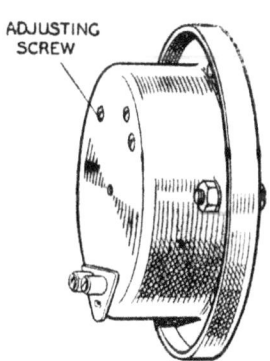

Fig. Y26.
Typical electric horn, showing adjustment screw.

After adjusting, note the current consumption, which must not exceed 3—4 amperes. A horn may give a good note, yet be out of adjustment and taking an excessive current. When adjusting do not attempt to unscrew the nut securing the tone disc or any other screw in the horn.

The adjustment is made by turning the adjustment screw, usually in a clockwise direction. The underside of the screw is serrated, and the screw must not be turned for more than 2 or 3 notches before re-testing. If the adjustment screw is turned too far in a clockwise direction, a point will occur at which the armature pulls in but does not separate the contacts.

B.S.A. Service Sheet No. 807 (contd.)

Some models have no adjustment screw at the back of the horn. Adjustment is carried out by means of the grub screw and locking collar which are revealed upon removal of the large domed nut on the front of the horn. Take care that the large nut securing the sounding disc is not disturbed. The locking collar requires a special tool, or a large screwdriver with the blade ground so as to leave two projecting prongs, in order that it may be undone. No attempt should be made to loosen the collar without a proper tool as it is very tight and may become damaged so that it cannot be removed. The adjustment should be carried out in a similar manner to that described for the other type of horn, but the locking collar should be firmly tightened after each adjustment as this affects the note.

B.S.A. MOTOR CYCLES LTD.,
Service Dept., Waverley Works,
Birmingham, 10.
Printed in England.

BSA SERVICE SHEET No. 808B

"D" GROUP MODELS

WIRING DIAGRAMS

Lucas D.C. Lighting

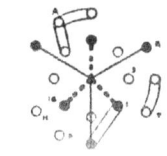

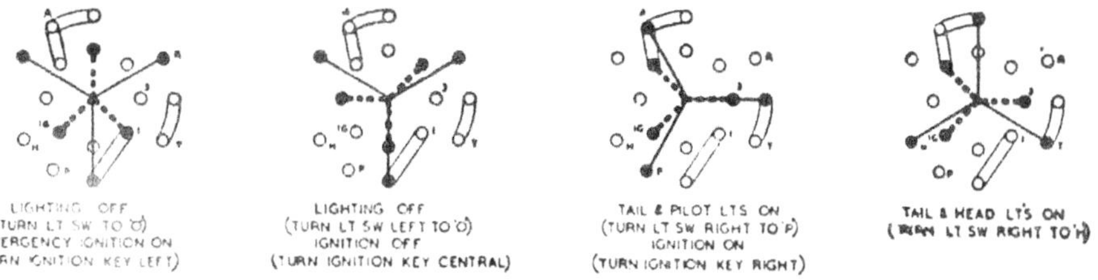

LIGHTING OFF
(TURN LT SW TO 'O')
EMERGENCY IGNITION ON
(TURN IGNITION KEY LEFT)

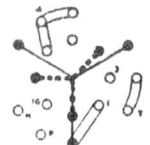

LIGHTING OFF
(TURN LT SW LEFT TO 'O')
IGNITION OFF
(TURN IGNITION KEY CENTRAL)

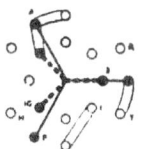

TAIL & PILOT LTS ON
(TURN LT SW RIGHT TO 'P')
IGNITION ON
(TURN IGNITION KEY RIGHT)

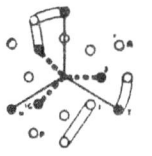

TAIL & HEAD LT'S ON
(TURN LT SW RIGHT TO 'H')

DIAGRAMS SHOWING SWITCH POSITIONS LOOKING ON TOP OF SWITCH

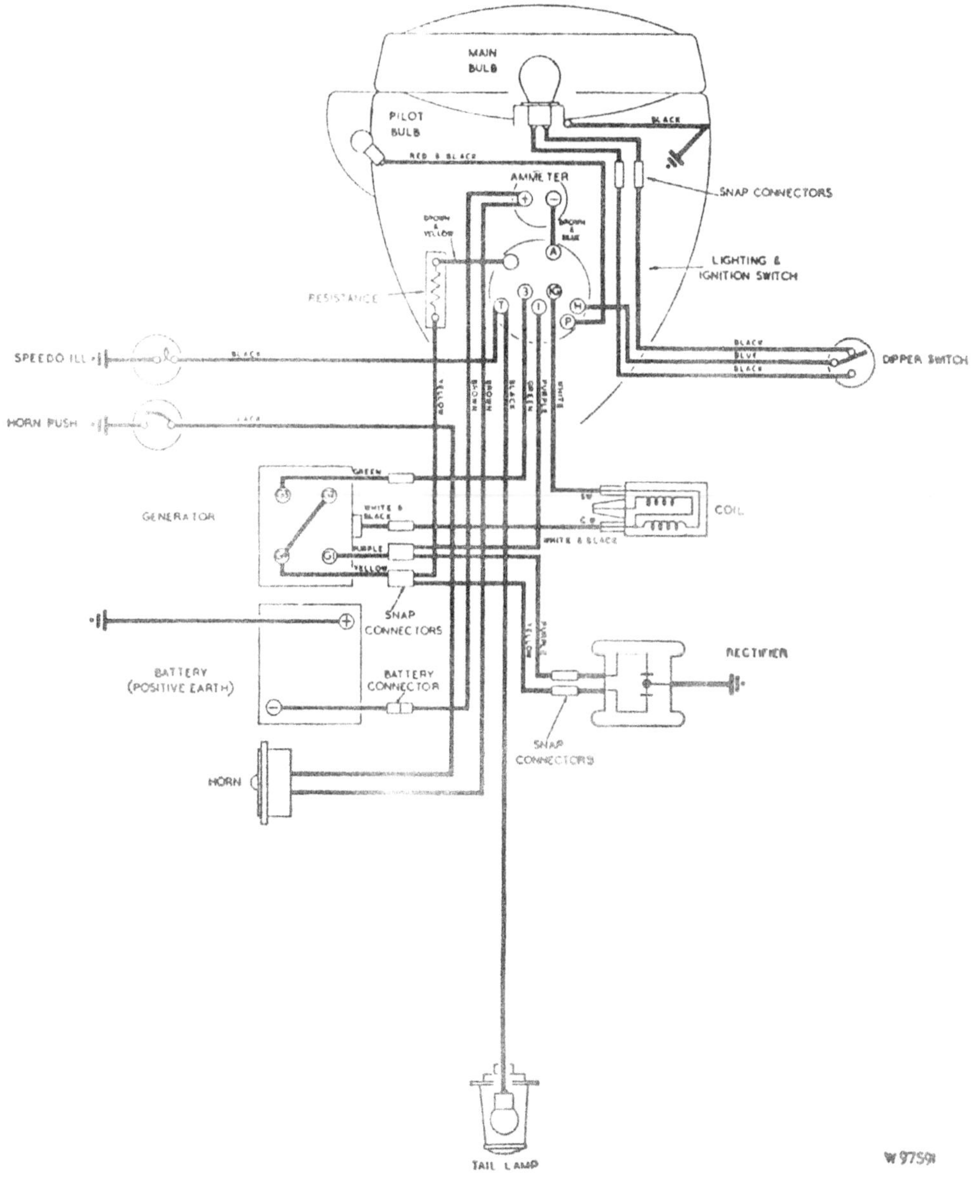

B.S.A. Service Sheet No. 808B (contd.)

Wipac A.C. Lighting

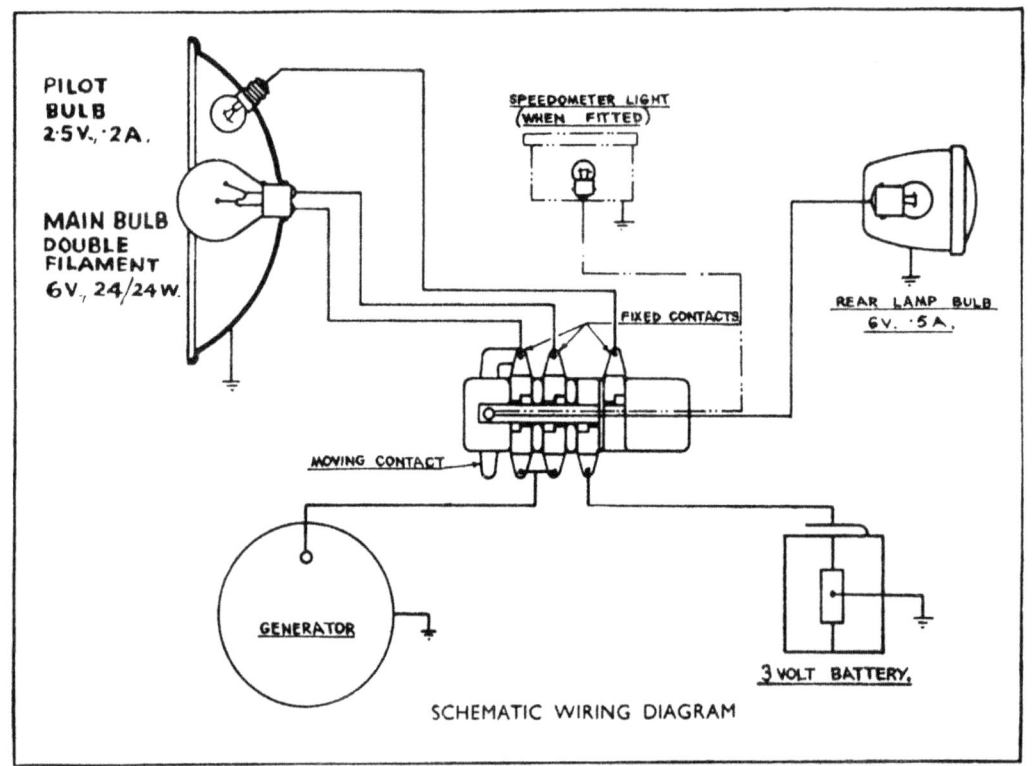

ABOVE: Wiring diagram for Wipac A.C. lighting when fitted with remotely controlled switch operated by handlebar lever.

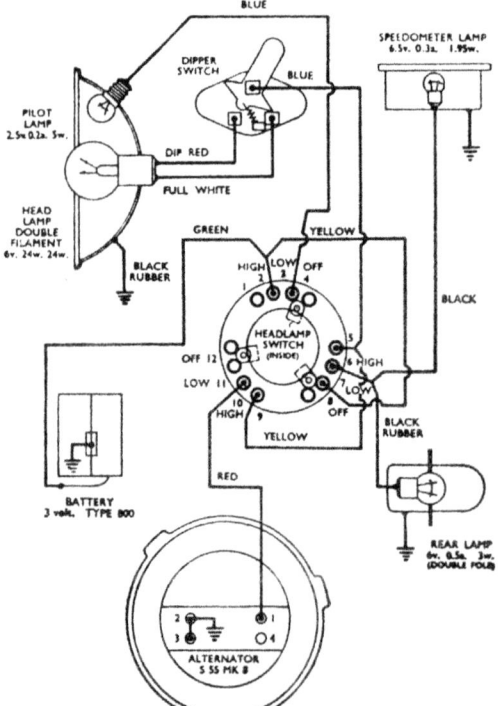

LEFT: Wiring diagram for Wipac A.C. lighting when switch is mounted on top of the headlamp shell.

B.S.A. Service Sheet No. 808B (contd.)

Wipac D.C. Lighting

(Negative Earth System)

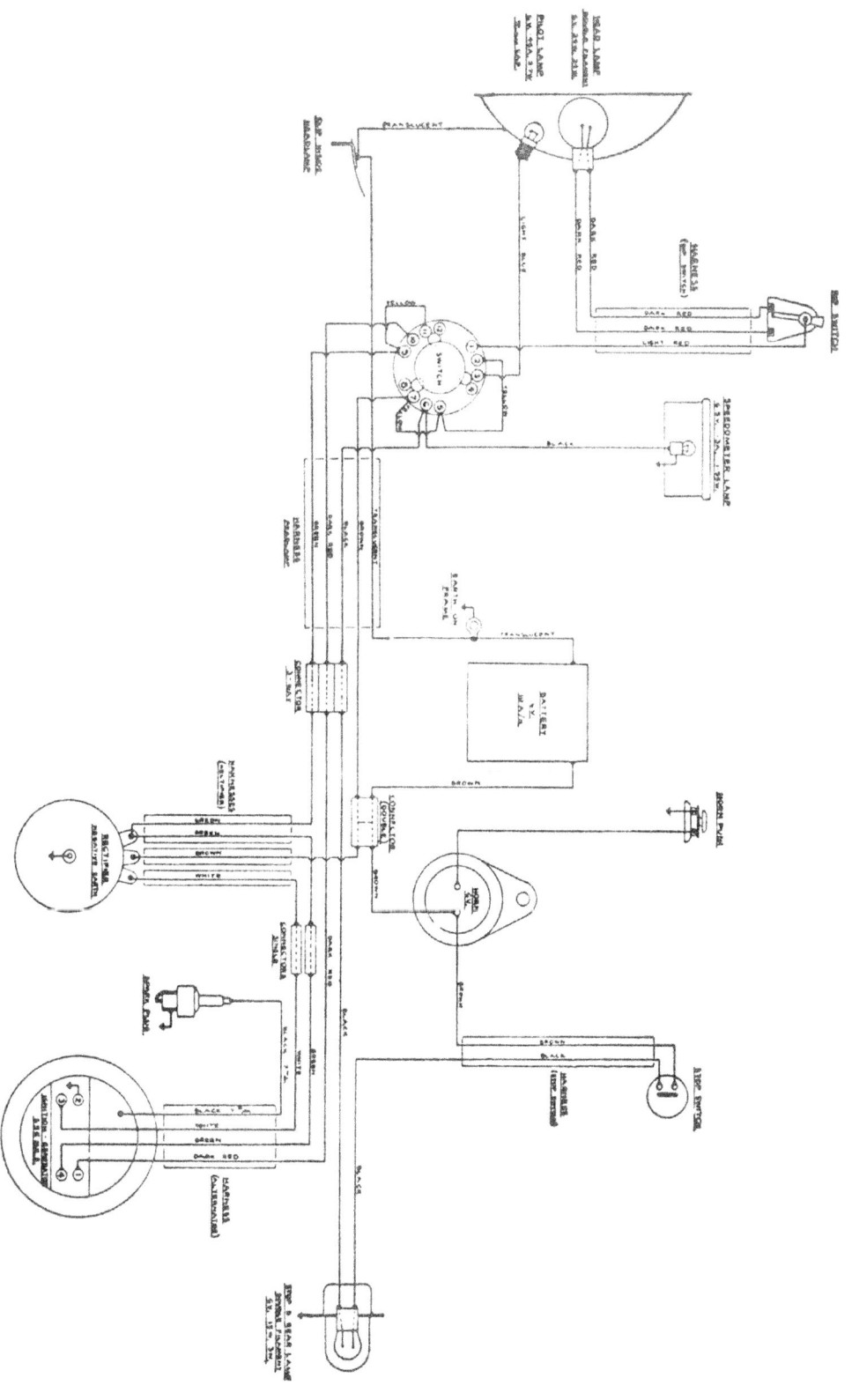

B.S.A. Service Sheet No. 808B (contd.)

Wipac D.C. Lighting
(Positive Earth System)

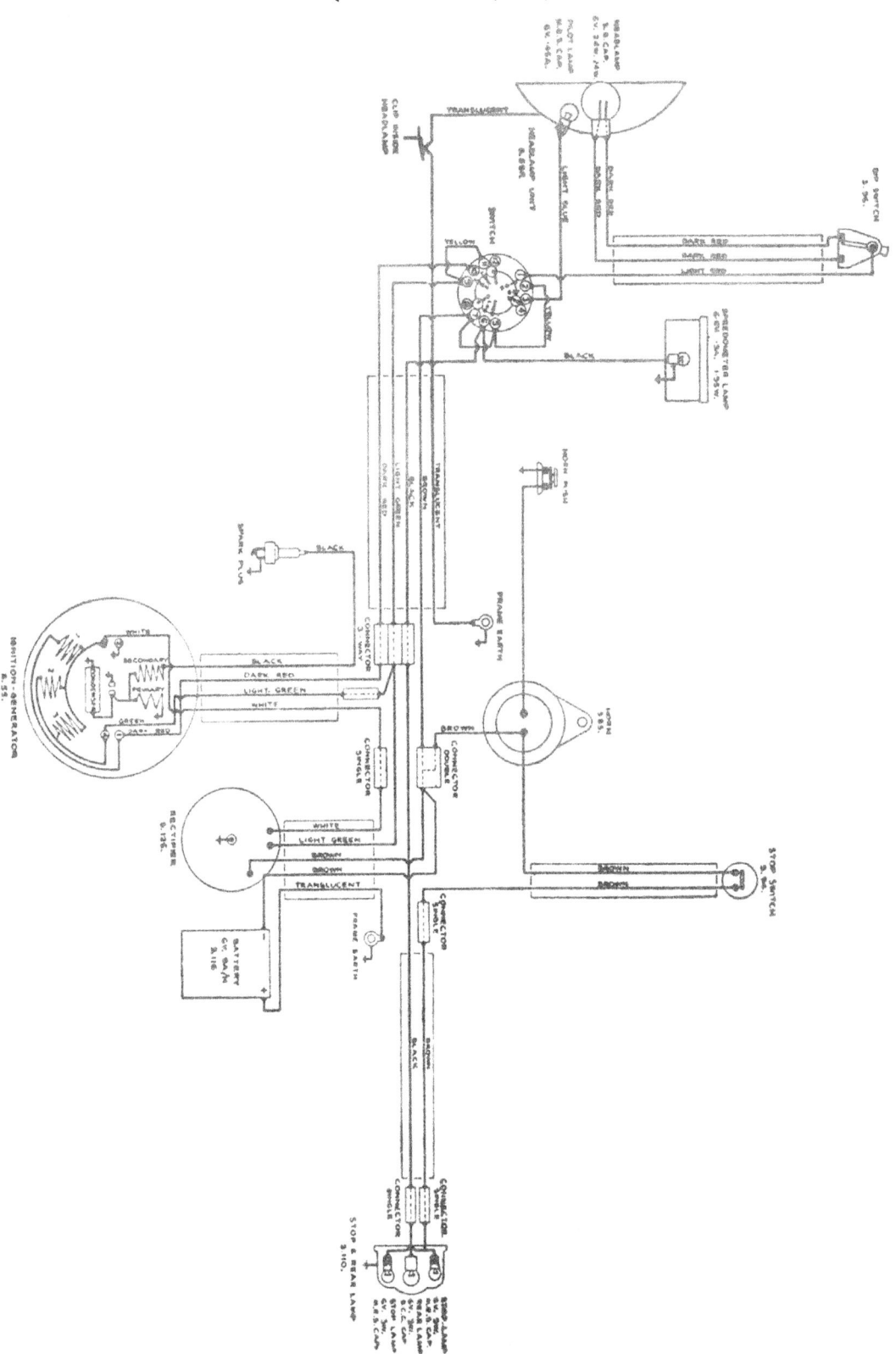

BSA SERVICE SHEET No. 808E

1956 D Group Models

WIRING DIAGRAMS

Wipac A.C. Lighting

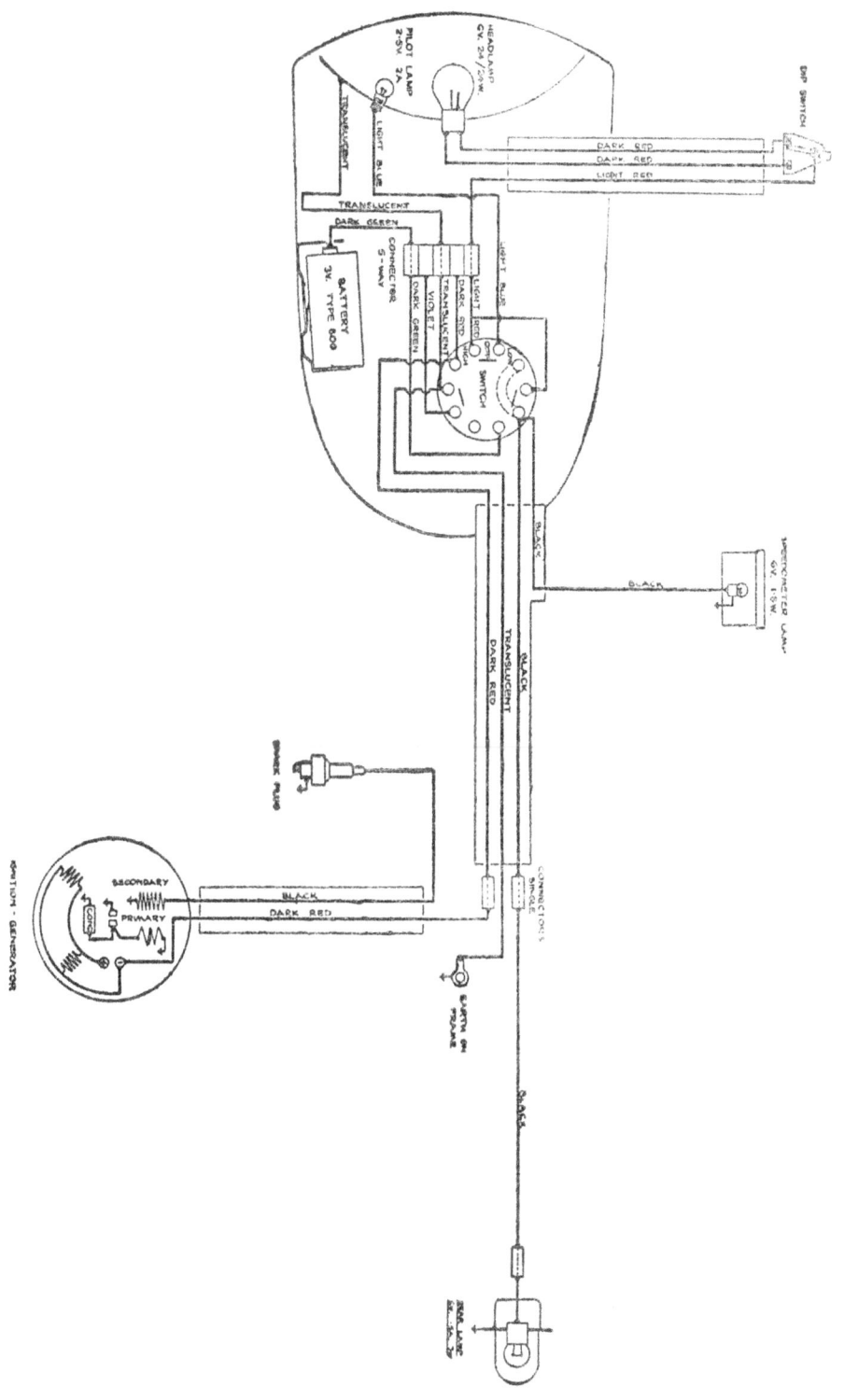

B.S.A. Service Sheet No. 808E—*continued*

Wipac D.C. Lighting
(Positive Earth System)

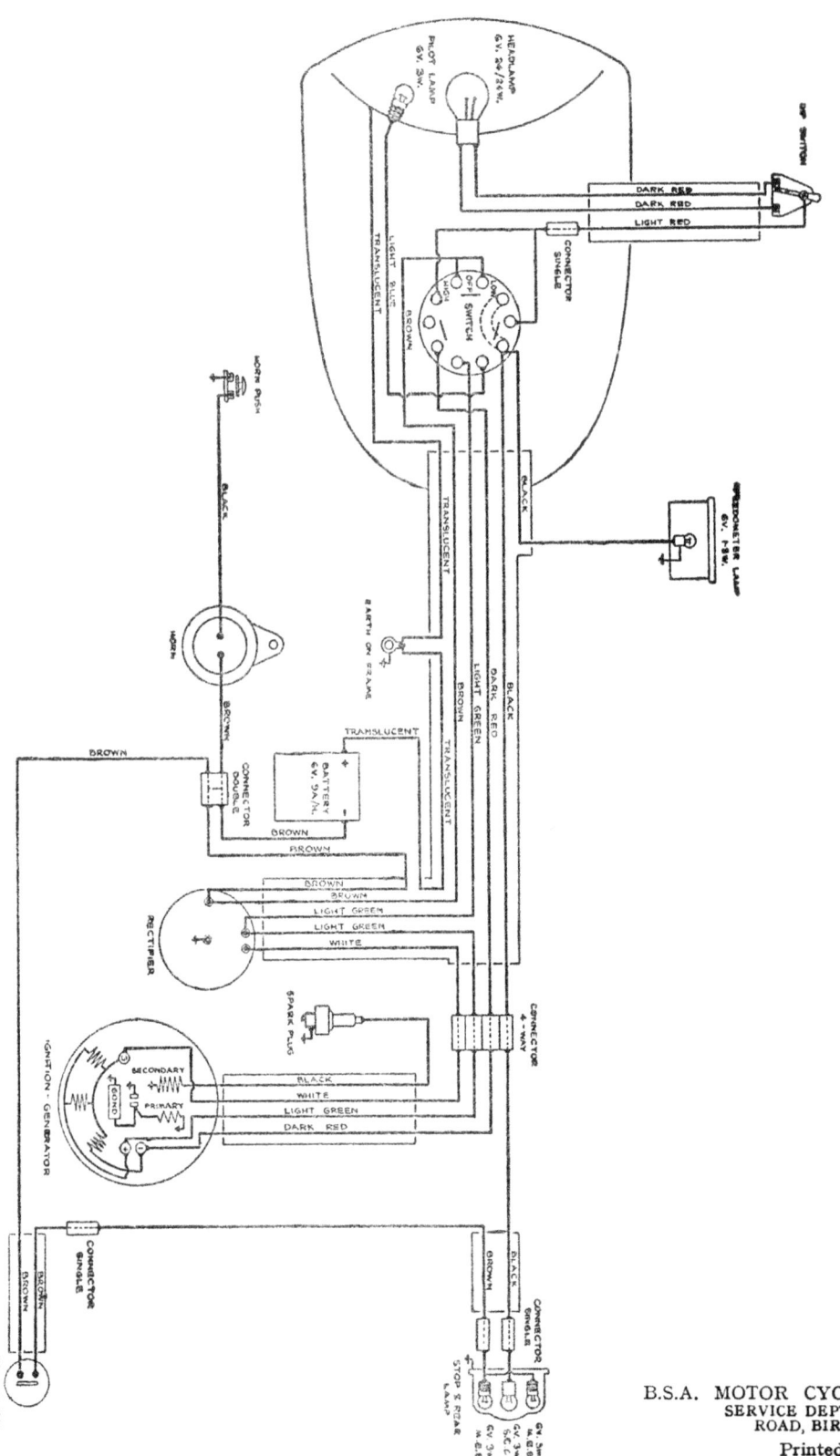

BSA SERVICE SHEET No. 808L
MODEL D7 (COIL IGNITION) WIRING DIAGRAM

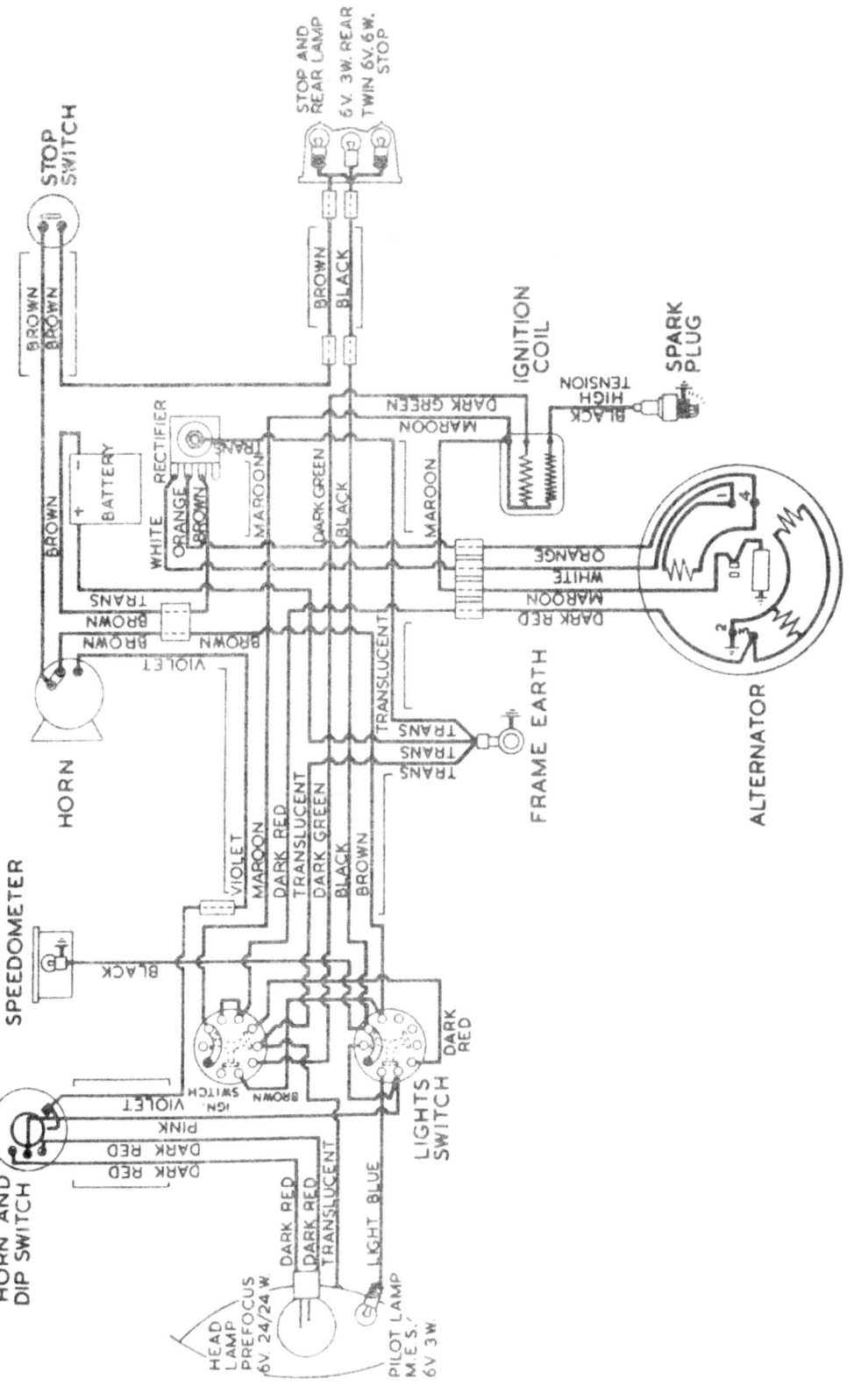

B.S.A. Service Sheet No. 808L (cont.)

MODEL D7 (COIL IGNITION) WIRING DIAGRAM

1965/66 MODELS

B.S.A. MOTOR CYCLES LTD., Service Department, Armoury Road, Birmingham. 11.

B.S.A. Press

BSA SERVICE SHEET No. 810

Model D1
(up to Engine number YD1-40660)

WICO-PACY "GENI-MAG" EQUIPMENT

DESCRIPTION

The 30-watt "Geni-mag" ignition and lighting unit embodies two assemblies, namely the flywheel and the stator which carries the ignition coil, lighting coils, contact breaker unit and condenser. The cam is fitted to the extended crankshaft of the engine and is located by a keyway.

The "Geni-mag" ignition unit provides a high performance spark output over a very wide range of speeds, special attention having been paid to the needs of the modern light-weight motor-cycle of the 125 c.c. class and of the motorised bicycle. While an excellent spark performance of about 8,000 volts at only 500 r.p.m. rising to 14,000 volts at 6,000 r.p.m. is obtained, it has yet been found possible to maintain an exceptionally large air gap between rotor and stator, thus considerably increasing the probability of a trouble-free system. Additional support is provided for the end of the crankshaft by the inclusion of a self-oiling bearing located in the centre of the stator housing.

A characteristic of the magneto is that its spark output will not vary over a wide timing range, thus rendering frequent adjustment of the contacts unnecessary, and at the same time allowing a fair tolerance for the accuracy of the setting. A further feature of the magneto is the accessibility and ease of adjustment of the contact breaker and other parts without the necessity of removing the flywheel at any time.

No engine timing is necessary; fit the stator housing slots central over the studs on the crankcase, tighten up the nuts, fit the cam which locates on a key in the engine shaft, set the contacts to .015 in., and the engine is timed. Any minor adjustment can be carried out while the engine is running. To advance the magneto, slacken off the stator housing nuts and slightly rotate the magneto in the opposite direction to the rotation of the flywheel.

The lighting coils are energized by the three magnetic units which concentrate a powerful magnetic charge within a small space and volume, the characteristic being such that brilliant lighting is obtained without flikering at low speed, while the rise of output above the rated wattage is sufficiently low as not to allow the lamps to be seriously over-loaded at maximum engine speeds, which are in the region of 6,000 to 7,000 r.p.m. One of the three magnet units also energises the ignition coil.

RUNNING MAINTENANCE

The magneto requires very little maintenance and if the following notes are observed the life of the machine should prove trouble-free.

Check and if necessary re-adjust the contacts once every 5,000 miles (see Service Instructions).

Occasionally clean the contacts by inserting a dry smooth piece of paper between them and withdrawing while the contacts are in the closed position. Do not allow the engine to run with oil or petrol on the contacts or they will start to burn and blacken, and if they do, lightly polish with a piece of smooth emery cloth.

Moisten the cam lubricating pad with a few drops of thin oil every 5,000 miles.

Do not run with a faulty or damaged high-tension lead and clean away mud and dirt from around the high-tension insulator when necessary.

B.S.A. Service Sheet No. 810 (contd.)

If the magneto requires any attention beyond the replacement of contact points and condenser, it is recommended that the complete machine should be sent to us or to an authorised Wico service station. The following information is given for the benefit of those unable to do so:—

SERVICE INSTRUCTIONS

Checking the Magneto for Spark

If the engine fails to start and there is an indication of the magneto causing trouble, the spark can be checked by holding the high-tension lead 3/16 in. away from a point on the frame. When the engine is kicked over in the usual way, a spark should jump this gap. If no spark is visible, see that the high-tension lead is in good condition and examine the contact breaker. Make sure there are no metallic particles inside the housing and that the contacts are perfectly clean, and the gap is correct to the recommended setting. If the contacts are found to be in a burnt or badly pitted condition, a faulty condenser is indicated. If the contact breaker appears to be in order the stator plate may be removed from the engine complete with coils and the leads of the ignition coil should be examined to ensure that there is no break in the wiring. One lead will be found to be joined to a tab which is clamped underneath one of the nuts which anchor the stator to the stator housing. If this is in order check the other end of the primary ignition coil which is connected to the back of the insulated post which projects into the contact breaker recess at the front of the magneto. The screw which locks this in position will be found underneath the lighting coil on the right-hand side looking at the inside of the stator housing when in its upright position. The condenser lead is also joined to this point. If both these are connected and the tabs are not earthing on the stator plate the ignition coil should be in working order. In the unlikely event of the high-tension insulation of the secondary coil breaking down, it should be possible to detect signs of charring either on the binding tape of the coil, the insulating gaskets or the high-tension insulator.

Replacement of Coil

To remove the coil, the high-tension insulator which is held by two screws outside the housing must be taken off. The removal of the stator is effected by unscrewing the three clamp nuts. The stator may then be gently eased off the three stator plate studs. Care must be taken not to jerk it, otherwise the lead which connects the lighting coils to the terminal on the stator may be broken. The live end of the primary ignition coil lead must then be disconnected from the contact breaker terminal post. In order to slide the coil from the iron limb, it is necessary to straighten the small brass tab which will be found on the side of the coil which faces the stator housing. If the coil is grasped firmly in one hand with the fingers under the insulator gaskets and on either side of the core, it may be quite easily pulled off. To refit the ignition coil proceed as follows:—

(a) Hold the coil in the left hand with the brass contact pointing away from the line of vision and the lead wires projecting downwards from the underside, and drop the leads through the rectangular hole in the two insulating gaskets, the extended end of which must point in the same direction as the coil tab.

(b) With the other hand push the coil core through the coil making sure that the brass locking tab riveted to the iron is on the same side as the coil contact. Drive the fibre wedge provided in between the core and the coil on the same side as the locking tab and bend over the tab.

(c) Connect up the sleeved lead to the terminal post placing the other parts in the following order:—
Screw, shakeproof washer, condenser tab, coil lead tab, thick metal washer and insulating washer. Then holding the outer end of the contact breaker terminal post in the square hole, with the finger of the other hand, drop the screw complete with washers into the round recess at the inner end of the square hole and drive the screw home.

B.S.A. Service Sheet No. 810 (contd.)

(d) Finally, bend both tabs slightly upwards to ensure that they do not make contact with the metal housing, screw down the stator anchoring the lighting and ignition coil earthing leads under the clamp nuts making sure at the same time that the coil insulator gaskets are bent upwards towards the high-tension insulator hole in the stator housing.

(e) Make sure that all tabs are clean and all clamped connections are tight, and before lowering the stator see that none of the coil leads become clamped in between the stator and the housing.
Important.—Bend in all stray loops of wire to behind the radius of the stator and push down the condenser wire into the well of the stator housing to ensure that they do not foul the rim of the flywheel. The flywheel rim reaches to within about 1/16 in. of the head of the insulated lighting terminal stud, and it is important to see that the live wire which is soldered to it is pushed down to well below this level.

(f) Refit the high-tension insulator.

Removal of Condenser

To change the condenser it is necessary to lift the stator as before described, and disconnect the lead from the terminal post and unscrew the clamp nut which is located on the contact breaker cover spring post. When replacing, make sure that the condenser lead is pushed down as far as possible into the well formed by the stator housing otherwise there is a danger of the flywheel rubbing and possibly severing it.

Adjustment and Replacement of Breaker Points

The only adjustable part of the magneto is the breaker plate which provides for the setting of the breaker points.

To set these points proceed as follows:—

Turn the engine over until the breaker points are fully open and insert the feeler gauge. Slacken off the locking screw which is to be found immediately above the points and if the gauge is tight rotate the eccentric adjuster in an anti-clockwise direction until the correct setting of .015 in. is obtained. Tighten up the adjusting screw.

The breaker point setting should only be adjusted in the manner described and at no time should the fixed contact be bent to provide adjustment.

The moving contact is integral with the breaker arm. If the points need replacement it is recommended that both fixed and movable points be replaced at the same time.

The breaker arm bearing is of the self-lubricating type and it is only necessary to lightly prime the pivot pin with oil or soft grease when assembling. Care must be taken to put in the correct number of thin spacing washers behind the breaker arm, in order to bring the contacts in line with one another. The end of the contact breaker spring is then anchored to the terminal post with a screw and shakeproof washer. Place one of the spacing washers over the pivot on the outer side of the breaker arm and insert the spring clip in its groove.

The Lighting Coils

In the unlikely event of any fault developing with these coils, the removal and replacement of them is a simple operation and may be performed without disturbing the ignition coil. The windings are in series and are made up in pairs complete with earthing tab and insulated terminal screw. To remove the lighting

B.S.A. Servce Sheet No. 810 (contd.)

coils, take off the high-tension insulator and unscrew the three stator clamp nuts. Take out the insulated terminal screw which projects from one of the cavities on the face of the stator plate. Straighten with a pair of pliers the two outer laminations on each coil core, which are bent outwards to hold the coils in position, and slide off the coil formers after slightly raising the stator on the studs in the stator plate. Replace in the following order:—

With the coil which carries the insulated terminal screw on the side nearest to the screw hole in the stator housing, and the slotted flanges of the two coil formers pointing towards the centre of the stator and the slots downwards, slide the two coils on to their cores. Insert the fibre wedges provided into the arc formed between the cores and the coil formers, and bend out the two outer laminations on each leg, taking care not to split the bakelite former on which one of the coils is wound. Push down the stator on to its locating spigot. See that neither the ignition leads nor the lighting coil leads become clamped between the flange at the base of the spigot and the stator. Reassemble the insulated terminal screw into the stator housing. Finally, tighten up the clamp nuts with the tabs in position and push any wire loops well back behind the working faces of the stator legs to prevent them from fouling the flywheel.

The Flywheel

The robust construction of the flywheel reduces the possibility of any faults on this unit to a minimum. The three powerful magnet inserts are cast in the rim of the wheel and it is not possible to demagnetize them by ordinary usage. No keepers are necessary when the magneto housing and stator are removed. The boss of the flywheel is located on the crankshaft by a keyed taper and locked by a nut and shakeproof washer. It is unnecessary to remove the flywheel unless at any time the engine has to be dismantled. A thread cut on the outside of the flywheel boss enables the wheel to be removed by use of a special extractor. When replacing, the flywheel must be perfectly clean inside and outside.

CAUTION

The 27-watt "Geni-mag" which is purely an A.C. unit, has now been superseded by the S55/KM8 ignition generator.

As the new unit incorporates extra magnets in the flywheel, all users should make careful note, that although similar in appearance the **flywheels of the two units are not interchangeable.** The flywheel of the new type generator can easily be identified because it is clearly marked "WIPAC AC/DC."

Care must also be taken to use the correct flywheel with the appropriate stator plate, as if the new flywheel is used with the old type "Geni-mag" plate, trouble will be experienced with lamps blowing or alternatively if the new stator plate is used with the old type "Geni-mag" flywheel, insufficient lighting output will be obtained.

B.S.A. MOTOR CYCLES LTD., Service Department, Armoury Road, Birmingham 11.

Printed in England.

BSA SERVICE SHEET No. 810A

February 1953
Revised 1958

MODELS D1, D3 and D5

Wipac Flywheel Ignition Generator Series 55 Mark 8

SPECIAL NOTES

The Series 55 Mark 8, Spec. No. IG 1130 A.C./D.C. generator superseded the 27 watt "Genimag," which was purely an A.C. unit. This change took place on and after engine number YD1–40661. As this unit incorporated extra magnets in the flywheel, all users should make careful note of the fact that, although similar in appearance, the *flywheels of the two units are not interchangeable*. If the latter type flywheel is used with the "Genimag" stator plate, trouble will be experienced with bulbs blowing. Alternatively, if the "Genimag" flywheel is fitted with a later type stator plate, insufficient lighting output will be obtained.

On machines manufactured after August 1955, different generators are used for A.C. and D.C. equipment. These are marked Spec. No. IG 1452 for A.C. only (D1, D3 and D5 models), Spec. No. IG 1454 for D.C. only (D1 models), and Spec. No. IG 1450 for D.C. only (D3 swinging arm models). The two D.C. units are the same, except for the lengths fo the leads.

When the generator complete, or the stator plate Spec. No. IG 1130, is replaced by one of the later D.C. units, the yellow link between terminals 9 and 11 in the headlamp switch must be removed in order to limit the charge rate in the "Low" position.

As the later type A.C. and D.C. stator plates are not interchangeable, it is necessary to specify A.C. or D.C. when ordering spares.

From 1950 onwards (engine number YD1–40661) the flywheels are the same for A.C. and D.C. For models prior to this, the complete generator should be changed when renewing the stator plate.

The A.C. generator Spec. No. IG 1452 cannot be converted to D.C. by means of a Wipac "Converta-kit," unless a new three-coil stator plate is also fitted.

DESCRIPTION

This ignition and power unit consists of two assemblies, namely the flywheel rotor, and the stator plate which carries the ignition coil, low-tension coils, contact breaker and condenser. The cam is fitted to the extended crankshaft of the engine and is located by a key.

Additional support is provided for the end of the crankshaft by the inclusion of a self-oiling bush in the centre of the stator housing.

The unit provides a high performance spark out put over a very wide range of speeds. While approximately 10,000 volts at only 500 r.p.m. rising to 15,500 volts at 6,000 r.p.m. is obtained, it has been found possible to maintain a large air-gap between rotor and stator to ensure a trouble-free unit.

A characteristic of the ignition generator unit is that its spark output will not vary over a wide timing range, thus rendering frequent adjustment of the contacts unnecessary, and at the same time allowing a fair tolerance for the accuracy of the setting.

A further feature of the magneto is the accessibility and ease of the contact breaker and other parts, without the necessity of removing the flywheel rotor. In fact, it is unlikely that, at any time it will be necessary to remove more than the stator cover plate; the stator being so designed that all adjustments, and even condenser replacement, can be made from the front of the unit.

No engine timing is necessary; fit the stator plate slots central on the fixing screws and tighten up these screws, locate the cam on the key in the engine shaft, set the contacts to .015 in. and the engine is timed. Any minor adjustment can be made while the engine is running. To advance the magneto, slacken off the stator plate fixing screws and slightly

B.S.A. Service Sheet No. 810A (contd.)

rotate the magneto in the opposite direction to the flywheel rotor.

Accasionally, it may be found that an engine will not start nor run unless the contact breaker points setting is about .006 —.008 in., instead of the correct figure of .015 in. This is caused by the points opening before the magnetic flux has been broken, so that no voltage is produced.

The first remedy to try is to reverse the small Woodruff cam key. Should this effect no improvement, a special cam, ground 5° late, can be obtained from the makers.

The low-tension coils are energised by the three magnetic units, which concentrate a powerful magnetic charge within a small space. One of these units energises the ignition coil. The generator has been designed to produce A.C. current directly into a 6-volt 30 watt load or, with the aid of a metal plate rectifier in the external circuit, produce D.C. current for battery charging.

With the IG 1130 generator, a maximum day charge of 2.5 amps is allowed to pass through the battery. During night use with a 6-volt 30 watt lamp load, a generated balance against this battery drain is accomplished at approximately 3,000 r.p.m. of the engine. A charge of ¾ amp is allowed at maximum engine speed.

The IG 1450 and IG 1454 generators have a higher rate of charge, giving slightly more than 3 amps at maximum engine speed. At night, the full lamp load is balanced at approximately 2,800 r.p.m., and a charge of 1.5 amps is obtained at 4,500 r.p.m. Batteries of 5, 10 or 12 amp-hour rating are equally suitable for use with these generators, the higher capacities being recommended.

RUNNING MAINTENANCE

The magneto requires very little maintenance and if the following notes are observed the life of the machine should prove trouble-free.

Check and if necessary re-adjust the contacts once every 5,000 miles (see "Service Instructions").

Occasionally clean the contacts by inserting a dry smooth piece of paper between them and withdrawing while the contacts are in the closed position. Do not allow the engine to run with oil or petrol on the contacts or they will start to burn and blacken, and if they do, lightly polish with a piece of smooth emery cloth.

Moisten the cam lubricating pad with a few drops of thin oil every 5,000 miles.

Do not run with a faulty or damaged high-tension lead and clean away mud and dirt from around the high-tension insulator when necessary.

If the magneto requires any attention beyond the replacement of contact points and condenser, it is recommended that the complete machine should be sent to us or to an authorised Wico service station. The following information is given for the benefit of those unable to do so:—

SERVICE INSTRUCTIONS
Checking the Magneto for Spark

If the engine fails to start and there is an indication of the magneto causing trouble, the spark can be checked by holding the high-tension lead $\frac{3}{16}$ in. away from a point on the frame. When the engine is kicked over in the usual way, a spark should jump this gap. If no spark is visible, see that the high-tension lead is in good condition and examine the contact breaker.

Make sure there are no metallic particles inside the housing, and that the contacts are perfectly clean, and the contact breaker gap is correct to the recommended setting.

If the contacts are found to be in a burnt or badly pitted condition, a faulty condenser is indicated. If the contact breaker appears to be in order, the stator plate may be removed from the engine, complete with coils.

To do this the following procedure should be adopted:—

Unscrew the two cover securing screws and remove the cover, unscrew the cam screw and withdraw the cam free of the shaft. The small cam key in some instances may leave its keyway, so care should be taken to make sure of this point when taking the cam from the shaft. Next remove the three stator plate securing screws. The stator can now be withdrawn clear of the engine.

The leads of the ignition coil should be examined to ensure that there is no break in the wiring. One lead will be found to be joined to a tab which is clamped underneath one of the nuts which anchor the stator coil assembly to the stator housing. If this is in order, check the sleeved lead of the primary ignition coil which is connected to the front of the insulated post, which also carries the condenser lead and contact breaker return spring.

B.S.A. Service Sheet No. 810A (contd.)

The screw which locks the insulated post in position will be found underneath the low-tension coil on the right-hand side looking at the inside of the stator housing when in its upright position.

There is, however, no need to remove this screw for any of the investigations recommended in these instructions. The second screw lying at a larger radius and appearing over the top of the coil is the earthing screw for the number 2 terminal on the front of the machine.

If the leads joined to the insulated post are in order and firmly clamped and the tags not earthing in any way, the ignition coil should be in working order. Should it be necessary to completely remove the stator plate entirely the low and high-tension leads should be freed from the insulated terminal boards on the front of the unit and the plugs respectively, the former by the loosening off of the grub screws and withdrawing the low-tension leads which are coloured through the rubber insulator. The stator plate assembly should then be entirely free of the engine.

In the unlikely event of the high-tension insulation of the coil breaking down, provided this is not internal, it should be possible to detect signs of charring on the binding tape of the coil. If the absence of spark is due to tracking, track burns may be visible on the insulator gasket.

Replacement of Ignition Coil

The removal of the stator coil assembly is effected by first disconnecting the ignition lead from the coil, then freeing the white, red and green low-tension leads from the terminals marked 3, 1 and 4 respectively, and unscrewing the two clamp nuts. The live lead of the primary winding of the ignition coil must then be disconnected from the insulated post by removing the securing screw. The stator coil assembly may then be gently eased off the two plate studs.

In order to slide the ignition coil from the iron limb, it is necessary to straighten the small brass tab which will be found on the side of the coil which faces the stator housing. If the coil is grasped firmly in one hand with the fingers under the insulator gasket and on either side of the core, it may be quite easily pulled off.

To refit the ignition coil proceed as follows:—

(a) Hold the coil in the left-hand with the brass contact pointing away from the line of vision and the lead wires projecting downwards from the underside, and drop the leads through the rectangular hole in the insulating gasket, the extended end of which must point in the same direction as the coil tab.

(b) With the other hand, push the coil core through the coil, making sure that the brass locking tab rivetted to the iron is on the same side as the coil contact. Drive the fibre wedge provided in between the core and the coil, on the same side as the locking tab and bend over the tab.

(c) Replace the stator coil assembly in position on the stator plate and before pushing right down on the studs, bring the sleeved low-tension lead of the ignition coil inside the base of the right-hand stator core stud. This keeps the lead clear of the flywheel rotor. Pass the low-tension leads through to the front of the unit. Note also that none of the coil leads become clamped in between the stator and the housing.

(d) Press the core down firmly and tighten down the two clamp nuts anchoring the ignition coil earth lead tab underneath the left-hand nut.

(e) Reconnect the sleeved ignition coil lead to the insulated post together with the condenser lead tab and the contact breaker return spring. Firmly screw home the securing screw.

(f) Reconnect the ignition lead to the high-tension terminal of the ignition coil, and reconnect the low-tension leads to the appropriate terminals as follows:—
The white lead to number 3, green to number 4 and red lead to number 1 terminal on the front of the unit.

(g) Make sure that all tabs are clean and all clamped connections are tight.

IMPORTANT:—*Bend all stray loops of wire to behind the radius of the stator to ensure they do not foul the rim of the flywheel rotor.*

Removal of Condenser

To replace the condenser, remove the condenser terminal nut and free the condenser lead. Unscrew the condenser bracket fixing screw and withdraw the condenser.

B.S.A. Service Sheet No. 810A (contd.)

Adjustment and Replacement of Breaker Points

The only adjustable part of the magneto is the breaker plate which provides for the setting of the breaker points. To set these points proceed as follows:—

Turn the engine over until the breaker points are fully open and insert the feeler gauge. Slacken off the locking screw which is to be found immediately above the points, and if the gauge is tight, adjust the fixed contact plate, by means of a suitable screwdriver engaged in the recess provided, in an anti-clockwise direction until the correct setting of 0.035 in. is obtained. Tighten up the fixed contact plate locking screw. The breaker point setting should only be adjusted in the manner described and at no time should the fixed contact platform be bent to provide adjustment. The moving contact is integral with the breaker arm. If the points need replacement it is recommended that both fixed and moving points be replaced at the same time.

When assembling the moulded breaker arm to the magneto it is necessary to lightly prime the pivot pin with oil or soft grease and an occasional priming throughout its life will be found to be advantageous.

Care must be taken to put in the correct number of thin spacing washers behind the breaker arm in order to bring the contacts in line with one another. The free end of the contact breaker spring is then anchored to the insulated terminal post with a screw and shakeproof washer. The condenser and primary ignition coil sleeved lead is secured by the same screw and washer. Place one of the spacing washers over the pivot on the outer side of the breaker arm and insert the spring clip in its groove

The Low-tension Coils

These coils are robust in character and are most unlikely to develop fault. In the event of a fault developing in the coil group, the removal more so than the replacement, of the coil or coils may not be an easy operation, and it is likely that further damage to the windings will occur during the removal process. It is advisable before any steps are taken to remove the low-tension coils, that the coils be thoroughly checked and proved beyond doubt to be at fault. The coils are secured to the iron core by means of a varnish adherent assisted by a fibre wedge. Paper formers are used, so damage to the winding can occur when being taken off.

In view of this, it is strongly recommended that should a fault occur in the low-tension coil group, that application be made for a coil group replacement already secured to the iron core.

The ignition coil can be removed from the stator assembly as previously described and replaced on the new stator core and coil group replacement. Having completed the coil assembly, proceed as instructed under paragraph "Replacement of Ignition Coil".

Care should be taken to see that the wire connections face toward the front of the machine when assembling the stator coil assembly into the housing.

Any wire loops or wires that could come into contact with the flywheel rotor should be pushed back clear to prevent any fouling or electrical breakdown.

Finally, when connecting the low-tension leads of the frame wiring to the magneto generator, make sure that the white, red and green leads are placed on the machine terminals already carrying that colour of lead. This is part of a colour coding scheme, the complete scheme of which is given with the wiring diagram.

The Flywheel Rotor

The robust construction of the flywheel rotor reduces the possibility of any faults on this unit to a minimum. The three powerful magnet inserts are cast in the rim of the rotor and it is not possible to demagnetise them by ordinary usage. No keepers are necessary when the magneto housing and stator are removed. The boss of the flywheel rotor is located on the crankshaft by a keyed taper and locked by a nut and shakeproof washer. It is unnecessary to remove the rotor unless at any time the engine has to be dismantled. A thread cut on the outside of the rotor boss enables it to be removed by the use of a special extractor. When replacing, the rotor must be perfectly clean inside and out.

B.S.A. MOTOR CYCLES LTD.,
Service Department, Armoury Road,
Birmingham 11. B.S.A. Press.

BSA SERVICE SHEET No. 811

Models D1, D3, D5, D7 and C10L
LAMPS
(Wipac Lighting)

Headlamp.

Two types of headlamp have been employed but they differ only with regard to the headlamp switch. Early models have the body of the switch mounted inside the headlamp shell but remotely controlled through a cable and a lever mounted on the handlebars. Later models have a switch mounted in the top of the headlamp so that it can be reached from the normal riding position

The reflector and bulb holder assembly are housed in the front rim and to obtain access to the bulbs, loosen the screw situated at the bottom of the lamp rim and lift the rim outwards and upwards. To remove the bulb holder, bend down the small tab which projects from the base of the reflector. The holder can then be removed, after turning it anti-clockwise, making the main and parking bulbs easily accessible. When replacing the main bulb be sure that the word "TOP" on the bulb is uppermost.

If the bulb is not marked, assemble as illustrated:—

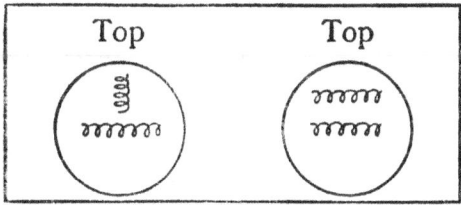

Correct way to fit double-filament bulbs.

The correct focus has been incorporated in the design of the headlamp and therefore no provision for adjustment has been necessary.

Tail Lamp.

To remove the rim of the lamp, undo the small 6BA screw and turn the rim slightly to the left, it can then be easily withdrawn. On later models a bayonet fitting is employed and it is merely necessary to push the lamp cover in, twist it to the left and then pull it away.

B.S.A. Service Sheet No. 811 (continued).

The bulb holder is of the bayonet pattern and the bulb is removed by the usual push and turn method. When a stop light is fitted a double filament bulb is used. Ensure that the bulb is the right way up. The portion marked "TOP" should be uppermost when the bulb is inserted, but if the bulb is not marked, check that it is located correctly by operating the foot brake and ensuring that the brighter filament is illuminated.

Switching.

No adjustment of the later type switch is necessary but it may occasionally be required to synchronise the earlier type of switch with the handlebar lever. This can be easily carried out after slackening the locknut on the adjuster which connects the Bowden cable to the lever assembly. Screw the adjuster in or out until the switch positions are synchronised with the lever positions, then tighten the locknut. Four positions are provided on the lever and these correspond to Parking, Head Dipped, Head Full On and Off.

Parking Battery.

Where D.C. lighting is employed a Varley accumulator is fitted. On models employing A.C. lighting a dry battery is fitted inside the headlamp shell. This is a 3-volt bicycle battery, type 800. To fit a new battery, hold it so that the vertical contact strip faces towards the lamp, the battery should then be positioned in the holding bracket in such a manner that the vertical contact connects with the metal battery holder at the rear of the lamp, while the horizontal contact fits inside its corresponding contact.

Replacement Bulbs.

Headlamp (main)	...	D1, D3, D5 and D7	24/24 watt, double filament, 6/7 volt.
		C10L	30/30 watt, double filament, 6/7 volt.
Headlamp (parking)	...	A.C. lighting ...	.25 amp. 2.5 volt M.E.S.
		D.C. lighting ...	6/7 volt, 3 watt, M.E.S.
Tail lamp (single filament)	... ...		6/7 volt, 3 watt S.B.C.
(with combined stop light)		...	6/7 volt. 18/3 watt, S.B.C.
(with separate twin stop lights)		...	6/7 volt, 3 watt, M.E.S.
Speedometer	... ...		6.5 volt, .3 amp.

B.S.A. MOTOR CYCLES LTD., Service Department, Armoury Road, Birmingham 11.
B.S.A. Press.

BSA SERVICE SHEET No. 812

Model D.1

LUCAS ALTERNATING EQUIPMENT

Alternator Model 1 A 45

DESCRIPTION

Inductor Type Alternator

The Lucas Model 1A45 unit, which has a nominal output of 45 watts, makes use of a generator of the inductor type. This consists of a 6-pole laminated steel rotor and a stator, the latter comprising two permanent magnets, a laminated field system and two coil windings housed in an aluminium casing. The rotor, with which is combined the contact breaker Cam, is bolted direct to the engine crankshaft. The Alternator body, which carries the Stator Coils and Contact Breaker Plate, is spigotted into the Crankcase. The Contact-breaker Plate is located by two fixing Screws passing through radial slots, Fig. Y.41.

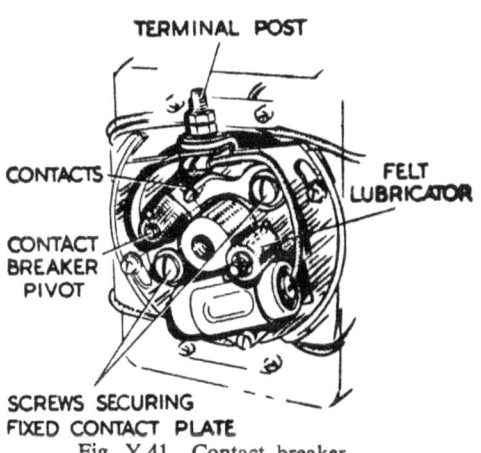

Fig. Y.41. Contact breaker.

The principle of operation of the induction alternator is the same as that of other generators, that is, the reversal of magnetic flux through the coil core which generates an EMF or voltage in the coil winding. In the normal generator, the reversal of flux is achieved by rotating either the magnet or coil, but in this design the coils and magnets are stationary and a laminated steel rotor is used to cause the flux reversals. The rotor is of 6-pole design in order to give as many flux reversals as practicable during one revolution.

Thus the windings are stationary, so avoiding the use of commutator, slip rings or collector brushes, making for greater robustness of construction and hence increased reliability.

The generator reaches its rated voltage at a low engine speed and the voltage is then maintained within close limits over a very wide speed range.

Coil Ignition—and Easy Starting with a Flat Battery

In addition to supplying the current required by the lamps (which, incidentally, have an increased headlamp bulb wattage of 30, with consequently greater light output than hitherto), the 1A45 unit also supplies power for the coil ignition equipment. The long standing objection to coil ignition on motor cycles, namely inability to start if the battery is run down, is overcome by providing 'emergency start' switching for use on these occasions. By means of this arrangement the battery is temporarily disconnected so that all the available energy from the permanent magnet alternator is applied to the coil, with the result that a slow speed performance approaching that of a magneto enables a 'kick-start' to be achieved. Thus the simplicity and economic benefits of this form of ignition can be utilised to the full.

B.S.A. Service Sheet No. 812 (continued)

Battery Charging

Since batteries can be charged only by direct current, a Selenium metal rectifier is incorporated in the system, and all components then run off direct current from the battery source. Two plates are used in the rectifier assembly to provide full-wave rectification in conjunction with the centre-tapped generator. The rating of the rectifier plates has been thoroughly investigated both in temperate climates, and in the high ambient temperatures of the Middle East. The rectifier is of robust construction and is sealed against water ingress, making it suitable for mounting in a semi-exposed position where it will receive adequate air cooling.

With this equipment there is no need to fit a cut-out as the reverse current through the rectifier is very small, and is a negligible drain on the battery. To avoid even this slight drain, which is very little more than the usual surface discharge across the top of the battery, the ignition switch is arranged to disconnect the battery and alternator when the ignition is switched off.

The ignition switch has three positions: 'Off', 'Emergency Start', and 'Normal Start'. 'Emergency Start' position enables the engine to be started and run with a flat battery.

The alternator has an ample margin of safety but should not be run with the battery removed and/or the ignition switch in the emergency position any longer than is necessary.

NOTE:— SWITCH OFF THE 'HEAD' AND 'PILOT' LAMPS BEFORE STARTING THE ENGINE WITH THE IGNITION. SWITCH IN THE 'EMERGENCY START' POSITION. FAILURE TO OBSERVE THIS PRECAUTION MAY RESULT IN BLOWN HEADLAMP BULBS.

IMMEDIATELY THE ENGINE IS RUNNING TURN THE IGNITION SWITCH SMARTLY BACK TO THE NORMAL RUNNING POSITION THEN SWITCH ON THE 'HEAD' OR 'PILOT' LAMPS AS REQUIRED.

Two Charging Rates

Reduced charge switching is coupled to the lighting switch so that full output is obtained from the generator only when the lamps are switched on, whilst during day running, a reduced charge resistance is inserted into the circuit.

Since the excitation is by means of permanent magnets, the wattage output for a given speed is limited and a higher battery voltage results in a decrease of charging current rather than an increase, so that the system is to a certain extent self-regulating.

The lighting switch is similar to the standard Lucas U.39 motor cycle lighting switch and provides positions for 'Lights off—Half charge', 'Pilot and Tail lights and Full charge', and 'Head and Tail lights with Full charge'.

Performance Data

Output 7—10 amperes. Half-charge rate 5 amperes. (With coil ignition the battery will be charged at the rate of 3 amperes when running normally with lights off). Alternator will commence to charge the battery at 600 engine revolutions per minute. Maximum output is attained at approximately 2,000 r.p.m. and is substantially maintained to maximum engine revolution.

Running Maintenance

Maintenance is restricted to occasional inspection and lubrication of the contact-breaker parts, and normal routine attention to the battery. No adjustment is necessary (or possible) to either alternator or rectifier. Every 1,000 miles (or monthly, whichever is the lesser period) remove the contact-breaker inspection cover for inspection of the contact points.

B.S.A. Service Sheet No. 812 (continued)

The contacts must be free from grease or oil. If they are burned or blackened, clean them with a fine carborundum stone or very fine emery cloth, afterwards wiping away any trace of dirt or metal dust with a petrol-moistened cloth. Reset contact-points to .010 — .012 ins. A few drops of good quality engine oil should be applied to the cam lubricating wick if it is dry. Place a small amount of Mobil grease No. 2 or clean engine oil on the contact-breaker pivot.

If the alternator requires any attention beyond the replacement of contact points and condenser, it is recommended that the complete machine should be sent to an authorised Lucas service station. The following information is given for the benefit of those unable to do so:

SERVICE INSTRUCTIONS,

Removal of Alternator

Remove alternator cover. Disconnect all wires at the 'Snap' connectors under the front of the petrol tank. Remove rotor retaining bolt. Insert special rotor extracting bolt supplied with machine and withdraw the rotor until it is just free of the crankshaft. Remove the nuts and spring washer from the through-studs securing the alternator body to the crankcase and lift the complete alternator bodily from the machine.

Important

THE ROTOR SHOULD ON NO ACCOUNT BE REMOVED FROM THE ALTERNATOR BODY. IF THE ROTOR IS WITHDRAWN IT WILL BE NECESSARY TO RETURN THE COMPLETE ALTERNATOR TO THE MAKERS FOR RE-ASSEMBLY AND RE-MAGNETIZING.

Stator Coil Removal

Disconnect the four leads from the terminal plate by unsoldering the terminals. Remove the two coil clamp fixing screws at the top and bottom of each coil. Remove clamps. Remove the insulation from the front of the body and the complete coil assembly can be lifted away from the alternator.

Contact-Breaker Removal

Unscrew the contact-breaker base fixing screws, then lift up the contact plate complete with the condenser. The position of the contact-breaker base relative to the alternator body should be noted and marked to obviate the need for resetting the ignition timing on reassembly.

INSPECTION AND TEST

Stator Coils

Replace coils if (a) the insulation is frayed or damaged, leads broken, or open-circuited windings (b) if the coil laminations are damaged and will not fit satisfactorily on to the Stator magnets. A preliminary test of the coil assembly should be made with an OHM-METER which should give a reading of 0.4 ohms. The two coils are not symmetrical and in the event of a fault in one coil, it will be necessary to replace the complete coil assembly consisting of the pair of coils.

During the re-fitting of coils, the laminations should be carefully inspected to make sure they are free of all traces of dirt, grease and especially any magnetically attracted particles such as swarf or filings.

Rotor

The rotor has no moving parts and is not subject to any wearing process. IT SHOULD NOT UNDER ANY CIRCUMSTANCES BE REMOVED FROM THE ALTERNATOR BODY or loss of magnetism will result. The alternator is designed in such a way as to prevent accidental removal of the rotor.

B.S.A. Service Sheet No. 812 (continued)

Contact Breaker Assembly

Deal with the contact-points as advised in Maintenance Instructions. The condenser is of normal Lucas design with a capacity of .2 microfarads.

Final Test and Assembly

Assembly of the unit should be carried out reversing the dismantling procedure. Refit the alternator to the engine as follows: Place the assembled alternator on the crankcase so that it locates on the register or spigot. Apply medium pressure to the rotor and rotate it until it registers with the driving key on the engine crankshaft. Insert the alternator body bolts and tighten down evenly.

The final test should be carried out as follows: Remake all connections. The engine should then be started up and run at medium speed—approximately 2,000 r.p.m. Use a moving iron or rectified type voltmeter and test the potential between G2 and G3. See Service Sheet No. 813. A reading of 17 — 18 volts should be obtained. Apply the same test between G1 and G3. A similar voltage reading should be obtained. A further test should be applied across the same terminals with a 6 volt 36 watt bulb, which should light up.

Switch off the ignition and remake all external wiring connections to the alternator in accordance with the Wiring Diagram. A further test should then be made with the rectified type voltmeter and a reading of approximately 20 volts should be obtained between terminals G1 and G2.

Finally when all leads are connected the headlamp should be switched on and the engine run at a speed sufficient to obtain maximum output. Taking into consideration the current consumed by headlamp, tail lamp and coil ignition, the total output of the generator should not exceed 10 amps. In the event of too high an output being given, it can be reduced by partially withdrawing the rotor from the alternator body. THIS WILL BE NECESSARY ONLY IN EXTREMELY RARE CASES, AND UTMOST CARE MUST BE EXERCISED IN WITHDRAWING THE ROTOR. NOT MORE THAN A QUARTER OF THE ROTOR LAMINATIONS SHOULD BE ALLOWED TO PROTRUDE BEYOND THE ALTERNATOR MAGNETS.

General Precautions

The set is designed for POSITIVE EARTH connection only. If the battery is connected with negative to earth, the rectifier unit will be burnt out or at least badly damaged immediately the ignition is switched on. The alternator set has an ample margin of safety, but should not be run with the battery removed and/or the ignition switch in the emergency position any longer than is necessary. Prolonged operation under these conditions will result in the ignition coil overheating due to higher operating voltage in the primary circuit and will lead to a shorter life of contact-breaker points. In the event of mechanical damage to the rectifier, or damage due to the unit becoming burnt out through incorrect fitting of the battery, it will be necessary to fit a new rectifier. It is not possible to repair a damaged unit.

The new rectifier must be fitted to the machine in the manner and place specified by the makers, i.e. spacer bushes must be used to allow the air free access to both sides of the rectifier, and if the rectifier is fitted to the machine in an inverted position it must be replaced in a similar manner.

Replacements

DESCRIPTION	NUMBER	
Headlamp (Main Bulb)	309	30/30 Watt (Export)
Headlamp (Main Bulb)	312	30/24 Watt (Home)
Tila Lamp	200	3 Watt
Pilot Bulb	988	3 Watt
Alternator 1A45	47077D	
Westalite Rectifier	2L985	

B.S.A. MOTOR CYCLES LTD.
Service Dept., Armoury Road,
Birmingham, 11

Printed in England.

BSA SERVICE SHEET No. 812A

SUPPLEMENT TO SHEET No. 812.

Lucas Alternator Equipment on B.S.A. Bantam Motor Cycles.

Type 1A45   **Service Reference 47077D.**

The 1A45 Alternator fitted to B.S.A. Bantam Motor Cycles is a development of the Standard Lucas design described in Service Sheet No. 812 and is specified for all Bantam machines fitted with Lucas equipment. A six-pole laminated rotating inductor and laminated stator coil assembly are used as in the standard machine but the modified unit now incorporates a roller steady bearing for the contact-braker end of the rotating inductor, and the alternator body is secured to the engine with four fixing bolts.

Workshop Instructions

Dismantling and re-assembly should be carried out as indicated in Service Sheet 812 but the following should be specially noted:—Provision is made for the easy removal and replacement of the steady bearing and bearing plate; the cam and steady bearing journal are both press fits on to the rotor shaft and can be removed by means of a suitable extractor of standard pattern. On re-assembly, it is imperative that the cam is correctly fitted in relation to the rotor shaft or the performance of the machine will be adversely affected when the engine is run with the ignition switch in the "emergency start" position.

The general procedure for re-fitting the Alternator to the motor cycle is the same as is given in Service Sheet 812 but the following precaution must be taken in order that the steady bearing is correctly aligned. During the re-fitting operation, the four contact plate fixing screws ("A" Fig. 42) should be slackened off and should not be re-tightened until the remainder of the re-fitting operations are completed, i.e., the Alternator fixing bolts and the rotor retaining bolt should be fully tightened before finally tightening the contact-plate fixing screws. The fixing screw holes in the contact plate are drilled oversize and providing the foregoing precautions are observed, the contact plate will automatically align the steady bearing with the rotor shaft.

The final test of the machine should be carried out as detailed in Service Sheet No. 812.

B.S.A. Service Sheet No. 812A (cont.)

IA45 INDUCTOR ALTERNATOR — Parts Details.

Alternator complete type 1A45, clockwise rotation	47077D
Condenser	465817
Contact Set	407050
Coils, Stator set of two	465713
Cam	465800
Support Plate for Steady Bearing	465816
Bearing RLS5E	189243
Sundry Parts Set	465784

B.S.A. Service Sheet No. 812A (cont.)

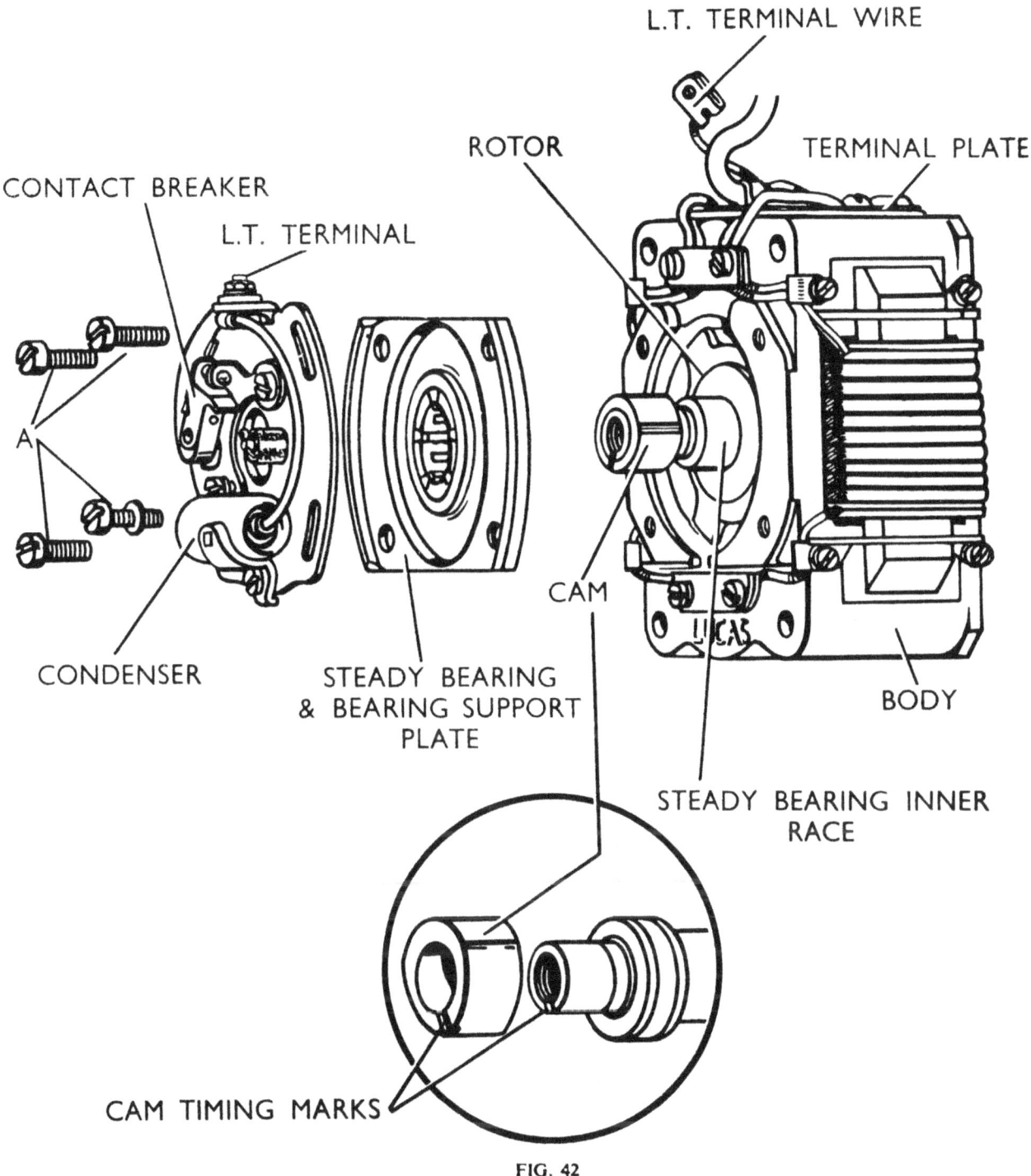

FIG. 42

GENERAL ARRANGEMENT OF IA45 ALTERNATOR
SERVICE REF. No. 47077D FITTED TO B.S.A. BANTAM MOTOR CYCLES

B.S.A. Service Sheet No. 812A (cont.)   B.S.A. "BANTAM" MOTOR CYCLE
(1949-52)

WIRING DIAGRAM

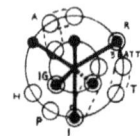 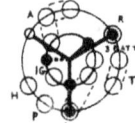 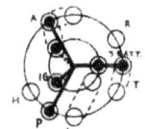 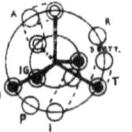

LIGHTING OFF
(TURN LT. SW. TO 'O')
EMERGENCY IGN. ON
(TURN IGNITION KEY LEFT)

LIGHTING OFF
(TURN LT. SW. LEFT TO 'O')
IGNITION OFF
(TURN IGNITION KEY CENTRAL)

TAIL & PILOT ON
(TURN LT. SW. RIGHT TO 'P')
IGNITION ON
(TURN IGNITION KEY RIGHT)

TAIL & HEAD ON
(TURN LT. SW. RIGHT TO 'H')

DIAGRAM SHOWING SWITCH POSITIONS LOOKING ON TOP OF SWITCH

KEY TO CABLE COLOURS

1. BLUE
2. BLUE with RED
3. BLUE with YELLOW
4. BLUE with WHITE
5. BLUE with GREEN
6. BLUE with PURPLE
7. BLUE with BROWN
8. BLUE with BLACK
9. WHITE
10. WHITE with RED
11. WHITE with YELLOW
12. WHITE with BLUE
13. WHITE with GREEN
14. WHITE with PURPLE
15. WHITE with BROWN
16. WHITE with BLACK
17. GREEN
18. GREEN with RED
19. GREEN with YELLOW
20. GREEN with BLUE
21. GREEN with WHITE
22. GREEN with PURPLE
23. GREEN with BROWN
24. GREEN with BLACK
25. YELLOW
26. YELLOW with RED
27. YELLOW with BLUE
28. YELLOW with WHITE
29. YELLOW with GREEN
30. YELLOW with PURPLE
31. YELLOW with BROWN
32. YELLOW with BLACK
33. BROWN
34. BROWN with RED
35. BROWN with YELLOW
36. BROWN with BLUE
37. BROWN with WHITE
38. BROWN with GREEN
39. BROWN with PURPLE
40. BROWN with BLACK
41. RED
42. RED with YELLOW
43. RED with BLUE
44. RED with WHITE
45. RED with GREEN
46. RED with PURPLE
47. RED with BROWN
48. RED with BLACK
49. PURPLE
50. PURPLE with RED
51. PURPLE with YELLOW
52. PURPLE with BLUE
53. PURPLE with WHITE
54. PURPLE with GREEN
55. PURPLE with BROWN
56. PURPLE with BLACK
57. BLACK
58. BLACK with RED
59. BLACK with YELLOW
60. BLACK with BLUE
61. BLACK with WHITE
62. BLACK with GREEN
63. BLACK with PURPLE
64. BLACK with BROWN

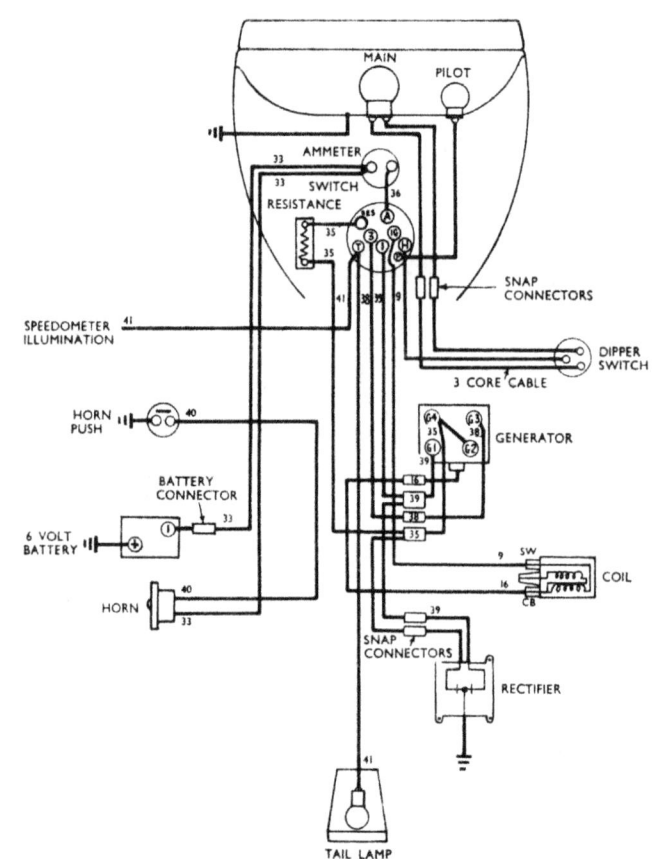

LUCAS ELECTRICAL EQUIPMENT

B.S.A. MOTOR CYCLES LTD.
Service Dept., Armoury Road,
Birmingham, 11.
Printed in England.

BSA SERVICE SHEET No. 815

Models D1, D3 and C10L
VARLEY BATTERY. TYPE MC5/9.

The Varley battery differs in several ways from the conventional form of lead acid battery and the following description of its construction and the maintenance required will assist in ensuring that its maximum capacity is maintained.

The battery has the same general characteristics of the free-acid lead battery, but is unspillable and less sensitive to vibration by virtue of its construction. The acid in the battery is fully absorbed in the porous material which fills the space between the lead plates, and therefore, there is no free acid which can flow from the vents if the battery is overturned.

Maintenance

Whilst in service on the machine, the only maintenance required is to add the equivalent of a teaspoonful of distilled water to each cell at intervals of approximately once a month or six weeks. This small addition is to replace the moisture lost by evaporation and electrolysis, and it is essential that excess liquid is not added. All the added liquid should be absorbed within 20 minutes, and if any remains in the vents after this period, it must be removed by syphoning or shaking out. Topping up should not be carried out immediately before a journey.

An overflow of liquid from the Varley battery (usually indicated by a milky white substance on top of the battery) can only be caused by the addition of excess liquid and failure to remove the surplus, or by overcharging, or a combination of both.

As long as the overflow is not excessive and remains white in colour, the battery will probably remain completely unharmed. It should, therefore, be cleaned and any surplus liquid still remaining should be drained off. After spilling of this nature has taken place it may be advisable to add weak battery acid instead of distilled water when next the battery is due for topping up.

If the overflow develops a brown colour it is an indication of very heavy overcharging, and the battery has probably been damaged beyond repair.

In the event of the battery capacity being reduced after a considerable period of service it may prove advantageous to use weak battery acid instead of distilled water for topping up on one or two occasions.

State of Charge

The state of charge of Varley batteries should be determined by the following voltage readings. It is not possible to use a hydrometer.

Fully discharged	5.7 volts or under.
Partially discharged	6.15 volts or under.
Fully charged	6.3 volts or over.
On charge, fully charged	7.8 volts or over.

Charging the Battery from a Separate Source

All Varley batteries fitted to B.S.A. machines have already been filled and charged before despatch from the Works. A glance at the battery will show exactly when the battery was initially charged as a date code is stamped into each individual battery case.

A letter 'C' on the left-hand bottom corner of the positive side of the battery denotes that the battery has been fully charged by the manufacturer.

On the opposite bottom corner of the same side a letter and figure denote the month and year of the initial charge ('A' for January; 'B' for February; 'C' for March, etc., and '3' for 1953, '4' for 1954, '5' for 1955, and so on). As an example, a battery coded 'C' 'J4' denotes that the battery was filled with acid and initially charged by the manufacturer in October, 1954.

B.S.A. Service Sheet No. 815 (contd.)

If the battery is subsequently left idle for any length of time without being put into service then it should be given a boost charge in accordance with the table below:

Battery idle for 1—2 months	Charge at 1 amp. for 6 hours.
Battery idle for 3—6 months	Charge at 1 amp. for 12 hours.
Battery idle for more than 6 months ...	Charge at 1 amp. for 12 hours. Discharge the battery at 1—2 amps. then immediately recharge at 1 amp. for 12 hours.

Under normal conditions the battery should never be allowed to stand idle for more than a month without charging.

Charging the battery on the bench is carried out in exactly similar manner to that adopted for free acid batteries. Add distilled water as necessary and if the battery has been allowed to get abnormally dry it should be topped up before and during charging. When the voltage reading on charge reaches 7.8 volts, continue charging for a further three hours. All surplus moisture should be absorbed into the battery within half an hour of switching off the charging current. If any liquid does remain in the vents it must be removed by syphoning or shaking out.

Charging a New Battery

If a new battery is to be installed on a machine and it has not already been filled and given its initial charge, then the following procedure must be carried out.

Remove the vent stoppers and fill the battery with pure accumulator acid of a specific gravity which agrees with the table below:

Temperate Climate	1.270
Warm Climate	1.250
Tropical Climate	1.235

The acid will be steadily absorbed into the battery and acid should be added to each cell in turn until the levels remain unchanged for several minutes.

Allow the battery to stand for a period of 2—8 hours. If any of the cells are dry after this period they should again be topped up with acid. It is particularly important that the battery absorbs sufficient acid during this initial period, if it is to give a long life and satisfactory performance. The battery must be put on charge within fifteen hours of the commencement of filling.

For the initial charge the input should be 60 Ah. at a rate not exceeding 1 amp. (i.e., 60 hours at 1 amp. or 80 hours at .75 amp.). During this first charge top up with distilled water only.

The charge should be continuous and it is not advisable for the current to be switched off until completion. If, for any major reason, the charging has to be stopped, the open circuit standing time should be allowed for.

During the final stage of charge, the voltage of the battery should read at least 7.8 volts (i.e., 2.6 volts per cell) and every cell should be gassing freely.

After completion of charge any liquid remaining in the vents should be removed by syphoning or shaking out. The battery should then be cleaned and thoroughly dried. Before replacing the vent stoppers, remove the sealing tape, if any. Grease the terminals slightly with vaseline before connecting up.

B.S.A. MOTOR CYCLES LTD.,
Service Dept., Armoury Road, Birmingham 11.
Printed in England.

VELOCEPRESS MANUALS - MOTORCYCLE

1930'S BRITISH MOTORCYCLE CARBS & ELEC COMPONENTS (BOOK OF)
1930'S BRITISH MOTORCYCLE ENGINES (OVERHAUL & MAINTENANCE)
1930'S BRITISH MOTORCYCLE GEARBOXES & CLUTCHES (BOOK OF)
AJS 1932-1948 SINGLES & TWINS 250cc THRU 1000cc (BOOK OF)
AJS 1945-1960 SINGLES 350cc & 500cc MODELS 16 & 18 (BOOK OF)
AJS 1955-1965 SINGLES 350cc & 500cc (BOOK OF)
ARIEL UP TO 1932 (BOOK OF)
ARIEL 1932-1939 PREWAR MODELS (BOOK OF)
ARIEL 1933-1951 (WORKSHOP MANUAL)
ARIEL 1939-1960 4 STROKE SINGLES (BOOK OF)
ARIEL 1958-1964 LEADER & ARROW (BOOK OF)
BMW R26 R27 (1956-1967) FACTORY WORKSHOP MANUAL
BMW R50 R50S R60 R69S (1955-1969) FACTORY WORKSHOP MANUAL
BRIDGESTONE 90 SERIES FACTORY WSM & PARTS CATALOGUE
BRIDGESTONE 175 SERIES FACTORY WSM & PARTS CATALOGUE
BRIDGESTONE 350 SERIES FACTORY WSM & PARTS CATALOGUES
BSA BANTAM D1 TO D7 1948-1966 FACTORY SERVICE SHEETS MANUAL
BSA BANTAM ALL MODELS FROM 1948 ONWARDS (BOOK OF)
BSA SINGLES & V-TWINS UP TO 1927 (BOOK OF)
BSA SINGLES & V-TWINS UP TO 1930 (BOOK OF)
BSA SINGLES & V-TWINS UP TO 1935 (BOOK OF)
BSA SINGLES & V-TWINS 1936-1939 (BOOK OF)
BSA C10, C11 & C12 1945-1958 FACTORY SERVICE SHEETS MANUAL
BSA OHV & SV SINGLES 250-600cc 1945-1959 (BOOK OF)
BSA C15 & B40 1958-1967 FACTORY SERVICE SHEETS MANUAL
BSA OHV & SV SINGLES 250cc (ONLY) 1954-1970 (BOOK OF)
BSA B31, B32, B33 & B34 1945-60 FACTORY SERVICE SHEETS MANUAL
BSA OHV SINGLES 350 & 500cc 1955-1967 (BOOK OF)
BSA M20, M21 & M33 1945-1963 FACTORY SERVICE SHEETS MANUAL
BSA TWINS A7 & A10 1948-1962 FACTORY SERVICE SHEETS MANUAL
BSA TWINS A7 & A10 1948-1962 (BOOK OF)
BSA TWINS A50 & A65 1962-1969 (SECOND BOOK OF)
CYCLEMOTOR (BOOK OF)
DOUGLAS 1929-1939 PREWAR ALL MODELS (BOOK OF)
DOUGLAS 1948-1957 POSTWAR ALL MODELS FACTORY SHOP MANUAL
DUCATI 160cc, 250cc & 350cc OHC MODELS FACTORY SHOP MANUAL
HONDA 50 ALL MODELS UP TO 1970 INC MONKEY & TRAIL (BOOK OF)
HONDA 90 ALL MODELS UP TO 1966 (BOOK OF)
HONDA 125-150cc TWINS C/CS/CB/CA FACTORY WORKSHOP MANUAL
HONDA 250-305 TWINS C/CS/CB FACTORY WORKSHOP MANUAL
HONDA 450 CB/CL 1965-1974 K0 TO K7 WORKSHOP MANUAL
HONDA C100 SUPER CUB FACTORY WORKSHOP MANUAL
HONDA C110 SPORT CUB 1962-1969 FACTORY WORKSHOP MANUAL
HONDA TWINS & SINGLES 50cc THRU 305cc 1960-1966 (BOOK OF)
HONDA TWINS ALL MODELS 125cc THRU 450cc UP TO 1968 (BOOK OF)
INDIAN PONYBIKE, BOY RACER & PAPOOSE ILL PARTS LIST & SALES LIT
J.A.P. ENGINES 1927-1952 & MOTORCYCLES 1934-1952 (BOOK OF)
LAMBRETTA 1947-1957 ALL 125 & 150cc MODELS (BOOK OF)
LAMBRETTA 1957-1970 LI & TV MODELS (SECOND BOOK OF)
MATCHLESS 1931-1939 ALL MODELS 250cc THRU 990cc (BOOK OF)
MATCHLESS 1945-1956 350 & 500cc SINGLES (BOOK OF)
MATCHLESS 1955-1966 350 & 500cc SINGLES (BOOK OF)
NEW IMPERIAL ALL SV & OHV FROM 1935 ONWARDS (BOOK OF)
NORTON 1932-1939 PREWAR MODELS (BOOK OF)
NORTON 1932-1947 (BOOK OF)
NORTON 1938-1956 (BOOK OF)
NORTON 1955-1963 MODELS 19, 50 & ES2 (BOOK OF)
NORTON 1955-1965 DOMINATOR TWINS (BOOK OF)
NORTON 1960-1970 TWIN CYLINDER FACTORY WORKSHOP MANUAL
NORTON 1970-1975 COMMANDO FACTORY WORKSHOP MANUAL
NORTON 1975-1978 MK 3 COMMANDO FACTORY WORKSHOP MANUAL
NSU PRIMA 1956-1964 ALL MODELS (BOOK OF)
NSU QUICKLY 1953-1963 ALL MODELS (BOOK OF)
PANTHER 1932-1958 LIGHTWEIGHT MODELS 250 & 350cc (BOOK OF)
PANTHER 1938-1966 HEAVYWEIGHT MODELS 600 & 650cc (BOOK OF)
RALEIGH MOPEDS 1960-1969 (BOOK OF)
RALEIGH MOTORCYCLES 1919-1933 (BOOK OF)
ROYAL ENFIELD 1934-1946 SINGLES & V TWINS (BOOK OF)
ROYAL ENFIELD 1937-1953 SINGLES & V TWINS (BOOK OF)
ROYAL ENFIELD 1946-1962 SINGLES (BOOK OF)
ROYAL ENFIELD 1958-1966 250cc & 350cc SINGLES (SECOND BOOK OF)
ROYAL ENFIELD 736cc INTERCEPTOR FACTORY WORKSHOP MANUAL
RUDGE 1933-1939 (BOOK OF)
SUNBEAM 1928-1939 (BOOK OF)
SUNBEAM 1946-1957 S7 & S8 (BOOK OF)
SUZUKI 50cc & 80cc UP TO 1966 (BOOK OF)
SUZUKI T10 1963-1967 FACTORY WORKSHOP MANUAL
SUZUKI T20 & T200 1965-1969 FACTORY WORKSHOP MANUAL
SUZUKI TWINS 1962 ONWARDS 125-500cc WORKSHOP MANUAL
TRIUMPH 1935-1939 PREWAR MODELS (BOOK OF)
TRIUMPH 1935-1949 (BOOK OF)
TRIUMPH 1937-1951 (WORKSHOP MANUAL)
TRIUMPH 1945-1955 FACTORY WORKSHOP MANUAL
TRIUMPH 1945-1958 TWINS (BOOK OF)
TRIUMPH 1956-1969 TWINS (BOOK OF)
VELOCETTE 1925-1970 ALL SINGLES & TWINS (BOOK OF)
VESPA 1951-1961 (BOOK OF)
VESPA 1955-1963 125 & 150cc & GS MODELS (SECOND BOOK OF)
VESPA 1955-1968 GS & SS (BOOK OF)
VESPA 1963-1972 90, 125 & 150cc (THIRD BOOK OF)
VILLIERS ENGINE UP TO 1959 INC. 3 WHEELERS (BOOK OF)
VILLIERS ENGINE UP TO 1969 (BOOK OF)
VINCENT 1935-1955 (WORKSHOP MANUAL)
YAMAHA 1961-1967 YA5 & YA6 (WORKSHOP MANUAL & ILL PARTS LIST)
YAMAHA 1971-1972 JT1 & JT2 (WORKSHOP MANUAL & ILL PARTS LIST)

VELOCEPRESS TECHNICAL BOOKS – MOTORCYCLE

CATALOG OF BRITISH MOTORCYCLES (1951 MODELS)
LUCAS ELECTRONICS BRITISH M/CYCLES REPAIR & PARTS (1950-1977)
MOTORCYCLE ENGINEERING (P.E. Irving)
MOTORCYCLE ROAD TESTS 1949-1953 (Motor Cycle Magazine UK)
SPEED AND HOW TO OBTAIN IT (Motor Cycle Magazine UK)
TUNING FOR SPEED (P.E. Irving)

VELOCEPRESS MANUALS - THREE WHEELER'S

BSA THREE WHEELER (BOOK OF)
VINTAGE MORGAN THREE WHEELER (BOOK OF)

VELOCEPRESS MANUALS - AUTOMOBILE

ALFA ROMEO GIULIA WORKSHOP MANUAL 1300 TO 2000cc 1962-1975
ALFA ROMEO GIULIA TECH MANUAL CARBURETED CARS FROM 1962
ALFA ROMEO GIULIA TECH MANUAL FUEL INJECTED CARS FROM 1969
ALFA ROMEO GIULIETTA & GIULIA 750 & 101 SERIES 1955-1965 WSM
AUSTIN-HEALEY SPRITE & MG MIDGET WORKSHOP MANUAL 1958-1971
BMW 600 LIMOUSINE FACTORY WORKSHOP MANUAL
BMW 600 LIMOUSINE OWNERS HAND BOOK & SERVICE MANUAL
BMW 2000 & 2002 1966-1976 WORKSHOP MANUAL
BMW ISETTA FACTORY WORKSHOP MANUAL
CORVAIR 1960-1969 WORKSHOP MANUAL
CORVETTE V8 1955-1962 WORKSHOP MANUAL
FIAT 500 FACTORY WORKSHOP MANUAL 1957-1973
FIAT 600, 600D & MULTIPLA FACTORY WORKSHOP MANUAL 1955-1969
JAGUAR E-TYPE 3.8 & 4.2 SERIES 1 & 2 WORKSHOP MANUAL
JAGUAR MK 7, 8, 9 & XK120, 140, 150 WORKSHOP MANUAL 1948-1961
METROPOLITAN FACTORY WORKSHOP MANUAL
MGA & MGB OWNERS HANDBOOK & WORKSHOP MANUAL
MG MIDGET TC, TD, TF & TF1500 WORKSHOP MANUAL
PORSCHE 356 1948-1965 WORKSHOP MANUAL
PORSCHE 911 2.0, 2.2, 2.4 LITRE 1964-1973 WORKSHOP MANUAL
PORSCHE 911 2.7, 3.0, 3.2 LITRE 1973-1989 WORKSHOP MANUAL
PORSCHE 912 WORKSHOP MANUAL
TRIUMPH TR2, TR3, TR4 1953-1965 WORKSHOP MANUAL
VOLKSWAGEN TRANSPORTER, TRUCKS & WAGONS 1950-1979 WSM
VOLVO 1944-1968 ALL MODELS WORKSHOP MANUAL

VELOCEPRESS TECHNICAL BOOKS - AUTOMOBILE

FERRARI 250/GT SERVICE AND MAINTENANCE
FERRARI GUIDE TO PERFORMANCE
FERRARI OWNER'S HANDBOOK
FERRARI TUNING TIPS & MAINTENANCE TECHNIQUES
HOW TO BUILD A FIBERGLASS CAR
HOW TO BUILD A RACING CAR
HOW TO RESTORE THE MODEL 'A' FORD
MASERATI OWNER'S HANDBOOK
OBERT'S FIAT GUIDE
PERFORMANCE TUNING THE SUNBEAM TIGER
SOUPING THE VOLKSWAGEN
SOLEX CARBURETORS (EMPHASIS ON UK & EU AUTOMOBILES)
SU CARBURETORS (EMPHASIS ON UK AUTOMOBILES)
WEBER CARBURETORS (EMPHASIS ON ALFA & FIAT)

VELOCEPRESS BOOKS & GUIDES - AUTOMOBILE

ABARTH BUYERS GUIDE
COMPLETE CATALOG OF JAPANESE MOTOR VEHICLES
FERRARI 308 SERIES BUYER'S AND OWNER'S GUIDE
FERRARI BERLINETTA LUSSO
FERRARI BROCHURES AND SALES LITERATURE 1946-1967
FERRARI BROCHURES AND SALES LITERATURE 1968-1989
FERRARI OPP, MAINTENANCE & SERVICE H/BOOKS 1948-1963
FERRARI SERIAL NUMBERS PART I - ODD NUMBERS TO 21399
FERRARI SERIAL NUMBERS PART II - EVEN NUMBERS TO 1050
FERRARI SPYDER CALIFORNIA
HENRY'S FABULOUS MODEL "A" FORD
MASERATI BROCHURES AND SALES LITERATURE

VELOCEPRESS BOOKS – RACING

CARRERA PANAMERICANA - MEXICAN ROAD RACE (BOOK OF)
DIALED IN - THE JAN OPPERMAN STORY
IF HEMINGWAY HAD WRITTEN A RACING NOVEL
VEDA ORR'S NEW REVISED HOT ROD PICTORIAL

AUTOBOOKS WORKSHOP MANUALS & BROOKLANDS ROAD TEST PORTFOLIOS

FOR A COMPLETE LISTING OF THE AUTOBOOKS & BROOKLANDS TITLES THAT WE CURRENTLY HAVE AVAILABLE, PLEASE VISIT OUR WEBSITE.

www.VelocePress.com

Please check our website:

www.VelocePress.com

for a complete up-to-date list of available titles

www.ingramcontent.com/pod-product-compliance
Lightning Source LLC
Chambersburg PA
CBHW080435230426
43662CB00015B/2283